Public-Private Policy Partnerships

Public-Private Policy Partnerships

EDITED BY
PAULINE VAILLANCOURT ROSENAU

The MIT Press
Cambridge, Massachusetts
London, England

All of the chapters in this book with the exception of chapters 1 and 6 were published in a special issue of *American Behavioral Scientist* entitled "Public/Private Policy Partnerships" (*American Behavioral Scientist,* Volume 43, Number 1, September 1999). Copyright © 1999 by Sage Publications, Inc. Reprinted by permission of Sage Publications, Inc.

This book was set in Times Roman by Wellington Graphics, Westwood, MA.
Printed and bound in the United States of America.

Library of Congress Cataloging-in-Publication Data

Public-private policy partnerships / edited by Pauline Vaillancourt Rosenau.
   p. cm.
  Includes bibliographical references and index.
  ISBN 0-262-18198-3 (hc : alk. paper)—ISBN 0-262-68114-5 (pbk : alk. paper)
  1. Policy sciences. 2. Privatization. I. Vaillancourt Rosenau, Pauline.
H97 .P84 2000
320′.6—dc21

                                    99-089689

The author wishes to acknowledge the work of Jesssica Neal in preparing the index.

Contents

1

Mapping the Terrain of the Public-Private Policy Partnership

STEPHEN H. LINDER
PAULINE VAILLANCOURT ROSENAU

Western industrialized nations have almost thirty years of experience with public-private policy partnerships. It is time to make an assessment. But first, some definitions. We cast a broad net. The title, *Public-Private Policy Partnership,* speaks to a division of labor between government and the private sector across policy spheres as much as to any specific collaboration between government and the private sector on particular policy projects. Concrete experience is accumulating in the policy fields of education (private sector, mostly nonprofit schools), health care (Medical Savings Accounts, Medicaid managed care, Medicare managed care), energy policy (proposals for new institutional forms for nuclear power), criminal justice (for-profit incarceration facilities), transportation (roads, rail projects, public and commercial mobility infrastructures), environmental policy (market incentives to reduce pollution), welfare (private delivery of services to the poor), technology policy, and many more. Experiments of a similar nature are likely in the future with trial balloons about public-private policy partnerships regarding Internal Revenue Services, the U.S. Census, and Social Security (Georges, 1998). While our focus is on North America, international experience is important too. Countries around the world are interested in public-private policy partnerships. Both the United Nations and the World Health Organization are experimenting with them too (United Nations Development Programme, 1998).

This volume explores the intersectoral relationships between public and private organizations across several different policy arenas. The goal is to clarify and to review experience in a wide range of issue areas regarding public-private policy partnerships and their advantages and disadvantages. We seek to specify the conditions in which they work best and indicate when they might be expected to fail. The pace of experience with partnerships is rapid. Partnerships between the public and private for-profit sector to fulfill public functions are on the increase.[1] But to date, organized assessments of partnering performance have been piecemeal and incomplete. Until scholarly research catches up, evidence will remain anecdotal and spotty. Together, the chapters in this volume constitute a step in the direction of systematic knowledge building. At this critical historical juncture, where old understandings are being called into question and new relationships are being forged between the public and the private sectors, we aim for broad-based conclusions that will provide insight across policy areas. But these are not easy to achieve.

THE CONTEXT IN BRIEF

While in the past, governments have defended their turf against the encrouchments of free enterprise, today some "governments are keen to shift more welfare provision into private hands to keep public spending under control and to avoid having to raise taxes or cut benefits" (Economist, 1998b). Faced with a new context, policymakers need broad-based conclusions with concrete relevance that could have an impact on policy formulation and implementation in the future.

Historically, the role of authority that "represented" the broad interest of society has implied a public sector—the idea of its separateness and distinction from the private sector involved the assumption that there is a societal interest, broader than that of individual members.[2] No matter what the form of government, or the appeal to legitimation, authority has implied societywide social responsibility. In feudal times, the lord of the manor held sway. The American Constitution initiated a new idea and assigned important responsibilities to the representatives of the people—with government assuring a greater public policy role, such as education.

Public-private policy partnerships were relatively rare in the past and the private sector hardly ever took on the admittedly few public responsibilities that did exist, not even for pay. The norm was a relatively clear separation of the private sector and the public sector. This does not mean that the definition of what was private and what was public has been stable over time. Some of what we consider public functions, today, were private in the past. As Anne Schneider points out in chapter 12, private, for-profit prisons are not an entirely new invention. They were the norm in the 19th century.

Government is our largest insurer, and very few of us would venture to say that we will never need the public programs that protect us from the unexpected, and the unanticipated. It is no surprise, then, that the state has taken an increasing responsibility for a minimal protection of the individual from the unforeseen and the irrational, because "such things could happen to anyone." But government is not an invisible hand. It represents all of us. We pay for it and we elect it, by voting. By choosing not to vote, we grant legitimacy to the choices made by those who do vote.[3]

In the end, we remain conflicted over individual responsibility and the obligation of society to its members. Despite this ambivalence about government and strong feelings about personal responsibility, broad public support exists for the role of government as a safety net in most Western industrialized nations. For example, almost everyone in the United States, Canada, and Western Europe agrees that "nobody . . . should be bankrupted by paying the cost of their medical care." Between 76% and 87% believe the government is responsible for seeing to it that "everyone gets the medical care they need" (Taylor & Reinhardt, 1991, p. 3). Government, to one extent or another, is viewed as responsible for fixing what is arbitrary, especially in conditions where the individual's personal responsibility is not clear. The modern state plays a huge role in national disaster management. Government set up Medicare, because getting old and getting sick are not conscious, personal choices. Even the best planners, the most thrifty, and those who exercise and eat well all the time cannot protect themselves against all the uncertainties of birth, life, and death. Even when it comes to "insuring American global competitiveness," people are more likely to look to government (49%) than to rely on the private sector (41%) (Calmes, 1998).

In the past, private-sector organizations were assumed to be less committed; they didn't do as good a job. An example illustrates this case. Private-sector armies, mercenaries, were common, but criticisms of their efficacy are legend. They were a resource of last resort for princes who had funds but no loyal citizens to defend domains. Mercenaries, a private-sector organization, only worked well in special situations when charged with a public responsibility. Loyalty to the prince, king, or nation would be higher due to ethnic identity (Hanover monarchs in England with mercenaries from Germany) or it could be increased by the promise of citizenship (the French Foreign Legion). But generally, a prince would prefer a volunteer army. The mercenary generally put individual interest first. "Anyone who relies on mercenary troops to keep himself in power will never be safe or secure, for they are factious, ambitious, ill-disciplined, treacherous. . . . In peacetime they pillage you, in wartime they let the enemy do it. This is why: They have no motive or principle for joining up beyond the desire to collect their pay. And what you pay them is not enough to make them want to die for you" (Machiavelli, 1995, p. 38). The volunteer might set aside personal interest (life itself) for societal interest or personal loyalty to the prince. This illustration is, of course, oversimplified—society is vastly more complex today. The modern state is less personal in character than that of the prince.

RETURN TO PRIVATE INITIATIVE

Beginning in the late 1970s and early 1980s, disenchantment with public-sector services loomed large in America. The public sector was criticized because of its monopoly and the absence of competition in the production of services. It was characterized by lack of choice, little innovation, low accountability to customers, and exposure to political interference (Economist, 1998a). For some, it was a matter of cost. The public sector was said to be inefficient and burdened with excessive bureaucracy. The private sector could deliver better quality for lower cost. For others, it was a broader philosophical matter. Government is "an inevitably dominant and coercive influence" that "should play only a minimal role in society" (Smith & Lipsky, 1992).[4] Stephen Linder discusses those differences in chapter 2. In the extreme, some argue that there are no civic responsibilities that the private sector couldn't do better (Machan, 1995). This includes "almost all civic policy functions including public safety, natural defense, health care, housing and urban development, social services, education, and recreation" (Savas, 1987, p. 223). Finally, others suggested the collapse of FDR's New Deal heritage and LBJ's Great Society and the legitimacy of a large role for the public-sector services and a broad safety net was simply the result of years of neglect. Systems developed problems, including waste, mismanagement, abuse, and fraud. There was a "failing to keep vigil over programs that did not change with the times" (Wines, 1995, p. 1).

If the public sector were less efficient than the private sector in the performance of society's business of public policy, it would be no surprise. In the United States, there is less of a historical tradition than in Europe for the "neutral civil service," the "bureaucracy staffed with career public servants." The Tammany Hall tradition, an American invention, employed public-service jobs as a political payoff (Riordon, Plunkitt, Riordan, & Quinn, 1963). In many cities, especially in the eastern United States, this was the equivalent of the Prince's mercenary army and its heritage remains today (see Purdy, 1996, for an example of a modern Tammany Hall).

For whatever reason, the enthusiasm for the private sector playing a greater role worldwide in the policy sector has been overwhelming over the last decades (Barker, 1996; Schultze, 1977). The drive to privatization of public services has been apparent at every level of government. This course of action involves deregulation, policy decentralization, downsizing of government, outsourcing of public services, and privatization of sectors previously assumed to be what economists called "natural monopolies" including gas, electricity, telephones, and so forth. For example, the trend has gone so far that, today, jury trials are being privatized in California (Jacobs, 1997), and utilities (electricity, water, gas, and transportation) are privatized around the world (Moffett, 1998). At the local level, outsourcing has been increasing enormously to include close to 600 cities by 1992 (Daley, 1996). It is in fact the wealthier, fiscally healthier communities that have been the quickest to privatize and have gone the furthest in this direction. State increases in privatization have been equally impressive since 1988 (Council of State Governments, 1997). It has even been suggested that the "promise" (read threat) to privatize be employed as a "stick" to improve public-sector performance even if there is no real plan to carry through such a proposal (Korosec & Mead, 1996; Osborne & Gaebler, 1992).

The rationale for privatization (Daley, 1996) can then be attributed to a wide range of factors that range from cost reductions to ideological preference (Starr, 1990). Costing out privatization may be extremely complex in every case. Implementation is often carried out in the absence of cost information (Lifsher, 1998; Xiong, 1997) with estimated data (U.S. General Accounting Office, 1998). Therefore, it is little surprise that much research on the topic simply assumes that privatization reduces costs (Greene, 1996, for example). Evidence in support of this proposition, generally based on case studies, is mixed and, on balance, evidence is simply contradictory (Handler, 1996, chap. 4). The chapters in this book attest to the wide variations across policy sectors as regards relative cost of public and private provision of services.

An unequivocal commitment to privatization in all circumstances may be too great a reaction to poor performance of the public sector and too naïve a trust in the private sector. The private sector brings attributes that mollify some, but not all, of the public sector's weaknesses. There are policy areas where weakness is simply structural and contextual, inherent in the act of providing a public service. In these cases, it makes little difference whether the public sector or private sector provides the service, alone or in a partnering format. For example, the private sector has incentives to increase services and expand the need for its product just as the public-sector government bureaucracy does. It should be no surprise, then, if private prisons don't have effective rehabilitation programs, or if they lobby for increasingly long prison terms (see Schneider, chap. 12). It is human nature, in both the private and public sector, to seek to increase the demand for whatever one is providing.

THE WORLD OF PARTNERSHIPS

Our title, *Public-Private Policy Partnerships,* speaks to the formation of cooperative relationships between government, profit-making firms, and nonprofit private organizations[5] to fulfill a policy function. Working together, they seek to meet the objectives of each while, hopefully, performing better than either one acting alone. Among advocates, partnerships represent the second generation of efforts to bring competitive market discipline to bear on government provision of goods and services. As distinct from the first generation of privatizing efforts, partnering involves a sharing of both responsibility and financial risk (United Nations Development Programme, 1998). Rather than shrinking government in favor of private-sector activity through a devolution of public responsibility, or other forms of load-shedding, in the best of situations partnering institutionalizes collaborative arrangements where the differences between the sectors become blurred. This should not involve turning a policymaking responsibility over to the private sector entirely. For example, private prisons that become "partners" with a state's Bureau of Prisons in the discretionary use of force may constitute too much of a delegation of the policymaking power that is usually reserved for government (diIulio, 1988; Starr, 1990).

Partnerships are complex organizations, and they may include for-profit companies, private nonprofit organizations (in a competitive environment or a monopoly situation), as well as public-sector nonprofit organizations (government). Government contracting with private nonprofit organizations is a form of partnership with advantages and disadvantages (Smith & Lipsky, 1992). (See Lovrich, chap. 11.) Each involves different levels and types of conflict of interest and different ethical responsibilities. Ironically, there is a risk that these types of partnerships involving private-nonprofit relationships require so much social capital that it will be exhausted (see Lovrich, chap. 12). Partnerships between the government and the nonprofit sector may be less susceptible to some forms of conflicts of interest than the alternative, but they still present problems (Smith & Lipsky, 1992).

Partnerships between government and for-profit enterprises have advantages and disadvantages as well. The private sector can often provide a service at less cost, but the short-run savings can lead to increased costs in the long run. For example, employees may not have pension plans when public institutions contract with private companies to provide services. This cost shifts back to the public sector years later if these employees end up on welfare when they are too old to work. The complexity of private-public policy partnerships is likely to be greater when the long-term view is taken into account.

Terminology is a significant problem when considering public-private policy partnerships. For some, partnering with for-profit organizations is just short of privatizing (Handler, 1996, p. 11). For others, it means a shared commitment to agreed-upon goals that take shape in projects requiring financial investment and human capital of both partners. Such projects share risk, authority, responsibilities, and accountability between public and private partners (United Nations Development Programme, 1998). They involve both the public and the private sector *planning* together for mutual advantage. Little agreement exists as to what "planning" means. For some, it may be implicit, informal, or even unintentional and accidental. For example, James Dunn points out, in chapter 5, that partnerships, defined broadly, might even include public development of roads through long-term investment with the private partners being prudent motorists, truckers, and so forth, who invest in vehicles, fuel, insurance, and so forth. For others, partnerships require close, explicit, and formal cooperation between the public and private sectors involving more than using public money for private goods and services. In addition, there may be many different types of public-private policy partnerships in the same policy sector, even in the same institutions—for example, in the prison system one can pay private companies for incarcerating prisoners, and one can also partner in the sense of having other private firms set up production plants in a prison, where prisoners provide the labor. Anne Schneider discusses both types of partnerships.

The distinctions between partnerships, public or private provision of services, and privatization can be understood in several different ways. A case can be made, for example, for generalizing the partnership notion to include almost any combination of public funding and private provision of services for public purposes. From this perspective, partnerships come in many forms and shapes, with new forms proliferating under governmental auspices (Muschell, 1995). The trend here is toward the inclusion of for-profit providers as contractual "partners" in the provision of human and non-defense public services, tasks once the exclusive preserve of government and nonprofit providers. A number of authors in this volume follow this convention, preferring "partnership" to "privatization," since the latter is understood to exclude most forms of joint funding and provision and still retains an ideological connotation of being antigovernment. To clarify whether partnerships in the 1990s resemble those that emerged in the 1970s, we need to pay closer attention to the role of the nonprofits and their transformation throughout the 1980s.

THE NONPROFITS AND INTERSECTORAL RELATIONSHIPS, INCLUDING PARTNERING

Following the trajectory of the welfare state from the 1960s onward, nonprofits expanded their revenue base beyond their traditional core sources in donations and subscriptions to include a substantial share of tax-based income through direct and indirect government funding. As government's role in public-service provision expanded through the early 1970s, so did the role of the nonprofits, increasing their relative dependence on public funding. As Salamon notes, "The central fact of life of the American welfare state as it had evolved by the 1970s was a widespread pattern of partnership between government and the voluntary sector. Facing major new responsibilities in a context of continued public hostility to the bureaucratic state, government at all levels turned extensively to existing and newly created private, nonprofit organizations to help it carry out expanded welfare state functions" (1995, p. 204).

The idea that somehow the state's expansion had been inimical to the nonprofits or had displaced their efforts in community affairs led some to posit that a contraction of the state would bring a corresponding increase in non-profit activity. A type of *substitution logic* is implied. As Bendick and Levinson point out, the experience following the Federal retrenchment in the 1980s did not bear this out (Bendick & Levinson, 1985). Nonprofits were left to find ways of making up for the shortfall in revenue, and did so, according to Weisbrod, principally by expanding into commercial activities (Weisbrod, 1997). Rather than the substitution effect posited by simplistic notions of antagonism between public and private sectors, the evidence points to symbiosis, especially between government and the nonprofit organization, committed to service delivery in community settings.

A similar form of substitution logic pervaded the discussion of "private initiatives" during the early 1980s. Again, the growth in non-defense spending was linked to a stifling of private economic activity, from crowding in the capital markets to a punitive regulatory presence undermining profitability. The Neo-Classical synthesis in liberal economics provided the theoretical rationale for separating sectors and for framing government activities as "interventions," justified only when private markets failed. Substitution between sectors dictated that deregulation, tax cuts, and dramatic expediture reductions would revitalize the nonprofit sector and, at the same time, stimulate growth in the for-profit sector (Bendick & Levinson, 1985).

Ironically, the rigid division of sectoral responsibilities underlying the anticipated substitution would also work to undermine the division itself. Government's departure would leave a "gap" in societal problem-solving that would need to be filled by the other two sectors. Here, private initiatives were seen as an alternative to government, with business filling the gaps in public-service provision, once they were free from government interference. The old lines of responsibility were redrawn implicitly as the logical consequences of substitution became more obvious. Treating government's role as a substitute for private activity now demanded that private activity substitute for government. The federal government, during the Reagan and Bush administrations, became the chief promoter of this kind of substitution.

A second view involving a more *pragmatic logic* emerged in the decade of recession that preceded this period. It implies a continuum of public-private policy relationships. In practice, the sectors were found to be mixed and cooperative, not antagonistic and substitutive. Some responsibilities were divided, and some were shared. Accordingly, as fiscal austerity began to reduce government's capacity to provide services, the emphasis shifted to finding ways to leverage public resources with private. Berger traces the reference to "partnerships" between sectors to the Carter administration's efforts to enlist the private sector's financial participation in urban redevelopment projects (Berger, 1985). Here, the government offered a wide range of subsidies, both direct and indirect, to create profit-making opportunities under the rubric of collaboration. Eventually, this partnership logic would subsume the substitution notion as a way of characterizing intersectoral relationships in the United States. Once it did, the term "partnership" would extend all the way from public subsidies for commercial activity to direct service provision by for-profit firms.

There is a third form of logic for constructing the complex relations across sectors, drawn largely from Catholic social doctrine and the Western European, conservative tradition. The principle of *subsidiarity* posits a hierarchical relationship across levels of social and political organization, ranging from the family to the state (Anheier, 1992). It creates a presumption in favor of independence at each lower level of organization from the higher ones; for example, the family should be able to pursue its life plans, without interference by secular authorities. This presumption is suspended, however, in cases of need. The presumption then shifts, assigning responsibility to the next higher level to provide support first, before still higher levels can be involved. A variation of this doctrine was imported to the United States by the sociologist/theologian Peter Berger, under the rubric of "mediating institutions." Here, local, non-profit organizations are thought to be best suited to both the assessment and satisfaction of community needs. This puts the federal government at the end of a long chain of providers and favors local initiative in problem solving. In contrast to the substitution logic mentioned above, the role of the for-profit organization in subsidiarity is largely a supportive one; they offer sources of voluntarism and charitable contributions. As with many normative ideas in our hybridized political culture, these three kinds of logic have been conflated over time. Substitution arguments creep into pragmatic depictions, and either can defer to subsidiarity. When we add to these sometimes conflated constructions of intersectoral relationships, an enthusiastic promotion of partnering in all possible forms, the conceptual picture is further muddied.

Consider how the partnership idea fares under each. First, from the point of view of *substitution logic,* if private or public provision of goods and services for the community are viewed as competing alternatives locked in conflict, then partnering appears to offer a flexible compromise to an either/or formulation of provider responsibilties. They are a means to finance and deliver publicly demanded services, qualitatively different from private and public, and superior to either one alone. For example, they may be structured to get around the deficiencies of extreme privatization that include important conflicts of interest. They may be structured to overcome, as well, public sector difficulties with lackadaisical performance and inefficiency due to monopoly status. Under this scenario, public-private policy partnerships may then be embraced as a corrective against overcommitment to privatization in recent years and citizen rebellion against this trend (Salpukas, 1998). Recent attention to a "Third Way," especially in Germany and Britain, uses this image of market-government antagonism as a rationale for its appeal. The Third Way is supposed to escape the public-private dualism altogether by encouraging collaborative ventures and partnerships of all sorts. Nonetheless, according to its critics, its content consists largely of promoting global economic expansion while indemnifying its local consequences, hardly an escape from the Postwar sectoral division.

Second, from a *pragmatic view* of intersectoral relationships, the private and public sectors, or the government and the market, can be envisioned as poles along a continuum (Mintzberg, 1996). Privatization and collectivization represent movement from one end to the other.[6] Traditional public financing and provision of services would be at one pole, and private at the other. Partnering would span the points between the two, with each location representing a slightly different mix between the two. Within this model, an infinity of possible compromise positions exists between a singularly government-oriented approach and the handing over of full responsibility to individuals acting in the private sector. Vouchers would be closer to privatization, while contracting out would constitute a "partnership" with the balance depending on the exact nature of the responsibilities assigned to the public and private partners under the terms of the contracts (Savas, 1987, p. 90; Smith & Lipsky, 1992, pp. 250–251). Not all writings on the topic share this perspective, and public-private policy partnerships are, of course, multidimensional; thus, it is impossible to capture their variety along a single continuum. Still, the idea of mixed government draws implicitly on this dimensional version of the classic market versus government dualism.

A third view associated with *subsidiarity* suggests that privatization and the increase of public-private partnerships signal not a decline of one sector relative to another but rather a reassumption of service responsibilities by local, community-based entities, acting in concert with the state and with the private sector. Viewing the public and private as sectors drifting apart "leads to an underestimation of the bonds which unite." The sectors, if anything, appear to be moving in the direction of greater interdependence. The private sector, for example, even in the global economy, is located in a concrete physical community subject to state supervision, and its markets are similarly grounded. "No enterprise can thrive sustainably in an impoverished and dangerous public environment. The fact that major enterprises have opened up to concerns of community interest and to the quality of their social and natural environment derives not from any particular virtue of citizenship but from the pursuit of their own interests" (Hanke, 1996; Supiot, 1996). From this perspective, partnering occurs most intensely within a given level in the hierarchy, for example, among local, private organizations. Partnering across levels, say, between government and private actors, is occurring more frequently, given the growing complexity of social problems and the resources that this complexity demands, but it is also more vulnerable to the strains of mixed motives and conflict.

WEAK AND STRONG PARTNERSHIPS—THE REVENUE CONNECTION

Building on the notion of intersectoral relationships, we can revisit the diversity of partnership terminology and usages mentioned earlier from a more analytical perspective and suggest some simple conventions for how best to view them. Following the approach taken in the literature on the nonprofit or voluntary sector, we can order ways of partnering based on revenue sources and the nature of the entities involved. First, assume that the function of the entities involved is to produce goods and services for the community and that all three sectors are involved in such provision—public, private, and voluntary. Note that we distinguish between these sectors which can be defined in formal legal terms and the revenue status of the entities (e.g. not-for-profit) that operate within them. This permits us to track the movement of these entities across sectors. Next, the source of revenue needs to be separated conceptually from the type of organization responsible for the provision of services. For our purposes only, three categories of revenue are necessary: taxes, commercial activities, and gifts. Each of these categories typically corresponds to one of three types of providers—government agencies, for-profit firms, or nonprofit organizations. Separating the revenue from the provider allows us to track the departure of a given provider from its traditional source of revenue. Recent literature on the voluntary sector considers the significance of the movement of nonprofits away from gifts as their primary source of revenue toward commercial activities of all sorts. Squeezed fiscally by falling government revenue, with no compensating increase in giving, nonprofits are finding ready sources of revenue in the market for theme-based items and services that bear their name or logo (Weisbrod, 1997).

A simple array of revenue sources by sectors is depicted in the following two figures. The first figure highlights the for-profits and the second, the nonprofits. Two directions of movement for these entites are of interest here. Horizontal movement in the figure represents changes in sources of revenue or income without altering the entity's basic functional orientation; accordingly, these are *intra*sectoral changes and are illustrated with dashed arrows. Vertical movement, in contrast, is *inter*sectoral; the principal income of the entity retains the same form but its functional orientation changes. Partnering is generally used to describe both kinds of movement. We will argue that the significance of partnering for the entities involved, and for the nature of the goods and services produced, will differ qualitatively depending on whether the changes were intrasectoral or intersectoral. In relative terms, intrasectoral changes entail weak partnerships, both in terms of commitment to entities outside one's own sector and consequences for service provision. Intersectoral changes, by way of contrast, entail strong ones.

Consider the depiction of intersectoral relations in figure 1. For-profit firms, appearing at the center of the figure, typically operate within the conventions

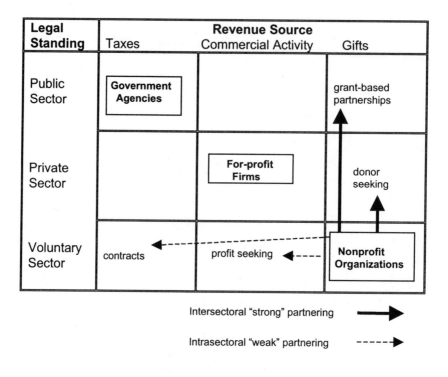

Figure 1: The Movement of For-Profit Firms Across Revenue Sources and Sectors

of profit-making practice and obtain their income primarily from commercial activity, that is, from buying and selling in the marketplace. They may supplant, or merely supplement, this income with noncommercial kinds of transactions when they contract with government to provide certain goods and services (horizontal movement to the left) and are compensated with tax dollars. They may also seek to attract community support for image-enhancing events, form coalitions to improve business conditions, or become affiliated with local institutions through voluntarism on the part of their employees. When either government or nonprofit organizations enlist for-profit firms to transport their public or voluntary functions, respectively, into the private sector, we term this, privatization. The original meaning of this term, now lost, was limited to government engagement in commercial activities, such as the auctioning of assets or equity sales, as a substitute for tax revenue. Typically, it is government or the nonprofit organization that favors the term "partnership" over privatization for this kind of horizontal movement.

Vertical movement finds the for-profit firm continuing to rely on commercial activity, but doing so under a different set of conventions. Movement into the public sector depicts a channeling of the firm's profit motive to public purposes. This includes efforts by the government to offer a range of incentives, from direct loans and tax subsidies to regulatory relief, for firms to participate in certain markets where profit-making opportunities would not otherwise exist. More recent examples of infrastructure projects entail joint activity and funding on the part of both government and for-profit firms; we consider these to represent the prototypical public-private partnership. The European Union, for example, has launched a multiyear project to improve the network of highways linking its member countries. Because of the cost involved, its strategy is to enlist the support, not only of governments at all levels, but of private firms willing to invest capital and know-how in this project.

Movement into the voluntary sector, while keeping its commercial aspects, typically involves a joint venture of some sort, where the for-profit firm stands to gain reputational capital for contributing to a "good cause" while making a profit on the sponsored activity or enterprise. For some firms, the best way to accomplish this without affecting their short-term profits is to "spin off" a foundation as a medium for collaboration with nonprofits. Upper management continues to control the direction for such collaborations, ensuring their eventual contribution to profitability, while cultivating an image of public-spirited activity. This strategy is perhaps best known in research circles, where universities and nonprofit "think tanks" obtain corporate funding to generate new knowledge, ultimately relevant to the competitive advantage of their sponsor.

The second of our two figures, figure 2, shifts attention to the movement of the nonprofits. As noted above, the horizontal movement of the nonprofits, first to tax dollars and then to commercial ventures, characterizes the changes in nonprofit income over the last two decades. Unlike the case with the for-profit firm, however, neither of these horizontal moves tends to evoke partnership rhetoric. There is little to be gained, at least by the nonprofit organization, from calling attention to its entrepreneurial forays into the market; such attention can easily undercut the organization's appeal to wealthy or corporate donors. Of course, among small donors, purchases of the nonprofit's products may be perceived primarily as a donation; here, the public display of the product signifies one's support.

Similarly, it is difficult to understand the relationship of nonprofits to government (especially the federal government) as a partnership between equals, when so many of these organizations were created to respond to government's program responsibilities and depended on tax money and public service contracts to function. Accordingly, when "partnership" is applied to either of these instances, it represents a weak version, common to intrasectoral movement more generally. It should also be noted that government contracts with nonprofits can be quite different from contracts with for-profits, since, in the

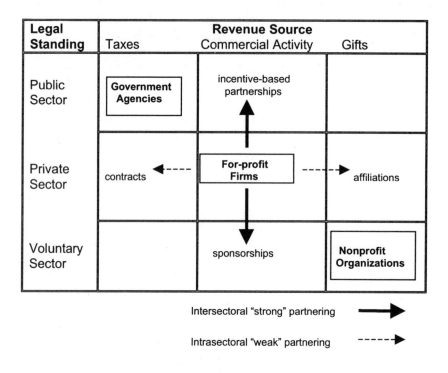

Legal Standing	Revenue Source		
	Taxes	Commercial Activity	Gifts
Public Sector	**Government Agencies**	incentive-based partnerships	
Private Sector	contracts	**For-profit Firms**	affiliations
Voluntary Sector		sponsorships	**Nonprofit Organizations**

Intersectoral "strong" partnering   ➡

Intrasectoral "weak" partnering   ----➤

Figure 2: The Movement of Nonprofit Organizations Across Revenue Sources and Sectors

absence of profit seeking, the missions and motives of the former can vary widely. For example, nonprofits affiliated with organized religion may not only employ their own standards of eligibility for services but may restrict the range of services they provide, based on religious doctrine (see Rom, chap. 10). Reproductive planning services are perhaps the most controversial in this regard.

In contrast, vertical movement by the nonprofits into the other two sectors tends to generate strong partnerships. Here, the nonprofit is appealing to potential donors, granting agencies and collaborators willing to contribute funds and know-how to shared purposes. And while the nonprofit is sticking to its traditional revenue base, it is expanding, or perhaps tailoring, its purposes to coincide with the functional expectations of private and public donors. This kind of strong partnership clearly predates the intersectoral movement of the for-profits by decades. Hence, when the advocates of partnering across sectors claim that this is all very new and somehow a refreshing departure from what went on before, they are only partly right. The entry of the for-profits into strong partnerships, as we term them, is new; the partnerships themselves are not. Further, whether this entry represents a refreshing departure is very much the focus of the research presented in this book.

IN PROSPECT

The purpose of this volume is to neither recommend nor criticize public-private policy partnerships in the abstract. It is rather to explore their advantages and disadvantages with a goal of isolating factors that explain success and failure. The hope is that this effort will contribute to an enhanced understanding of when partnering between sectors should be encouraged and pursued and in which cases it is best avoided (see Rosenau, chap. 13). Most chapters focus on an evaluation of past experience combined with qualitative and quantitative evidence in the hope of basing general conclusions on results from a number of different policy sectors. Authors report not only on their own research contribution but on the recognizable trends in their specific policy field. Collectively, these chapters point to the policy arenas where direct government provision does the best job. For example, economists Stiglitz and Wallsten argue that due to market failure, government support for socially optimal levels of research and development (R & D) in technology are desirable (Stiglitz and Wallsten, chap. 3). We identify those where the private sector has demonstrated superior results, such as filling the demand for education in narrow market niches (religious, educational philosophy, special value-oriented schools) (Levin, chap. 8). The private sector appears effective in providing services where an increased demand (for example, an increase in incarceration facilities) cannot be met by government (Schneider, chap. 12).

Whatever the place of the policy partners on the public-private policy map, whether bipolar ideal types, points on a continuum, or simply redefinition of terms, they all involve the private sector carrying out public policy purposes (Starr, 1990). There are philosophical and political consequences, as we will see. There is no obvious increase in the private sector's adopting voluntary accountability and responsibility. However, there may be increased legal bounds that are generated when the private sector undertakes a policy-relevant project with public exposure. The chapters that follow will also suggest where public-private partnering works best. The development of fuel efficient vehicles is one example (Dunn, chap. 5). We also point to areas where the evidence about partnering is not yet clear, as is the case for welfare services for the poor (Rom, chap. 10). These are, as well, policy functions of private-public partnerships that are relatively new and original. For example, Rosenbaum suggests authentic policy partnering could increase citizen participation in the nuclear energy sector, which could, in turn, revitalize an institutional context (Rosenbaum, chap. 4). These energy partnerships have, in the past, been characterized as weak and inefficient with low communication between the public and private partners. While Linder traces a range of partnership possibilities that merit skepticism (Linder, chap. 2), there is a sense in which "partnerships point to an essential task of democratic life: citizen empowerment and the need to create and espouse strategies to achieve it" (Stephenson, 1991).

NOTES

1. Osborne and Gaebler (1992) describe 36 alternative ways to deliver public service (p. 31). Public-private policy partnerships are described as having "exploded" since the 1980s (p. 335).

2. Such assumptions do not go unquestioned today (Machan, 1995 #1170). Governor Bush in Texas proposed to privatize administration of welfare, Medicaid, and food stamps (Roth, 1997 #1171).

3. Public-sector contributions to society affect us all though sometimes only indirectly. For example, even those without children need schools for several reasons. Most important, we need a highly educated citizenry to vote in elections and preserve our democracy, to make wise decisions through the vote, especially if we choose not to vote, as is the case with so many of us today.

4. On the other hand, government is not the only powerful force in human affairs. Others include "corporate bureaucracies, the great institutions of the media, banks and financial institutions, trade associations and lobbying groups" (Brinkley, 1996 #1267).

5. Nonprofit organizations, sometimes called the "third sector," are defined as "organizations that are privately owned and controlled, but that exist to meet public or social needs, not to accumulate private wealth. By this definition, large nonprofit firms that exist primarily to accumulate wealth would not qualify. But for-profit institutions that exist to meet social or public need (development banks, for instance) would qualify" (Osborne & Gaebler, 1992 #1233).

6. Privatization is "any process that is aimed at shifting functions and responsibilities in whole or in part from the government to the private sector through such activities as contracting out or assets sales" (U.S. General Accounting Office, 1998 #1183). "If viewed as the sharing or delegating of authority to nongovernmental agents, then privatization, both formally and informally, is a common practice in both civil and criminal regulatory regimes. . . . At the other end of the spectrum, privatization means the public sale of assets—government withdrawing, or 'load shedding.' Although a favorite of the conservatives, this form of privatization has never really amounted to much in the United States (Handler, 1996 #1241, p. 78).

REFERENCES

Anheier, H. (1992). An elaborate network: Profiling the third sector in Germany. In B. Gidron, R. Kramer, & L. Salamon (Eds.), *Government and the third sector* (pp. 31–56). San Francisco: Jossey-Bass Publishers.

Barker, C. (1996). *The health care policy process*. London: Sage Publications.

Bendick, M., & Levinson, P. (1985). Private sector initiatives or public-private partnerships? In L. Salamon & M. Lund (Eds.), *The Reagan presidency and the governing of America* (pp. 455–479). Washington, DC: The Urban Institute Press.

Berger, R. (1985). Private sector initiatives in the Reagan era: New actors rework an old theme? In L. Salamon & M. Lund (Eds.), *The Reagan presidency and the governing of America* (pp. 181–211). Washington, DC: The Urban Institute Press.

Brinkley, A. (1996, August 18). Big government is a check. *The New York Times Magazine,* p. 37.

Brinkley, A. (1996, August 18). Big government is a check. *The New York Times Magazine,* p. 37.

Calmes, J. (1998, December 10). Despite buoyant economic times Americans don't buy free trade. *The Wall Street Journal,* p. A10.

Council of State Governments (1997). *Private practices: A review of privatization in state government.* Lexington, KY.

Daley, D. (1996). The Politics and Administration of Privatization: Efforts Among Local Governments. *Policy Studies Journal, 24*(4), 629–631.

diIulio, J. J. (1988). What's Wrong with Private Prisons. *The Public Interest* (92), 66–83.

Economist (1998a, June 13). The end of privatisation? *The Economist, 347* (8072), pp. 53–55.

Economist (1998b, October 24). A survey of social insurance; Privatising peace of mind. *The Economist, 349* (8019), pp. 3–22.

Georges, C. (1998, June 22). Social-Security "privatization" effort makes headway. *The Wall Street Journal,* p. A24.

Greene, J. D. (1996). How much privatization? A research note examining the use of privatization by cities in 1982 and 1992. *Policy Studies Journal, 24*(4), 632–640.

Handler, J. F. (1996). *Down from bureaucracy: The ambiguity of privatization and empowerment.* Princeton, NJ: Princeton University Press.

Hanke, B. (1996). *Travail, capital et Etat: Relations de travail et ajustement economique dans l'Europe des annees 1980.* Paper presented at the Perspectives on Work, Maison des sciences de l'Homme, Ange-Guepin, Nantes, France.

Jacobs, M. A. (1997, July 7). Private jury trials: Cheap, quick, controversial. *The Wall Street Journal,* pp. B1, B5.

Korosec, R. L., & Mead, T. D. (1996). Lessons from privatization task forces: Comparative case studies. *Policy Studies Journal, 24*(4), 641–647.

Lifsher, M. (1998, May 27). Busting into the prison business. *The Wall Street Journal,* p. B10.

Machan, T. (1995). *Private rights and public illusions.* New Brunswick, NJ: Transaction Publishers.

Machiavelli, N. (1995). *The prince* (Wootton, David, Trans.). Indianapolis: Hackett Publishing.

Mintzberg, H. (1996). Managing government, governing management. *Harvard Business Review, 74,* 75–83.

Moffett, M. (1998, April 27). Sour juice: In Brazil, a utility dims public's enthusiasm for privatization. *The Wall Street Journal,* pp. A1, A10.

Muschell, J. (1995). *Health Economics technical briefing note: Privatization in health.* Geneva: WHO Task Force on Health Economics.

Osborne, D., & Gaebler, T. (1992). *Reinventing government: How the entrepreneurial spirit is transforming the public sector.* New York: Addison-Wesley.

Purdy, M. (1996, May 14). Web of patronage in schools grips those who can undo it. *The New York Times,* pp. A1, B15.

Riordon, W. L., Plunkitt, G. W., Riordan, W. L., & Quinn, P. (1963). *Plunkitt of Tammany Hall; A series of very plain talks on very practical politics.* New York: Dutton.

Roth, B. (1997, May 25). Wage levels, privatization nettle state implementing welfare law. *Houston Chronicle,* p. 12A.

Salamon, L. (1995). *Partners in public service.* Baltimore, MD: Johns Hopkins University Press.

Salpukas, A. (1998, October 25). A California vote could rewrite U.S. electric bills. *The New York Times,* pp. A1, B13.

Savas, E. S. (1987). *Privatization: The key to better government.* Chatham, NJ: Chatham House Publishers.

Schultze, C. L. (1977). *The public use of private interest.* Washington, DC: The Brookings Institute.

Smith, S. R., & Lipsky, M. (1992). Privatization in health and human services: A critique. *Journal of Health Politics, Policy and Law, 17*(2), 233–253.

Starr, P. (1990). The new life of the liberal state: Privatization and the restructuring of state-society relations. In J. Waterbury & E. Suleiman (Eds.), *Public enterprise and privatization* (pp. 22–54). Boulder: Westview Press.

Stephenson, M. O. (1991). Whither the public-private partnership: A critical overview. *Urban Affairs Quarterly, 27*(1), 109–127.

Supiot, A. (1996). Work and the public/private dichotomy. *International Labour Review, 135*(6), 653–663.

Taylor, H., & Reinhardt, U. E. (1991). Does the system fit? *HMQ, Third Quarter,* 2–10.

United Nations Development Programme (1998). Public-private partnerships. [On-line]. Available: http://www.undp.org:80.

U.S. General Accounting Office (1998). *Privatization: questions state and local decisionmakers used when considering privatization options* (GAO/GGD-98–87). Washington, DC: United States General Accounting Office.

Weisbrod, B. (1997). The future of the nonprofit sector: Its entwining with private enterprise and government. *Journal of Policy Analysis and Management, 16*(4), 541–555.

Wines, M. (1995, September 24). The social engineers let welfare go unfixed. *The New York Times,* p. 1.

Xiong, N. (1997, July 13). Private prisons: A question of savings. *The New York Times,* p. 5.

2

Coming to Terms With
the Public-Private Partnership

A Grammar of Multiple Meanings

STEPHEN H. LINDER

The P-P partnership, as a rubric for describing cooperative ventures between the state and private business, currently enjoys remarkable acclaim in both official and scholarly circles. Organizations ranging from the European Union to Canadian Heritage not only endorse the partnership idea but actively employ it as a programmatic tool for adapting to what they perceive as changing needs and circumstances (Kinnock, 1998; Canadian Heritage, 1996). Further, its advocates tout it as the epitome of a new generation of management reforms, especially suited to the contemporary economic and political imperatives for efficiency and quality. Despite momentum gathered since the late 1980s, and its present status as a de rigueur reform, the partnership is not new to governance. More than a decade earlier, without the fanfare or reformist cachet, partnerships were deployed by the federal government in the United States as a tool for stimulating private investment in inner-city infrastructure. Likewise, partnerships were key to coordinating federal initiatives in regional economic development. The record of these devices through the 1970s is at best mixed (Stephenson, 1991). How can we account for its reincarnation in the 1990s as a reform on the bleeding edge?

The simple answer in this instance raises only an unsatisfying irony. The P-P partnership is frequently viewed as a derivative of the privatization movement, which captivated conservative leaders in western liberal regimes on both sides of the Atlantic throughout much of the 1980s. Public asset sales, outsourcing (e.g., procurement contracts), and load shedding (e.g., divestiture) that occurred in these regimes was nominally intended to discipline the provision of services with competitive market pressures (Kettl, 1993). The rationale was that private providers would provide higher quality goods and services at lower cost, and the government sector of public providers would shrink accordingly. Conversely, the hallmark of partnerships is cooperation—not competition; the disciplining mechanism is not customer exit or thin profit margins, but a joint venture that spreads financial risks between public and private sectors. Joint-venture arrangements actually stabilize volatile markets and work to mitigate competitive pressures, not exploit them. Rather than struggling to redefine the boundary between public and private, with the former typically ceding territory to the latter, partnering works to blur them (Starr, 1990). It remains, then, an anomaly relative to contemporary ways of separating public from private.

The idea of government and business partnering for some common purpose evokes images of wartime solidarity and memories of small town life in America, where business and local government shared talent and community responsibilities. It seems to draw on communal traditions of cooperation that are, at once, vaguely familiar and socially valued. Of course, when we scratch the surface of these arrangements over the past century, the spectacle of machine politics, of graft and corruption, shines through. Part of the impetus for the growth of the liberal state was to inhibit these kinds of cooperative ventures by carefully defining and then policing the boundaries between public and private (Starr, 1990). This entailed both an elaborate overlay of administrative law on public sector activity, and a burgeoning regulatory apparatus to protect the public interest from private ones. For some, notably the critics of interest-group pluralism, the overlay was inadequate to the task. Nevertheless, the resulting partisan alignments, at least in the Anglo-American experience, were basically contests over the hegemony of one sector over the other (Jacobs, 1997). In this context, the movement for privatization in the 1980s endorsed the existence of a clear boundary separating the two sectors by contesting the division of responsibility between them. The partnership idea represents a different set of conceptual premises altogether.

FROM PRIVATIZATION TO PARTNERSHIP

According to its proponents, partnerships (among other things) require actors from each sector to adopt characteristics and points of view that once defined and stabilized the identities of their counterparts. Government actors would need to think and behave like entrepreneurs, and business actors would need to embrace public interest considerations and expect greater public accountability. Here, the elaborate demarcations that defined roles and set the rules of engagement between business and government since the Progressive Era are, in large part, elided, removing the impetus for the adversarial character of their interactions. Moreover, the legal doctrine that professionalized the civil service in western liberal regimes and institutionalized public accountability through administrative procedure is being altered in certain states to support partnering arrangements. In Italy, for example, civil service reforms are eliminating many of the features of public sector careers that distinguished them from private sector employment (Supiot, 1996). Rulemaking procedures, once at the heart of command-and-control regulation in the United States, have been amended to center on negotiation among stakeholders (Negotiated Rulemaking Act, 1990). In short, the ground appears to have shifted under the postwar contest between the liberal state and its free-market opponents. Rapprochement of a sort lurks behind the partnership rhetoric.

More generally, the points of reference defining the binary separation of public from private, in welfare economics and liberal political doctrine alike, have been confounded by complex, variegated views of multiple sectors, including civil, intimate and dialogical realms, anchored to distinctive notions of social relations and political order. Use of the terms, public and private, now suggests any of a variety of social differentiations, not all of which translate into bipolar struggles for hegemony (Weintraub, 1997). To say that partnerships are yet another antiliberal effort to shrink the state by privatizing its functions is to misconstrue the significance of the partnership idea. First, figuratively stretching one sector by shrinking the other simply no longer applies (if it ever did) because the meaning of the sectors themselves is shifting (Feigenbaum, Hamnett, & Henig, 1998). Second, partnership advocates talk of new roles and innovative tools for the public manager, leveraging private capital for policy initiatives. The earlier privatization rhetoric of inefficient government and wasteful programs has largely faded from view, although its partisans remain active (Jack, Phillips, & The Robert Phillips Group, 1993). Part of the enthusiasm surrounding the rebirth of the partnership notion reflects a sense of new possibilities and changing alignments. As I will argue later, this sense reflects, albeit unconsciously, larger changes in the ideological, as well as the conceptual, landscape of governance.

The drive for privatization as a programmatic movement is typically attributed to free-market advocates and conservative politicians, joined in common cause against the liberal welfare state (Starr, 1988). Partnerships arise as a derivative reform in areas where full privatization seems less tractable, perhaps due to technical problems attending the assignment of property rights. If statist responsibilities must extend to certain goods and services, so the logic goes, then the delivery should be through business-mediated arrangements. Complications set in, however, once these ideologies are considered in detail. Part of the force behind privatization came from its status as a portmanteau idea, bringing together pragmatic reformers and ideologues of different stripes. As we unpack the various lines of reasoning among the constituent ideologies, we find distinctive commitments that partnerships are intended to embody. The more prominent among these ideologies draw upon neoconservative and neoliberal ideas. These will be explored as sources of meaning attached to partnerships. Consequently, the concept of the partnership itself will appear protean, making it less amenable to simple technical or programmatic definition.

Besides the loss of sector boundaries and its accompanying logic, and the ideological splits along new fault lines, the third influence on the rhetoric and significance of the P-P partnership comes from the advocates of management reform. They are providing the operational details and organizational processes for altering traditional governance in fundamental ways. The scope of these initiatives rivals the postwar efforts to reform the civil service. The Public Service Ministry in Britain refers to the partnership idea as central to the New Public Management, perhaps to distance itself from the ill-fated Tory experiment in quasi-autonomous governmental organizations (i.e., quangos; British Council, 1997). In the United States, the reform campaign underway is to reengineer government; the premises and rhetoric can be found in the promotional material of major management consultancies (Reijniers, 1994; Jack et al., 1993; Apen, Benicewicz, & Laia, 1994). Again, governmental and business organizations appear alike in their need to adapt to a global economy, new communications technologies, and growing client pressure for quality. The prescriptions are largely the same, flexible structure, results-oriented processes, and a client-service ethic (Canadian Council for Public-Private Partnerships, 1996; National Council for Public-Private Partnership, 1997). Partnering then becomes a vehicle for jointly overcoming the few remaining insoluble differences. Once we add an ideological backdrop, however, these forward-looking reforms appear less prescient and more instrumental and opportunistic.

My argument so far links the contemporary renewal of the partnership idea to three kinds of changes. At the most abstract level, there has been extensive theoretical work critically elaborating on, and extending the complexity of, the traditional binary division of sectors into public and private on economistic grounds. This thinking opens up public discourse on distinctive institutional realms and stimulates new ideas about social orderings. In effect, the old compartmentalization of public and private loses its natural appearance and assumes the features of an outmoded artifact of an earlier era (Wolfe, 1997). At a lower level of abstraction comes the influence of political values and commitments that animate contemporary ideological cleavages, at least among liberal constitutional regimes bordering the North Atlantic. The ascendancy of conservative leadership in these regimes throughout the 1980s added status and practical experience to their doctrinal base (Giddens, 1994). These, together with official responsibilities and error, helped splinter the movement into factions but, at the same time, multiplied the plausible alternatives to Progressive-era ideals and to the centrist methods of the postwar welfare state. Finally, at a pragmatic level, trends in management reform by the early 1990s had turned away from leadership and behavioral principles and toward more structural emphases on flexibility and innovation—reinforcing partnership ideals (Reijniers, 1994).

THE MULTIPLE MEANINGS OF PARTNERSHIP

With these contextual features in place, we can now attempt to sort out the welter of meanings that P-P partnership assumes in contemporary discussions. As the title suggests, a form of deconstruction is adopted here to unpack the various meanings of the term and expose at least some of their underlying premises and ideological commitments to critical scrutiny. A deconstructive strategy was implicit in the preceding argument's attention to contexts—conceptual, ideological, and pragmatic—to clarify the production of meaning. My intent in the remainder of the piece, however, is much more modest than a full-blown poststructuralist analysis would admit. I prefer to rely on discursive uses of the term by certain actors rather than on narrative images and stories that evoke the term, because my interest inclines more toward political ideas and policy tools than to representational strategies. Likewise, claims about partnership will receive attention rather than partnership practices, because, at this point at least, I am more interested in conceptual clarification than in the workings of power or patterns of exclusion that partnerships may entail (see Handler, 1996). Finally, my efforts at clarification will not extend much beyond the level of value commitments. Questions of ontology and metaphysical pedigree are left for another time.

To map the discursive terrain, we must first identify some landmark usages that can serve as reference points, and then orient them relative to several fixed ideological projections. The meaning of each usage, not to strain the metaphor too much, comes from clarifying its location relative to other usages and knowing its ideological bearings. For the term, P-P partnership, as a policy device, there are at least six distinct usages that can serve as reference points. These are not mutually exclusive, definitional categories that might serve some taxonomic purpose, but rather are simple meanings attached to the use of the term by certain actors in making claims for its application or adoption. The next step is to orient these relative to several ideologies and identify their most likely attachments.

THE IDEOLOGICAL REFERENTS

The two ideologies represented here both have *neo* prefixes, indicating a self-conscious split from their respective, institutionalized forms that have been well elaborated in the western political experience. Perhaps with a touch of irony, both neos are reversions to centuries older and, in their view, purer forms. Neoliberalism defines itself in opposition to, what it calls, welfare-state liberalism, the liberalism of the postwar European labor parties and New Deal democrats. Although aligned philosophically with Lockean individualism, it appears indebted to Scottish enlightenment notions (due to Smith and Hume) of moral regeneration through ownership and market exchange. Its faith in the spontaneous social coordination fostered by market incentives owes much to Hayek. Yet, it is distinguished from contemporary libertarianism by its apparent commitment to progress—material and technological—and a Deweyian pragmatist's sense of agency.

This sense of agency draws, not so much on the perfectibility notions espoused by the radical left and right, as on faith in human ingenuity and its role in social betterment. Although hardly collectivist and understandably wary of paternalism, neoliberalism bears an intriguing resemblance to the liberalism that Crowley (1987) found in the Progressive Era work of the Webbs, which was typically consigned to the ranks of utopian socialists. Progress, for the Webbs, depended upon innovation, and innovation would come from social experimentation. The neoliberals would agree that social change could be engineered through organizational means, but would prefer Hayek's entrepreneur in the marketplace to Beatrice Webb's industrial planner. Still, both see the devising of novel organizational mechanisms, not community solidarity, civic virtue, or individual training, as the key to progress. And both, in varying degrees of course, turn to government as the sponsor or referee.

The second ideology is neoconservatism, formed in part out of disaffection with the anticapitalist sentiments and religiosity of traditional conservatism. Although the neo view of conservatism shares Burkean roots with its parent, it represents an odd amalgam of deference to the sedimented knowledge that tradition conveys, with a Lockean liberal's faith in self-reliance and commerce as guarantors of human freedom. In doctrinal terms, this translates into an effort to strengthen the local cultural institutions that inculcate traditional values—the family, community churches, and civic associations—while opposing concentrations of power (economic or political) that undermine these values or the social order they reproduce. The liberal welfare state, in its substitution of entitlement for desert, of legalism for virtue, and of paternalism for self-initiative, effectively erodes the cultural basis of social order. Likewise, the mass marketing of large corporations to promote limitless consumption substitutes immediate gratification for self-restraint, celebrity lifestyles for prudent ways of living, and possessive egoism for community service. To be sure, either the state or the corporation can be an ally, should it choose to promote the appropriate cultural attachments and institutions or simply choose to withdraw its substitutions.

Both neo ideologies are typically lumped together under the banner of the New Right, as espousing traditional values and free markets. Ironically, the two claims are contradictory. In historical terms, the market, if anything, has been a de-traditionalizing force, advancing social change, not stability. Participants in unfettered exchanges in the global marketplace are likely to be exposed to sentiments and practices that prove corrosive to their values. Moreover, the sovereign consumer seeking to satisfy her appetites behaves quite differently than the citizen fulfilling community obligations. We expect the consumer to look outward for opportunities and price signals, and the citizen to look inward to a moral compass pointing the way. There is no guarantee that the two views will coincide. The New Right's formulation pits virtue against appetite and trusts that the former will triumph. In this context, the market can only make things tougher.

Certainly, one aspect of modernity is a belief that the self can be both citizen and consumer, that we adapt to complexity and social differentiation by proliferating ourselves to suit our social roles. Liberalism in the modern era offers two other solutions that complement this. First, moral sentiments can be fashioned from tastes rather than from virtues, deftly removing one side of the contradiction. This was Bentham's gift to the modern self. Second, social life can be divided into separate domains, a private one for money and consumption and a public one for power and citizenship; we appear to owe the genesis of this separation to natural law theories of contract (Gobetti, 1997). The New Right takes comfort in neither solution.

To simplify, neoconservatives split with neoliberals over which side of the traditional-values/free-markets contradiction they are willing to entrust with the task of securing a stable social order. Again, neoliberals side with Hayek and the invisible hand; neoconservatives prefer to rely on Berger's mediating institutions. Contrasting views about the role of the state follow. Collective activity, planned and undertaken by the state, appears to be the antithesis of the private orderings of the market; accordingly, neoliberals presume that it typically interferes (the exception occurs when the state acts to prop-up a failing market or to police market agreements). Similarly, to the extent that state transactions fail to mimic market ones, they are presumed to be inefficient. For neoconservatives, the state has a legitimate role to play in the acculturation of its citizens. The problem with the welfare state is not that it tried to instill a regime of social discipline on the needy, but rather that it was inadequate to the task. Other institutions, especially local ones, in their view, are more suitable and competent. The problem with the state is that it is overextended and it tries to do too much, and consequently, it does not do many things well. Neoliberals want to privatize the state because it is intrinsically inefficient. Neoconservatives want to privatize because the state is perpetually overburdened and underdisciplined; it can control neither its giveaways to the undeserving, nor its appetite for more tax dollars.

SIX OF THE MEANINGS

Partnerships have been viewed as a retreat from the hard-line advocacy of privatization. From this perspective, they serve a strategic purpose, enlisting the support of more moderate elements that are less opposed to state action on principle. Partnerships are accommodationist; they hold back the specter of wholesale divestiture and, in exchange, promise lucrative collaboration with the state.

Unfortunately, this picture assumes that everyone sees partnerships in the same way—as a political tool—and that fear of privatization brings the state and its supporters to partner with the privatizers and their beneficiaries, whose successes of late have dwindled. Yet, once we deconstruct the partnership idea, attending to the discursive claims made on its behalf and to the premises that support them, the meanings proliferate. They convey not just strategic aims but normative ones as well.

There are at least six distinctive uses of the term, P-P partnership. Each use makes a claim about what partnerships are and conveys an understanding of their intended purpose and significance. Moreover, each use invokes certain premises about what the relevant problems are to be solved and how best to solve them. The premises of interest here are the ideological ones that form a coherent but largely unassailable set of beliefs and commitments. All six meanings, in my view, can be plausibly related to either neoliberal or neoconservative ideologies. This, of course, matters much more to those would-be supporters of partnerships, who take serious issue with these ideological premises, than it would to their ideological kindred. For those skeptical of partnerships, the discussion to follow may clarify the grounds for their skepticism.

1. P-P partnership as management reform. Partnerships, in this instance, are severed from their historical roots in community voluntarism and urban economic development and linked instead to the privatization movement's quest for efficiency gains. Accordingly, neither of these other roots will be explicitly treated here. (In fact, the link to voluntarism in the United States is quite complex; it typically evokes either traditionally conservative service obligations on the Right, e.g., the Junior League, or progressive ideals of citizen activism, e.g., Volunteers in Service to America, and not-for-profit community projects on the Left.) Nevertheless, as a management reform, partnerships are promoted as an innovative tool that will change the way government functions, largely by tapping into the discipline of the market. To do this, managers of government programs must formally enlist the collaboration of profit-seeking firms that (presumably) already enjoy the benefits of such discipline.

The collaboration, however, resembles more of a mentoring relationship than a joint undertaking. The flow of know-how appears asymmetric. Government managers are expected to become more like their business counterparts, than vice versa. This implies that business managers, at some earlier time, were reformed themselves, perhaps chastened by the fires of free-market competition or educated by management consultants in the ways of cost-efficiency and quality improvement. Government managers, in contrast, are taken to have grown flabby without competitive pressures and to be mired in the inefficiencies of red tape and bureaucratic organization. Such overstatement is typical of the rhetoric of the Reason Foundation, Coopers and Lybrand, or the Canadian Center for Management Development (Apen et al., 1994; Rodal & Wright, 1997; Gratias &

Boyd, 1995). The conduct of the promotion itself follows the regimen of the management consultancy. The National Council for Public-Private Partnerships (1997) in the United States and the Canadian Council for Public-Private Partnerships (1996) both have official government sanction (the former displays President Clinton's photograph in its materials). There are networks of prospects awaiting partners, databases of experienced exemplars, corporate underwriters, fee-for-service consultations, a speakers bureau, workshops, conventions, and of course, membership fees.

The imperatives for transforming government agencies to resemble profit-seeking businesses come from the hard lessons learned by firms that had their profits squeezed by more intensive competition, rapidly changing markets, and more demanding customers. The core presumption is that the skills needed to find new markets, enhance productivity, and stay ahead of the competition can also improve the way government works. Partnerships are viewed as the best vehicle for accomplishing this. Government managers learn by emulating their partners, as they adapt to the rigors of competition. If successful, they will become more entrepreneurial and flexible, occupied with deal making and attracting capital rather than with administrative procedure. The premises of this construction are prototypically neoliberal. The market stands as the superior source of production and service efficiencies, and its competitive character stimulates innovation and creative problem solving. Rather than divesting government altogether, however, its culture and operations can be changed with the right kind of intervention. Partnership, as management reform, is meant to serve this purpose.

2. P-P partnership as problem conversion. A variation on the management reform, partnerships are viewed from this perspective, not as a tool for changing managerial practices, but rather as a universal fix for most problems attending public service delivery. The task for government managers shifts from getting their own practices in line with entrepreneurial mores to reframing the problems they face in a way that will attract profit-seeking collaborators. In other words, commercialize problems to bait the marketplace. Here, the manager's duty is not to reform herself or himself but to induce others, wise to the ways of the market, to perform government's tasks for less money. The intent of the United Nations Development Program for the Urban Environment (1996), for example, is to accelerate private sector involvement by creating business opportunities out of gaps in infrastructure. Private firms bring their know-how and their capital. Government eases the regulatory and tax burdens and may add funds. The public gets its roads and water treatment. What distinguishes this venture from the machine politics of a century ago, in part at least, is the promoter's apparent obliviousness to the temptations of kickbacks and patronage. Will prospective partners be judged on noncommercial grounds? Where there is substantial money to be made, commercializing public problems can raise special difficulties with oversight. The other major difference comes from the partnering mechanism replacing the standard procurement-by-contract with some kind of joint-investment arrangement.

This commercialization idea bears some resemblance to the European Union's effort to attract private capital for a TransEuropean road network (Kinnock, 1998). The distinction between them becomes obvious only at the level of their premises. The European Union wants to supplement public funds to add projects that would otherwise not be affordable; it plans to take on partners, as it needs them, either for their expertise or for their capital. Nonetheless, government managers remain in charge. There is no effort to alter their public service ethic, or to change the way they manage. Instead, there is official sanction given for opportunistic partnerships as a supplemental tool for the financial management of complex, large-scale projects. In contrast, the United Nations depicts partnerships as the principal means of obtaining sustainable development in urban areas. Sustainability, in this context, appears to coincide with commercial viability; one must attract enough businesses that are not only willing to stay put, but able to shoulder the costs of infrastructure development largely on their own. Here, the government manager assumes the role of investment broker, putting deals together and attracting entrepreneurs and private capital to cooperative ventures on a project-by-project basis. Again, neoliberalism inspires confidence in the capital markets and enthusiastically propels the government manager beyond the bounds of contracting for services and into the promotion of private business growth and equity-based commercial transactions.

3. P-P partnership as moral regeneration. Each of the foregoing usages depicts partnership as a vehicle for bringing government closer to the market, either as a deal maker or as a pseudoentrepreneur. In both instances, competitive market exchanges appear as a model deserving emulation. The neoliberal's faith in the superiority of market-mediated relations helps reinforce whatever other influences are at work driving government to embrace market incentives. Similarly, it takes a neoliberal's sense of agency, holding that change for the better can be engineered through properly organized efforts, to inspire the confidence in partnership arrangements displayed here. Neoconservatives, in contrast, are more likely to view partnerships as a middle ground between public and private, rather than as a comprehensive tool for remaking government in the market's image.

A more subtle distinction becomes apparent when we consider the effects that partnerships are intended to have on the people involved. Performance aside, there are certain features of government provision that convey official sanction, desert, entitlement, or worth that are largely absent from anonymous market exchanges, mediated by money rather than eligibility. In rejecting government for some forms of the public's business, the neoliberal is implicitly also taking exception to the noncommercial differentiations that government programs rely upon. These are thought to have a corrosive influence on those served, as well as on those doing the serving. Of course, the opportunity costs of (unreformed) government programs and their tax implications are always a prominent concern. And yet, consider the efforts of the Clinton Administration to link welfare to work. Without work, the argument goes, welfare cultivates dependency and, at the same time, generates bureaucratic waste. Part of the impetus behind welfare reform can be found behind management reform. Commercial bases for doing the public's business are less fraught with moral judgments and are thus less corrosive to the human spirit. Hence, getting government managers involved as market participants, say through partnering arrangements, should have a salutary moral effect on them as well.

Taking this a step further, it is not just the relief of moving away from the effects of government service programs that matters to the neoliberal, it is the movement toward market-inspired traits of character. Self-reliance, initiative, hard work, integrity, prudence, and so on, all of which are familiar from Weber's characterization of the protestant ethic, are all thought to accompany participation in property holding and commercial enterprise. When Prime Minister Thatcher denationalized British utilities, shares were sold below par value with the intent of giving as many people as possible a chance for ownership. The idea was not to liberalize the industries (the regulatory regime remained in place), but to give the public a direct stake in an important national enterprise (and to raise some cash) (Starr, 1988). Like property ownership, partnerships accomplish this moral purpose in a way that direct privatization would not have. Government managers are drawn into entrepreneurial activities via partnerships that strengthen their characters and stimulate their creative problem-solving skills.

The interesting irony here is that although neoconservatives promote virtue and wish to nurture the institutions that do so, neoliberals are the ones who find virtues in the market. Character is built through self-initiative and entrepreneurship, that is, through market experience. The place of other institutions is less central. For the neoconservative, on the other hand, the market offers expression to certain values but cannot be their principal source.

For the three usages that follow, the tone and perspective shifts subtly. In place of the neoliberal's commitment to the market as the wellspring of social order, we have the neoconservative's more reserved endorsement of market incentives as a partial means of devolving and decentralizing public sector responsibilities.

4. P-P partnership as risk shifting. The usage here portrays partnering as a means of responding to fiscal stringency on the part of the government. The program's advocates are typically speaking from official positions within government and express concerns about leveraging public capital for infrastructure and other capital-intensive projects. From the government's perspective, the partnership arrangements are a means of getting private interests to sign on, and they promise profit potential for doing so. The British Treasury's Private Finance Initiative (1997) encourages government managers to refashion property-rights assignments to attract private capital to shoulder start-up costs. Through special lease-purchase arrangements, private investors assume the financial risks of ownership, once the projects are complete. The rhetoric in this instance is similar to that coming out of the European Union, as mentioned earlier. It follows the logic of load shedding but stops short of full privatization. In effect, government is exhorted to do more with less.

This usage fits squarely in neither one ideological camp nor the other, because we also find this kind of thinking in the New Deal liberal's support for funneling public money directly to cities for redevelopment partnerships with local developers and business interests. In the latter case, it represents a pragmatic coalitional strategy for ensuring sufficient support for these projects in business-dominated jurisdictions. In more colorful terms, it promises enough pork to go around. The neoconservative's construction, however, puts business on the check-writing side. When partnering works the way it is supposed to, business partners help bring fiscal restraint to these projects and insure their financial viability. Certainly, reinforcing the support that business traditionally offers conservative parties may play a role in the push for partnering. Nevertheless, the idea of heightened vigilance over public investments squares with the neoconservative's efforts more generally to restrain government spending, especially for service programs, and to scale back its service commitments.

On the surface, there are obvious parallels between risk shifting and problem conversion, both of which are depicted here as separate meanings assigned to partnership. The two meanings appear to differ more in degree than in kind; risk shifting might be seen as a prelude to more elaborate efforts to transform a public problem wholly into a private one. Nonetheless, as our deconstruction shows, their ideological premises differ. The rhetoric of problem conversion valorizes commercial activity and market discipline, placing government in a supporting, subordinate role. In contrast, risk shifting assigns the supporting role, not to government, but to commercial interests. Furthermore, the exhortation is for business to join in cooperative ventures of some sort to leverage government's resources, not displace them. The purposes remain public, even though the resources are eventually mixed.

5. P-P partnership as restructuring public service. Part of the neoconservative's objection to government reflects concerns about its growth. Recent thinking about the engines of this growth continues to owe a debt to Lowi (1979) for singling out interest-group liberalism as the culprit. In his scenario, government agencies are set upon by legions of interests demanding money and services. The agencies respond, having been given (in error) the discretion and authority to do so. The regrettable result is government out of control, overburdened and overextended. The two putative solutions are to take the discretion away (Lowi's) or to devolve the responsibilities to other levels of government more used to saying no. Several decades later, we have two unintended consequences of these fixes. First, the administrative procedures intended to structure agencies' discretion have restricted their ability to adapt to changing circumstances. Second, those local agencies, expected to say no, have been less able to cope with demands from the inside. Public sector employees in the United States have unionized in record numbers. Partnerships can address both.

In theory, partnerships can not only relieve projects of some of the weight of administrative procedures, at least on the private partners' side, they can also move from a public to a private workforce, one that is disciplined by the labor market. In conventional labor-management relations, the management's efforts to shift work outside a unionized plant to nonunion employees (also called outsourcing) is reason enough to strike. For public employees who are typically prohibited from striking in the United States, the recourse is less clear. Partnerships can serve as a means for effectively deregulating employment relations through the substitution of unorganized workers (Supiot, 1996). The approach of labor and liberal governments might well be the reverse. Partnerships could also be used to control labor standards via formal agreements on wages, as well as noncommercial features, such as gender and racial discrimination. This has been a recent trend in international trade agreements and contracting in some large cities. In this case, partnerships appear to provide a vehicle that can move in either direction.

6. P-P partnership as power sharing. Although privatization has been promoted by some as empowerment because it devolves control vertically downward toward the consumer, partnerships, according to this sixth usage, spread control horizontally, especially in regulatory matters where control has been concentrated in the government. Partnerships as power sharing can alter business-government relations in fundamental ways. First, an ethos of cooperation and trust replaces the adversarial relations endemic to command-and-control regulation (Ghere, 1996). Second, any relationship between partners will involve some mutually beneficial sharing of responsibility, knowledge, or risk. In most instances, each party brings something of value to the others to be invested or exchanged. Third, there is an expectation of give-and-take between the partners, negotiating differences that were otherwise litigated. For the neoconservative, power sharing can take the teeth out of regulation, making it less rigid, punitive, and arbitrary. Although the neoconservatives are not opposed to the government using force and coercion to preserve order, using coercion to force firms to change the way they make their business decisions is objectionable. The neoliberal typically goes further and supports commercialization of environmental problems, as opposed to the liberalization of compliance schedules and control requirements.

What kinds of control are shared in practice is another matter. The U.S. Environmental Protection Agency (EPA; 1998a, 1998b) operates extensive partnership programs for each of its major areas of responsibility. Some are promotions to provide technical assistance for recycling or waste disposal on a voluntary basis. Others enlist firms in programs that promise reductions in reporting and control requirements for those willing to demonstrate higher abatement levels and share their control strategies with their competitors. The market lure is cost savings, technical assistance, and flexibility in monitoring and enforcement. The agency, on the other hand, gains an opportunity for intensive social marketing, roughly analogous to the Salvation Army's exchange of soup for sermons. Here, the partnership falls under the rubric of reengineering government, stimulating innovation and cost savings. Nevertheless, regulatory control in EPA's case seems to be parceled out very sparsely and only to trusted firms. This seems to have little to do with the neoconservative's preference for loosening regulatory controls. As with the usage of partnerships as restructuring public sector employment, the power sharing idea can harbor a liberal's intent behind its neoconservative face.

TWO REMAINDERS

The grammar of meanings that has structured my treatment of partnerships assumes six distinct, but sometimes overlapping, ways of understanding and talking about partnering. Each of these six ways, in turn, depends upon a set of normative premises that have been linked to one of two major neo ideologies. Although many more ideologies are influential in the industrialized West, these two continue to play a central role in provoking and inspiring the reform of the welfare state before the century's end. There are, however, two significant remainders—meanings excluded from our grammar. Both entail very different takes on partnering. One connects it with traditional modes of not-for-profit collaboration, and the other treats it as simply a new face on conventional forms of privatization. A brief consideration of these remainders follows.

The grammar of partnerships fashioned in previous sections has purposely excluded the variety of day-to-day, public-spirited partnerships that have gone on in various localities for years, often with progressive intent. Partnerships among nonprofit organizations, schools, churches, and civic organizations, for example, often fill gaps in the social service safety net left by fiscal austerity and neoliberal thinking about government. Not-for-profit service organizations may partner with advocacy groups and local government to serve the needs of certain neighborhoods or vulnerable groups. Money may be raised locally, contributed by fund-raising organizations, such as the United Way, or charitable foundations; in the United States, this is indirectly subsidized by the tax code. These classes of service partnerships deserve their own deconstructive treatment for several reasons.

First, unlike the P-P partnerships discussed above, these *public-public* or *private-private* partnerships may have historical roots in their communities that extend across generations. In effect, they are woven into the fabric of civic life and may not easily be distinguished from the communities that they serve. Second, the ideologies that they are premised upon represent very different traditions in public thinking from the ones treated here. The rhetoric of these partnerships is typically a moral one tied to meeting communal needs. Finally, the absence of profit motives among the participants changes the dynamics of the partnership itself—who participates and why—as well as the bases of cooperation.

Among these local institutions, rights-based liberalism or communitarian notions direct objectives away from commercial interests and profit seeking, and toward service ideals and civic responsibilities. Traditional conservatism may play a role in directing aims, as in some organizations based on religious affiliation or upper-class voluntarism. From across the ideological spectrum, social democratic ideology may appear in grassroots organizations, partnering in coalitions to oppose for-profit corporate projects or practices. In either instance, opposition to a legitimate government presence or advocacy of market solutions—the core of our neo ideologies—play a negligible role.

The second remainder omitted from our grammar consists of those treatments that construct partnerships as a rubric to cover most ongoing forms of privatization. Here, the term seems to function as a euphemism for privatizing the functions of government without assailing its legitimacy. Attention to partnerships between government and for-profit firms, in North America at least, has intensified over the last decade, on the heels of the privatization campaigns of the 1980s. The central messages of these campaigns, their open animosity toward government and strident assurances of superior service and no waste, have been tempered somewhat in the promotional literature that disguises privatization as partnering. Hence, partnering appears as privatization's logical successor, but a more refined and domesticated version, perhaps one better adapted to the less doctrinaire 1990s. Partnerships in this genre seem to offer a more palatable, less prickly, form of packaging around the contents of a government's shifting functions to commercial enterprises.

The more circumspect academic pieces that attempt to assess the performance of contemporary partnerships as a policy tool can easily be caught up in this symbolic succession. Accordingly, partnering, in this literature, is distinct from privatization in name only. Further, what passes for partnerships, because of the term's connotation of cooperativeness and its reformist cachet, can extend from indirect subsidies to traditional procurement contracting. Lost to these treatments is the basic idea that partnering, in some of its guises, can represent a fundamental departure in the post-Cold War relationship between public and private sectors. This idea is the premise behind the grammar of multiple meanings presented here.

REFERENCES

Apen, P. G., Benicewicz, B. C., & Laia, J. R. (1994). A new model for public-private partnerships. *Technology in Society, 16*, 389-402.

British Council. (1997). Restructuring government. In *Issue 1: Law and governance* [On-line]. Available: http://www.britcoun.org/governance/briefing/iss1res.htm.

Canadian Council for Public-Private Partnerships. (1996). *About the council* [On-line]. Available: http://www.inforamp.net/~partners/index.html.

Canadian Heritage. (1996). *Partnership resource kit* [On-line]. Available: http://www.beyondgov. ca/kittoc.html.

Crowley, B. L. (1987). *The self, the individual, and the community: Liberalism in the political thought of F. A. Hayek and Sidney and Beatrice Webb.* Oxford, UK: Clarendon Press.

Environmental Protection Agency. (1998a). *Partners for the environment* [On-line]. Available: http://www.epa.gov/partners/.

Environmental Protection Agency. (1998b). *Review of the common sense initiative, executive summary* [On-line]. Available: http://www.epa.gov/epahome/.

Feigenbaum, H., Hamnett, C., & Henig, J. (1998). *Shrinking the state: The political underpinnings of privatization.* New York: Cambridge University Press.

Ghere, R. K. (1996). Aligning the ethics of public/private partnership: The issue of local economic development. *Journal of Public Administration Research and Theory, 6,* 599-621.

Giddens, A. (1994). *Beyond Left and Right: The future of radical politics.* Stanford, CA: Stanford University Press.

Gobetti, D. (1997). Humankind as a system: Private and public agency at the origins of modern liberalism. In J. Weintraub & K. Kumar (Eds.), *Public and private in thought and practice: Perspectives on a grand dichotomy* (pp. 103-132). Chicago: The University of Chicago Press.

Gratias, F.X.A., & Boyd, M. (1995). *Public/private partnerships: A tool to right-size government. Discussion notes.* [On-line]. Available: http://www.cyberus.ca/~ppp/ccmd.html.

Handler, J. F. (1996). *Down from bureaucracy: The ambiguity of privatization and empowerment.* Princeton, NJ: Princeton University Press.

Her Majesty's Treasury. (1997). *Private finance initiative* [On-line]. Available: http://www. treasury-projects-taskforce.gov.uk/contacts/pppp.htm.

Jack, M., Phillips, R., & The Robert Phillips Group. (1993). Public-private partnership organizations in health care: Cooperative strategies and models. *Hospital & Health Services Administration, 38,* 387-400.

Jacobs, B. (1997). Networks, partnerships and European Union Regional Economic Development Initiatives in the West Midlands. *Policy and Politics, 25,* 39-50.

Kettl, D. F. (1993). *Sharing power: Public governance and private markets.* Washington, DC: Brookings.

Kinnock, N. (1998). *Using public-private partnerships to develop transport infrastructure* [On-line]. Available: http://europa.eu.int/en/comm/dg07/speech/sp9837.htm.

Lowi, T. (1979). *The end of liberalism* (2nd ed.). New York: W. W. Norton.

National Council for Public-Private Partnership. (1997). *Partnership forum* [On-line]. Available: http://www.ncppp.org.

Negotiated Rulemaking Act of 1990, 5 U.S.C. § 561 *et seq.* (Lexis Law Publishing, 1999).

Reijniers, J.J.A.M. (1994). Organization of public-private partnership projects. *International Journal of Project Management, 12,* 137-142.

Rodal, A., & Wright, D. (1997). A dossier on partnerships. *Optimum, the Journal of Public Sector Management, 24,* 1-4.

Starr, P. (1988). The meaning of privatization. *Yale Law and Policy Review, 6,* 6-41.

Starr, P. (1990). The new life of the liberal state: Privatization and the restructuring of state-society relations. In J. Waterbury & E. Suleiman (Eds.), *Public enterprise and privatization* (pp. 22-54). Boulder, CO: Westview Press.

Stephenson, M. O., Jr. (1991). Whither the public-private partnership: A critical overview. *Urban Affairs Quarterly, 27,* 109-127.

Supiot, A. (1996). Work and the public/private dichotomy. *International Labour Review, 135,* 653-663.

United Nations Development Program for the Urban Environment. (1996). Program information. In *Public-private partnerships for the Urban Environment Program* [On-line]. Available: http://www.undp.org:81/undp/ppp/listserver/index.html.

Weintraub, J. (1997). The theory and politics of the public/private distinction. In J. Weintraub & K. Kumar (Eds.), *Public and private in thought and practice: Perspectives on a grand dichotomy* (pp. 1-42). Chicago: The University of Chicago Press.

Wolfe, A. (1997). Public and private in theory and practice: Some implications of an uncertain boundary. In J. Weintraub & K. Kumar (Eds.), *Public and private in thought and practice: Perspectives on a grand dichotomy* (pp. 182-203). Chicago: The University of Chicago Press.

3

Public-Private Technology Partnerships

Promises and Pitfalls

JOSEPH E. STIGLITZ
SCOTT J. WALLSTEN

The U.S. federal government has a long history of supporting private sector
R & D. Indeed, the Constitution gave Congress the right to grant patents to "promote the progress of science." Until recently, however, most federally funded
industrial R & D was directed at government needs, such as large weapons systems. Concerns about lagging U.S. productivity and increasing competition
from U.S. trading partners in the mid-1980s and the subsequent end of the Cold
War began to change the focus from government needs to government funding
of commercial R & D. The end of the Cold War posed a challenge. Previously,
Cold War research had funded a host of projects that eventually led to innumer-
able commercial projects of immense value. Although these projects were typically not undertaken to advance commercial technology, it was one of the clearly
beneficial byproducts. Indeed, popular support for federal research undertakings such as the space program was maintained, in part, by frequent references to
commercial spin-offs. With the end of the Cold War, the government began to
put even more emphasis on research leading to commercially viable outcomes.

In 1993, the newly-elected Clinton administration put technology—and public support of private R & D in particular—at the center of its economic agenda, stating that "government can play a key role in helping private firms develop and profit from innovations" (Clinton & Gore, 1993).

Many types of public-private technology partnerships have been implemented in the last decade. These range from direct public funding of industry-led R & D projects, to public funding of private research consortia, to collaborations at the national laboratories between industry and government scientists. All of these programs share the goal of generating research that yields commercial products and innovations. The economic justification for these programs is clear. Theory predicts, and many empirical studies confirm, that profit-maximizing firms invest less than the socially optimal level of R & D. Government support of private R & D can help rectify this market failure. Sound theory does not always translate easily into sound policies. These programs must overcome enormous technical and political challenges if they are to succeed. Indeed, preliminary evidence on the effectiveness of these programs is mixed, at best.

In this paper, we first discuss the theory behind government support of R & D in general, and government support of industrial R & D in particular. We then discuss the rise of public-private technology partnerships over the past decade. Next, we consider the types of research projects these programs must fund if they are to be successful and the obstacles they face in achieving this goal. After the theoretical discussion, we highlight the largest and most prominent of these programs. This section also discusses the available evidence on the effectiveness of these programs. Finally, we conclude with policy recommendations, recognizing that these programs have potential, but that they also must overcome significant hurdles in order to be successful.

WHY DOES GOVERNMENT FUND R & D?

Investments in R & D are crucial for economic growth, accounting for at least half of all increases in per capita output (Griliches, 1992). In fiscal year (FY) 1997, the United States spent about $205 billion on R & D. Industry provides the majority of R & D funds—approximately $133 billion in FY 1997. The federal government provides most of the remainder—about $67 billion in FY 1997, almost $20 billion of which went to industry. Table 1 provides a breakdown of U.S. R & D spending by performer and source of funds. Industry funds the majority of product-related research (i.e., applied R & D) whereas government funds the majority of fundamental (i.e., basic) research. Although much federal R & D is for specific government needs, government funding is crucial to economic growth because market failures cause firms, which act in their own best interests, to underinvest in R & D from society's perspective.

TABLE 1: Source and Performers of R & D in the United States, 1997 (all figures in millions of dollars)

	Source of Funds					
Performer	Federal Government	Industry	Universities and Colleges	Other Nonprofits	Nonfederal Government	Total
Government	16,450					16,450
Industry	20,787	130,631				151,418
Universities and colleges	14,285	1,710	4,457	1,759	1,821	24,031
Other nonprofits	2,900	967		1,653		5,520
Industry FFRDCs[a]	2,273					2,273
U & C FFRDCs[ab]	5,405					5,405
Nonprofit FFRDCs[a]	644					644
Total	62,744	133,308	4,457	3,412	1,821	205,742

SOURCE: National Science Foundation, 1998.
NOTE: Figures are preliminary estimates.
a. FFRDCs: Federally-funded R & D centers.
b. U & C: University and college.

THE PRIVATE SECTOR INVESTS TOO LITTLE IN R & D FROM SOCIETY'S PERSPECTIVE

Investments in R & D have very high returns and are a key component to economic growth. Under different assumptions, economic theory can explain why firms may underinvest or overinvest in R & D.[1] Empirical research, however, demonstrates that the private sector invests less than the optimal level in R & D. Jones and Williams (1997) estimate that actual total R & D spending in the economy is less than one quarter the optimal level. Underinvestment occurs because firms cannot appropriate all the returns to their R & D investments and because capital market imperfections may make financing R & D more expensive than other investments.

From the firm's perspective, R & D is like any other investment. The firm invests in R & D until the expected risk-adjusted private returns of the last research project equals its costs. Average returns on R & D to the firm are high—20% to 30%, on average—but the returns to society are even higher—often 50% or more.[2] These R & D spillovers occur as others use research results and extend them in directions the original innovator often could not have imagined. Spillovers mean that an innovator is compensated for only a fraction of the total returns on R & D. As a result, firms invest less in R & D than they would if they reaped all the rewards to their investments. In other words, some research projects that would yield positive net total benefits (i.e., the sum of private and social benefits less the project costs) are privately unprofitable because the investor does not see the social returns.[3] Without some intervention in the market, the private sector will not undertake these research projects, although it is in society's interest for them to do so.

In addition to investing in less R & D than society would like, firms may invest less than they want if they do not have sufficient access to capital for R & D. Capital market failures could arise if an innovator is reluctant or unable to provide financiers with enough information to evaluate a research project for fear of revealing too much about the proposed idea. Moreover, R & D cannot be collateralized, unlike investments in machines or buildings. Firms may therefore be forced to pay higher rates of interest on loans for R & D than charged borrowers financing other, collateralizable forms of investment, or they may have to rely more extensively on internal funds (see Hall, 1992; Himmelberg & Petersen, 1994). Because funds are fungible, firms with sufficient internal cash flow can, of course, resort to those funds for research, using collateral to finance investments in plant and equipment. The fact of the matter is that many high tech firms would like to invest more in research than they can finance through cash flow and collateralized loans. Schumpeter (1939) called attention to these constraints long ago. The evidence of the impact of changes in cash flow on R & D investment, however, must be interpreted with caution, because events that adversely affect cash flow may also adversely affect the firm's net worth and ability to bear risks (see, e.g., Greenwald, Salinger, & Stiglitz, 1991).

The fact that there is overall underinvestment in R & D does not mean that there may not be overinvestment in certain types of research. The most obvious example is alleged pharmaceutical research attempting to innovate around a patent. The objective of firms engaged in such research is not so much to produce a better drug (though that may be an unintended byproduct), but to divert the "monopoly rents" of an existing patent holder toward themselves. There can also be excessive expenditures in a patent race in which the marginal contribution—the earlier arrival of the innovation compared to when it would otherwise have arrived—may be small compared to the average return. This is a variant of the "common pool" problem. Some of the return represents the embodiment in the patent of commonly available knowledge.[4]

TRADITIONAL GOVERNMENT SUPPORT OF R & D

The existence of a market failure opens up the possibility that government can help mitigate the underinvestment problem. The government has traditionally used many tools to promote science and technology. Some methods, such as the patent system and research tax credits, are indirect. The patent system— enshrined in the Constitution and probably the oldest tool for promoting R & D—increases the potential profits from an innovation. Because an innovation is costly to develop but often inexpensive to duplicate, the patent system grants a temporary monopoly to an innovator. Temporary monopoly rights provide an incentive to invest in research by creating the potential to profit off an innovation before others can use it. Patents, however, entail a high social cost.

Knowledge is a public good in the sense that the marginal cost of an additional individual using that knowledge is zero. There is thus a trade-off between static inefficiency, associated with the underutilization of knowledge, and dynamic inefficiency, associated with the underproduction of knowledge. That is, once knowledge has been produced, it is inefficient to prevent others from using it, but if anyone can use it without cost, there will be little incentive to undertake the investments necessary to produce that knowledge. The rules for intellectual property rights attempt to strike a balance, for example, by choosing the length of the patent's life and the breadth of the discovery the patent covers.

Research tax credits—a much newer device, having been implemented in 1981—decrease the cost of doing research to the firm by giving the firm a tax credit for a portion of its R & D expenditures.[5] A credit provides an incentive to increase R & D investment by reducing the cost of any research project, making any given project potentially more profitable. The R & D tax credit is actually a credit on incremental expenditures. As such, its impact on the long-run level of expenditures might be expected to be more limited. There are also concerns about whether all expenditures qualifying for the incremental R & D tax credit really are research and development (e.g., should marketing research really qualify for the tax credit). The R & D credit, of course, does not attempt to distinguish between research that has a high level of spillovers and research that does not.

The government also directly funds R & D. As noted above, the government funds the majority of basic research, where market failures are presumably greatest. Much of government support for basic research goes to universities and colleges. Basic research is crucial for long-run growth and is a key ingredient in more applied R & D. Commercial products and innovations, however, are rarely the stimulus for basic research and often come years after the research is completed. For that reason, and because commercial applications of basic research are rarely obvious, firms have little incentive to fund basic research on their own. There is little disagreement that government must take the lead in funding basic research and training scientists (presumably because the total returns to society from their activities are in excess of the returns they appropriate).

Much of government-direct R & D funding goes to applied R & D in industry, although the extent to which government should support industrial R & D is more controversial. Traditionally, most of this funding has been to satisfy government objectives like space, defense, and, especially recently, health research directly. Although market failures may be less extreme in applied R & D than in basic research, they still exist. Even the most applied R & D is inherently risky and can generate large spillovers.

Government support of R & D has generally been successful in helping to mitigate the underinvestment problem. Each dollar in research tax credit appears to generate more than a dollar in private R & D spending (Hall, 1993). Direct government spending also seems to stimulate additional private spending on both basic and applied research (Hill, 1995; Levy & Terleckyj, 1983; Robson,

1993). Although most federal R & D was not intended to yield commercial products for civilian use, it would often spin off into commercial use. As the Council of Economic Advisers (1995) noted, in this manner the government "supported the development and diffusion of jet aircraft and engines, semiconductor microelectronics, computers and computer-controlled machine tools, pharmaceuticals and biotechnology, advanced energy and environmental technologies, advanced materials, and a host of other commercially successful technologies."

This system for supporting R & D worked well when national security concerns generated sufficient support for funding myriad types of R & D. The end of the Cold War, however, decreased the demand for defense research and made national security a less compelling reason to support R & D. In addition, in the mid-1980s, the slowdown in U.S. productivity growth and the increasing competitiveness of U.S. trading partners led to a belief that the federal government should do more to help firms transfer research results in the laboratory to products in the market. These conditions led to a new push for public-private partnerships intended to support commercial R & D. Much of the groundwork for these partnerships was laid in the 1980s. The Clinton administration seized on these ideas and expanded public-private commercial R & D partnerships greatly, making them the centerpiece of its technology program.

The next sections discuss the rise of these programs, the largest such public-private partnerships, and the promises and pitfalls associated with this new approach to funding R & D.

A NEW APPROACH: PUBLIC-PRIVATE TECHNOLOGY PARTNERSHIPS

Previously, we explained why some form of public support for research is desirable—without that support there will be underinvestment in R & D. There remains the question of what form that support should take. The concept of partnership has increasingly come into vogue. The concept suggests a relationship in which each partner is assigned specific responsibilities and given incentives and resources to fulfill those responsibilities. Partnerships work best when there are common shared objectives, but they may still be effective even when interests are disparate. When the partners have separate interests, however, more attention needs to be placed on the incentive-accountability structure. Public partnership policy is concerned with designing the terms of the partnership in ways that fulfill public objectives that are within the limits of available public resource constraints and that take into account private incentives and public political processes. The latter has received increasing attention. The government not only must have incentives to fulfill its commitments (responsibilities), but the public policy must be politically sustainable; that is, it must receive the necessary electoral support. (The problem of public commitment is especially important, because sovereign governments often cannot bind themselves with contracts in the same way that private parties, which rely on the government for contract enforcement, can).[6]

Partnerships in applied technology research generally take two forms. The first involves government funding of industrial R & D. The second involves government and industry scientists actually working together. The common theme of these two types of partnerships is promoting research, not necessarily to meet government objectives, but to help the private sector move research from the lab to the market. These programs are controversial. Proponents contend that they address a legitimate need—helping firms undertake research that is too risky or expensive for a firm to do by itself. Such research can lead to innovations that are net benefits to society, but would not have been profitable to the firm. Opponents contend that these programs result in government attempting to pick winners—second-guessing the market about which technologies will be successful.

Ironically, underlying the current drive for public-private partnerships is the widespread belief that government is not very effective in choosing good projects (i.e., picking winners) and managing research. The evidence for this perspective is far from clear. Certainly, government support and conduct (and dissemination) of agricultural and medical research is widely viewed as highly successful. Similarly, in the key area of telecommunications, government support has been vital, from the first telegraph line between Washington and Baltimore in 1842 to support of the Internet.

The close connection between firms that do research and firms that market gives some credibility to the view that the private sector may have a comparative advantage in the conduct of applied research. Today's technology partnership typically entails government support for research that is initiated and conducted primarily by the private sector. The point is that the rationale for government intervention is not that the government is better than the private sector at picking winners, but that there exist important spillovers, even for applied technology. The objective of the government is thus to identify winning projects that would be privately unprofitable but socially beneficial because of high spillovers.

Figure 1 can help us evaluate the effectiveness of a partnership. The figure shows the expected returns to research projects in two dimensions, social and private. The expected total returns to a project are the sum of the expected social and private returns. Government support can have several possible outcomes as follows:

- In some cases, government support goes to inframarginal projects—high return projects that would have been undertaken anyway (projects in Area C). In that case, the government support is just a transfer payment. It has no allocative effect (other than the distortions caused by raising the revenue).
- Some of the money may go to marginal projects (projects in Areas A and B—projects that firms will not undertake on their own). If the government cannot identify spillovers, then the subsidy causes firms to undertake some projects that are (at the margin) unproductive (i.e., projects in Area A, which have no positive spillovers), and also some projects that (at the margin) have a total return in excess of the

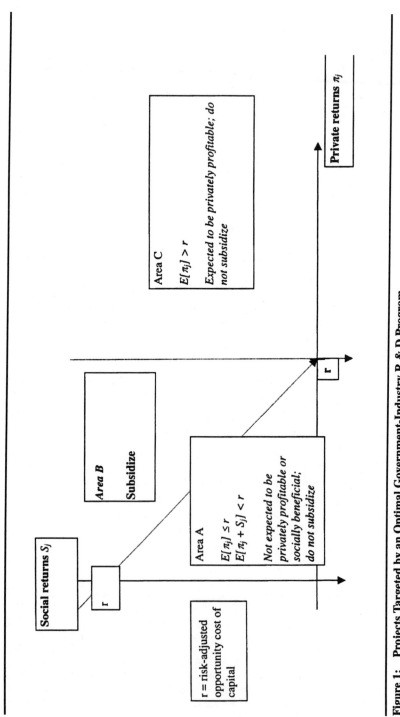

Figure 1:   Projects Targeted by an Optimal Government-Industry R & D Program

opportunity cost of capital and would not have otherwise been undertaken (i.e., projects in Area B). The net social benefit in this case is ambiguous.
- If the government is very effective in identifying projects with social returns not captured by the private sector (i.e., projects in Area B), then the support unambiguously increases economic efficiency.

There are further ambiguities in the effects of government support. If there were no spillovers, limited available resources (e.g., key research personnel) for research, and if the government were worse than the private sector in picking winners, then the government would distort the direction of research into less productive areas. On the other hand, the reward structure for government research managers or project selectors and those in the private sector may be markedly different. The private sector participates in the upside potential of research projects—when successful they can reap tremendous rewards. The upside potential for public officials, however, is far more limited. There is, not surprisingly, more of a culture of risk taking in the private sector than in the public, partly as a result of these reward structures. The consequence is not that the government is bad at picking winners, but that it places too much attention on picking projects that have a high probability of success, foregoing projects that have even higher expected returns, but have a lower probability of success. To the extent that this is true, and that there are limited resources for research, government research support may lower expected returns.

IMPLEMENTATION AND EVALUATION ISSUES

Consider again Figure 1. Recall that a government technology partnership program is more effective the better it can fund projects in Area B (projects with relatively high spillovers and low private returns). It is not clear how best to accomplish this goal. Most of these programs require industry to propose projects and the government to decide whether to subsidize them. Often, government subsidies are less expensive than capital from other sources, meaning that firms may be tempted to look to government before looking to other sources for financial support. In other words, there is no reason to believe that firms will propose only research projects in Area B (see Figure 1). Firms may be tempted to propose a project that falls anywhere in Figure 1 as long as they expect the subsidized project to be privately profitable. It is up to the government to determine which of these research projects would benefit society but would not be privately profitable without a subsidy. This means that government should not simply fund the best proposals it receives. Instead, it should fund the best among those that could not be funded elsewhere.[7]

Program managers who make funding decisions must reject not only projects of dubious scientific and technical merit, but also reject scientifically sound proposals that are very likely to yield commercial successes and therefore could be funded elsewhere. The obvious theoretical way to encourage this behavior is to build the proper incentives into these programs. Program managers should be rewarded for funding projects on the margin—those that are socially beneficial but would not be undertaken without a subsidy—and punished (or at least not rewarded) for funding inframarginal projects—those that firms would undertake without a subsidy.

In practice it is difficult to implement such a mechanism. First, observers must recognize that R & D is inherently risky, and any program that attempts to fund research projects that firms will not undertake will ultimately fund some projects that fail. Indeed, if the program funds only successful projects, it probably is not taking enough risks. But government-industry R & D programs—especially those aimed at commercialization—are controversial. Program supporters may be reluctant to allow many failures for fear that opponents will point to individual project failures as evidence of program failure. Likewise, managers may not feel comfortable rejecting the most promising proposals, either because they want to increase the chances of achieving commercial success or because it puts them in the position of rejecting proposals that are too good.

Second, the only way to implement an incentive mechanism of the sort mentioned above is to include a comprehensive evaluation mechanism as part of the program. That is, properly rewarding and punishing program managers is possible only if there is some way to detect what type of projects they fund. Evaluating technology programs is technically very difficult. A comprehensive evaluation would combine complicated scientific knowledge with economic analysis under conditions of uncertainty. In any event, as Adam Jaffe (1998) notes, technology programs have never been designed with economic evaluation in mind. Without some comprehensive evaluations, public debates on these programs tend to focus on easily measurable private returns and easily understandable anecdotal stories of project success and failure.

Even if the technical obstacles to conducting comprehensive evaluations can be overcome at a reasonable cost, political factors may decrease the likelihood that these programs can be implemented efficiently. The politics of technology spending are similar to those of other issues. Cohen and Noll (1991) point out that politicians face incentives to treat technology programs like they do any other government spending—as a way to reward constituents, not to correct market failures. Indeed, Cohen and Noll conclude that the "overriding lesson from the case studies is that the goal of economic efficiency—to cure market failures in privately sponsored commercial innovation—is so severely constrained by political forces that an effective, coherent national commercial R & D program has never been put in place" (p. 378). Politicians who favor allocating technology funds on the basis of constituencies may object to comprehensive evaluations, which have the potential to highlight funds allocated for reasons other than economic efficiency.

On the other hand, these programs cannot ignore constituency issues if they are to survive. Programs that attempt to select projects only on their economic and scientific merits may never develop a constituency and, thus, political support. Such programs may either be eliminated or changed to build support. This creates a potential Catch-22 situation: A program that allocates funds to reward constituencies may be popular, but will be less effective at correcting a market failure, whereas a program that attempts to correct a market failure may never develop a constituency and ultimately be canceled.

Finally, these programs raise other important questions that have yet to be dealt with fully. For example, how do we balance a firm's need for secrecy involving its research with society's desire to disseminate widely the results of publicly funded research and to evaluate the programs? Firms will not participate in these programs if results are immediately made available. On the other hand, making publicly funded research results available to only a few firms—which may profit enormously from them—puts the government in an awkward position. Moreover, the programs cannot be evaluated without access to information, and they are much more likely to be susceptible to political manipulation if not evaluated properly.

Another important question is how costs and benefits should be shared. Both to enhance private sector incentives and to enlist private sector judgments in making project selections, these partnerships are beginning to require greater equity contributions by the private sector. A common suggestion (e.g., Branscomb & Keller, 1998) is to require firms to bear costs in proportion to a project's expected private benefits. By requiring the private sector to put up considerable equity, it enlists the private sector in identifying winners, enabling government to focus on ascertaining the magnitude of spillovers. In addition, the reasoning goes, by contributing to project costs, the firm demonstrates its commitment to the project.

Although cost-sharing appears to be an attractive—and fair—proposition, in reality it raises many additional and as yet unanswered questions. First, estimating *ex ante* the private and social benefits of a project is a monumental task. The task is made even more difficult by information asymmetries. The firm will have far more information about the potential market success of an innovation than will the government, and the firm has an incentive to predict market success in a way that increases the probability of receiving a government subsidy. Second, cost sharing could have a perverse impact on the types of projects industry proposes to government. Although cost sharing may indicate a firm's commitment to a research product, it also indicates the firm's belief that the project is more likely to yield a commercial success. By requiring cost sharing, therefore, the government may actually be less likely to fund projects for which there is a market failure. Whether this hypothesis is true is yet to be seen. The point is that it is not necessarily true that cost sharing will increase program effectiveness. Cost sharing will affect incentives, but empirical analysis is necessary to determine precisely what the effects are.

In the following discussion, we will look more carefully at the impact of various government programs for the support of research. Unfortunately, many of these programs were started too recently and have funded too few projects to allow for reliable assessments. Moreover, although some of the analyses described below focus on the impact of the programs on the level of expenditure, few provide much insight into the more fundamental questions of the quality of research expenditures.

GOVERNMENT-INDUSTRY R & D PROGRAMS: EXAMPLES AND EVALUATIONS

Much of the legislative groundwork for today's public-private technology programs was laid in 1980. The Stevenson-Wydler Technology Innovation Act of 1980 "granted broad authority to the Department of Commerce 'to enhance technological innovation for commercial and public purposes . . . including a strong national policy supporting domestic technology transfer and utilization of the science and technology resources of the federal government.' In addition to leveraging the economic impact of federal R & D investments, Stevenson-Wydler directed the federal government to conduct a wide range of research and cooperative activities to assess and improve American technological competitiveness" (Brody, 1996, p. 26). The Bayh-Dole, or University and Small Business Patent Procedure Act, of 1980 reformed government patent policy. Bayh-Dole allowed government grant recipients and contractors to retain ownership rights to government-funded innovations. The act also encouraged universities to license innovations to firms (National Science Foundation, 1998).

Although those key pieces of legislation were put in place in 1980, it was not until the mid-1980s that public-private technology partnerships began to materialize, and not until the Clinton administration took office that they became a central part of federal technology policy. The new administration believed that "only the private sector has the skills and abilities to manage the complex process of developing new technologies and bringing them to market, while . . . [the] government plays a vital role in enabling the private sector's efforts" (Executive Office of the President, 1996, p. 42). Indeed, a central tenet of the administration's technology policy was that "the Federal government must encourage the development, commercialization, and use of technology" (Executive Office of the President, 1996, p. 42).

Technology partnership programs come in two forms, direct government funding of private R & D and direct collaboration between government and industry scientists. The most prominent of the first type are the Small Business Innovation Research Program (SBIR Program), the Advanced Technology Program (ATP), and Sematech (which stopped receiving funds in FY 1997, but then entered into a partnership of the second type). The second type includes Cooperative Research and Development Agreements (CRADAs), the Partnership for a New Generation of Vehicles (PNGV), and the Manufacturing Extension Partnership (MEP). Table 2 shows funding for the SBIR Program, ATP, MEP, and

TABLE 2: **Funding for Government-Industry Technology Programs—A Partial List**

Year	SBIR[a]	ATP[b]	MEP[c]	PNGV[d]
		Program (all figures in millions of current dollars)		
1983	44.5			
1984	108.4			
1985	199.1			
1986	297.9			
1987	350.5			
1988	389.1		5.0	
1989	431.9		7.5	
1990	460.7	10	8.7	
1991	483.1	37	13.8	
1992	508.4	49.4	17.0	
1993	698	67.9	18.2	
1994	717.6	199.1	30.2	Not available
1995	948.9	340.5	74.2	223
1996	974	221.0	80.0	241
1997	1,269	253	95.0	263
1998 (estimated)		199	113.5	281
1999 (estimated)		269	106.8	

a. Source: Small Business Administration and authors' calculations.
b. Source: ATP (1998), Office of Management and Budget (1998).
c. Source: MEP (1998).
d. Source: Office of Management and Budget (1996, 1997).

PNGV from their inception through the present. We will next describe these programs and discuss the available evidence on their effectiveness.

THE SBIR PROGRAM

The SBIR Program, established by the Small Business Innovation Development Act of 1982, was perhaps the first among the new wave of government programs intended to support private commercial R & D. This act required federal agencies with extramural (i.e., contract and grant) R & D budgets of over $100 million per year to set aside a certain percentage of that budget to SBIR Program grants. The set aside increased from 0.2% of the annual extramural budget in FY 1982 to 1.25% of the budget by FY 1986. By 1986, the SBIR Program budget was almost $300 million per year. The SBIR Program was renewed in 1992 and expanded dramatically. Congress increased the set aside to 2.5% of the agencies' extramural budget by FY 1997, causing SBIR Program funding to break the $1 billion mark that year.

SBIR Program grants are intended to encourage commercialization of innovations by small firms (i.e., firms with 500 employees or less). Eligible firms submit research proposals to participating federal agencies, which use a competitive review process to make funding decisions. Firms can first apply for up to

$100,000 to determine "the scientific and technical merit and feasibility of ideas." If successful, they can then apply for up to $750,000 to "further develop the proposed idea." Finally, the firm is expected to commercialize a product, although no additional SBIR Program funds are provided for that purpose.[8] The firm retains intellectual property rights to its innovation and all profits from commercialization, although the government retains a license for government use.

The U.S. General Accounting Office has reviewed the SBIR Program several times (e.g., U.S. General Accounting Office, 1989, 1992, 1995). These evaluations focus primarily on the commercialization rate of funded projects under the assumption that high commercialization rates imply a successful program. Such analyses ignore the possibility that some commercialized projects may not have required government support as well as the possibility that some projects that were not commercialized may have yielded large social returns. The focus on commercialization suggests that program managers may be rewarded for funding many successful projects. This system may induce managers to fund projects guaranteed to yield a commercial success. Firms may realize this and propose projects that they believe are more likely to yield a commercial success. As a result, the program could fund many very successful projects, but because they were selected on their expected probability of yielding a commercial success, these projects may not have needed government funding to begin with. Under that scenario, the program would support many successful projects, but would have no real economic impact.

Wallsten (1998a) found that firms that won SBIR Program grants reduced their own R & D expenditures by approximately the amount of the government grant, and that grants did not increase employment or sales. The results suggest that these government grants may crowd out a firm's R & D spending. That is, firms simply reduce their own R & D expenditures by the amount of the subsidy and put the money toward investments other than research. However, Lerner (1996) found that, for firms located in areas with high venture capital activity, those receiving SBIR Program awards increased employment more than those that did not receive the awards.

THE ATP

The ATP, although not the biggest government-industry commercial R & D program in the government's portfolio, has attracted the most attention. The ATP was established under the authority of the Omnibus Trade and Competitiveness Act of 1988 and implemented by the Bush administration in 1990. According to this act, the ATP was established "for the purpose of assisting United States businesses in creating and applying the generic technology and research results necessary to (1) commercialize significant new scientific discoveries and technologies rapidly, and (2) refine manufacturing technologies" (Hill, 1998, p. 146). The ATP was initially funded at a relatively modest $10 million, slowly increasing to $68 million by FY 1993. The Clinton administration seized the ATP as a key component of its technology policy and increased funding to approximately $340 million by FY 1995. The ATP has been controversial, and funding has fallen since 1995, with only $181 million appropriated for FY 1999.

Like SBIR, firms submit proposals to the ATP for research aimed at ultimately commercializing a product.[9] According to the ATP (1998), it attempts to "foster enabling technologies that will lead to new, innovative products, services, and industrial processes. For this reason, ATP projects focus on the technology needs of U.S. industry, not those of government. The ATP is industry driven, which keeps the program grounded in real-world needs. Research priorities for the ATP are set by industry: for-profit companies conceive, propose, cofund, and execute ATP projects and programs based on their understanding of the marketplace and research opportunities." The ATP also attempts to encourage firms to combine research efforts and thus funds many research joint ventures. Firms retain all intellectual property rights from any innovation.

The ATP is among the newest of these programs, and as such, few evaluations have been conducted. Preliminary evidence, however, is mixed. Yager and Schmidt (1997) examined the ATP's selection criteria and concluded that the ATP had no built-in mechanism to select projects that require government funding. The U.S. General Accounting Office (1996) surveyed firms that won awards and near winners firms that were rejected in the final stage of the competition. The U.S. General Accounting Office concluded that the ATP funded both marginal and inframarginal projects. Unlike many other government-industry R & D programs, however, the ATP has attempted to make economic evaluation a centerpiece of its implementation. The ATP holds regular conferences with economists and scientists in order to formulate ways to evaluate the program properly. In addition, recognizing that the program is new and itself an experiment, the ATP frequently rethinks the types of proposals it funds and how its funding should be allocated.

The ATP has faced more congressional opposition than any other technology program. In part, this opposition was simply the result of a Republican Congress attacking a program strongly identified with a Democratic president. But the opposition is not only the result of partisan politics. Some observers believe this opposition resulted, in part, because the ATP emphasized its role in mitigating market failure rather than in building a constituency. The ATP stated in 1996 that it aims to select "only those projects for awards for which it thinks the potential social rate of return . . . far exceeds the potential private rate of return on investment, and for which it thinks the private sector will either not do the project at all, or not within the critical time, or in the scale/scope necessary to realize the potential private benefits" (National Institute of Science and Technology, 1996, p. 4). In other words, the ATP's specific goal was to mitigate a market failure, not to reward or build a constituency. Because ATP had no natural constituency, it became an easy target for congressional critics of the administration, which had made ATP its flagship technology program.

The ATP's political problems also highlight another problem facing any government program that must reject some industry proposals and fund others. Although the program is sensitive to the problem of picking winners, by rejecting some proposals it ends up picking losers—firms that may be put at a disadvantage because they did not get government funds. This creates resentment between firms that did not receive funding. From 1990 to 1995, ATP received 2,210 applications and funded only 280 projects (ATP, personal communication, February 28, 1996). Even if all these projects were rejected on legitimate grounds, the large number of rejections creates a large number of potential program enemies.

SEMATECH

Sematech was the first prominent example of government support of an industrial research consortium aimed at commercialization. Sematech is a government-supported industry consortium founded in 1987 to help shore up America's once-declining position in the semiconductor industry. The National Cooperative Research Act of 1984 paved the way for this consortium by loosening antitrust restrictions on industrial research collaborations. Sematech began as a consortium of 14 leading U.S. semiconductor-manufacturing firms. By participating in Sematech, otherwise competing firms pooled semiconductor R & D efforts. Participating firms are required to contribute 1% of their semiconductor revenues to the consortium, with a minimum of $1 million and a maximum of $15 million. Firms are also required to send engineers to Sematech's facility in Austin, Texas for at least half a year.

The federal government, through the Defense Department's Advanced Research Projects Agency (ARPA), provided approximately half of Sematech's annual $200 million budget through 1996. This direct subsidy ended in FY 1997. Sematech now has 11 domestic members and, now that it no longer receives funds from ARPA, has established a wholly owned subsidiary, International Sematech, with five foreign firms as members. Although Sematech no longer receives a direct subsidy, it has maintained a connection with the federal government by entering a partnership with Oakridge National Laboratory (partnerships of this sort are discussed below).[10]

Sematech is often credited with reversing the fortunes of the U.S. semiconductor industry, but that hypothesis is difficult to test. The Sematech model may have promise. For example, it is consistent with Paul Romer's (1993) suggestion of creating self-organizing industry investment boards. Such boards could "combine the government's efficiency at solving free-rider problems with the market's effectiveness in selecting practical problems that offer the highest rates of return" (p. 361). Here, too, we see difficulties in implementing theoretically sound ideas. Irwin and Klenow (1996), for example, found that firms involved in Sematech reduced their R & D expenditures by approximately $300 million per year. This reduction has positive and negative interpretations. On one hand, firms may have reduced spending on duplicative research. On the other hand, firms probably did not increase spending on high-spillover research. In addition, no research projects are completely duplicative—more than one firm working on similar problems may develop very different solutions or directions for future research.

CRADAs

Government-industry partnerships in which government and industry scientists work together for the purpose of commercializing a product is a new approach. The largest of these are CRADAs. CRADAs are formal agreements between the national laboratories and private firms. CRADAs are intended to help the national laboratories in their primary mission by building their technical capabilities and to help private industry by commercializing innovations produced in the labs (Cohen & Noll, 1995). Traditionally, the national laboratories facilitated technology transfer to the private sector by publicizing research results. By contrast, information from CRADAs is closely held, and the private partner retains intellectual property rights to any innovation. The Clinton administration initially wanted the national laboratories to devote 10% to 20% of their budgets to cooperative work with industry (Clinton & Gore, 1993). Unfortunately, data about CRADAs are exceedingly difficult to obtain. Available information reveals that the number of new CRADAs increased from about 500 in 1992 to over 1,100 in 1994 before beginning to decline in 1995.

CRADAs have not been subject to any comprehensive economic analysis. In part, this lack of evaluation is the result of a lack of access to data. As Cohen and Noll (1995) note,

> The government has been especially closed in providing solid information about CRADAs—a policy that was deliberately set in motion by the provisions of the enabling statutes that protect the confidentiality of the agreements. CRADA proposals and reports are exempted from the Freedom of Information Act, and the agreements bind the parties not to reveal any proprietary information brought to the CRADA or any research results that emanate from it, without their mutual consent. Whereas some agencies make the titles and partner identities available and, in some cases, the cost, agencies are not obliged to do so and will not if their partner objects. Moreover, none of the agencies responsible for managing the CRADA program regularly collects information about the extent of its CRADA activity, much less performance data about the joint project. Hence, nearly all the available information takes the form of raw 'CRADA counts' that do not differentiate between small, narrowly defined projects and massive, broad agreements with large industrial consortia. (p. 230)

Although the idea of CRADAs was initially popular across the political spectrum, implementation has led to many controversies. Most of them arise when a CRADA appears to be too successful. For example, the AIDS drug, AZT, was developed by Burroughs-Wellcome in a CRADA with the National Institute of

Health (NIH). Burroughs-Wellcome initially priced the drug at $2,000 to $10,000 per year. This led the NIH to develop fair pricing clauses for its CRA-DAs, but has been unable to determine what "fair pricing" means.[11]

PNGV

Another large public-private partnership is the PNGV. This program began in 1993 as a collaboration between seven federal agencies, 20 federal laboratories, and the three big U.S. automobile manufacturers. The program's goal is "to develop an environmentally friendly car with up to triple the fuel economy of today's midsize cars—without sacrificing affordability, performance, or safety. The other two PNGV goals are (1) to significantly improve national competitiveness in automotive manufacturing, [and] (2) to apply commercially viable innovations to conventional vehicles" (PNGV, 1998). The PNGV has not received as much attention as other government-industry programs, although it receives over $250 million annually from the federal government.

The PNGV has not been subject to any economic evaluation. Although PNGV may have overcome many technological hurdles in its quest for a more efficient automobile, nobody has been able to investigate what the real effect of PNGV has been. Indeed, the National Academy of Sciences (1998) "found it difficult to assess the efforts and resources applied to the PNGV program because no funding plan was made available" (p. 11).

THE MEP

The MEP is another part of the new push toward public-private technology partnerships. MEP is different from other programs in that it is not intended to produce any particular product. Instead, MEP consists of regional offices that provide small- and medium-sized firms with technical, technological, and business advice and help them form partnerships with other businesses or government agencies (MEP, 1998). Like some other programs, MEP began in 1988, but was very small for several years. In 1992, there were only seven MEP centers. By 1997, MEP had 70 centers and an annual budget of almost $100 million. Like CRADAS and PNGV, there have been no economic evaluations of MEP.

CONCLUSIONS AND POLICY RECOMMENDATIONS

The end of the Cold War brought with it a need to rethink the way the United States funds science and technology. Support for basic research remains strong, and many have voiced their belief that government must continue to support R & D at universities and colleges. The question of how to support industrial R & D best has proven sticky. Government, and the Clinton administration in particular, has chosen to focus on government-industry R & D partnerships aimed at commercializing innovations. The administration has started a host of such programs and drastically increased funding to many others. These programs, however, remain controversial, and it is not yet clear that they can achieve their ambitious goal of mitigating a market failure.

The economics behind these programs is sound. Firms acting in their own best interests will invest less than the socially optimal level of R & D. By subsidizing some R & D, government can help mitigate this market failure. Sound theory, however, does not always translate easily into sound policy. Preliminary evidence on new government-industry technology programs suggests that they face a host of problems in terms of implementation, evaluation, and political support. Each of those issues impacts the other.

Checkered preliminary evaluations, however, should not necessarily be viewed as condemning either the programs or the idea behind the programs. Just as the outcome of R & D itself is inherently uncertain, so too is the outcome of an R & D program. Large firms undertake a portfolio of R & D projects, recognizing that some projects will pan out and others will not. Likewise, government programs to support industrial R & D should be viewed as a portfolio. Some of these programs may turn out to be successful whereas others will not. The failure of one program to generate benefits does not necessarily mean that another program cannot generate benefits.

RECOMMENDATIONS

The large gap between private and social returns on R & D suggests that government-industry R & D programs, if properly implemented, could potentially yield enormous benefits. These programs are new, which means that we have a lot to learn about how they should be run. If we are to determine what works and what does not, the programs must include evaluation mechanisms. Unfortunately, the government agencies in charge of these programs tend to resist efforts to conduct comprehensive evaluations. As a result, we know very little about whether the programs are meeting their objectives.

Federal agencies should be more open toward evaluation and should give more thought to what success really means in the context of government-industry R & D programs. Simply noting that funded projects have a high commercialization rate does not demonstrate that government funding had any real impact. Likewise, a failed project does not mean that the program is a failure and a spectacular commercial success does not necessarily mean that the government should not have funded the project. To our knowledge, no program has been willing to release data that would facilitate a proper evaluation, much less actually implement the program in a way that facilitates evaluation.[12] For example, most programs are unwilling to release even the names of firms that applied to the program and were turned down. Without that basic information, it is nearly impossible to determine whether government funding had any real effect.

Agencies should also think carefully about the incentives facing managers who run these programs. Too much emphasis on commercialization may cause a manager to fund the most commercially promising proposals, which may be the very proposals that do not need funding. On the other hand, criticism of very large commercial successes may make managers reluctant to fund research that they feel has some small probability of being a tremendous commercial success (but would not be funded by the private sector alone). Comprehensive evaluations may help on this score—if managers are not judged just on commercialization then perhaps the debate will shift away from focusing on simple anecdotes.

Government-industry R & D programs are an innovative approach to solving a serious market failure. Whether the problems facing government-industry R & D programs can be overcome is still an open question. Much research needs to be done to determine how these programs can accomplish their goals. More thought needs to be given to the incentives affecting the behavior of politicians, program managers, and firms involved in these programs. If the problems can be overcome, these programs could contribute significantly to economic growth.

NOTES

1. See Griliches (1992) for a discussion of underinvestment. See Reinganum (1989) for a discussion of factors that can lead firms to overinvest.

2. See Griliches (1992) and Nadiri (1993) for overviews of the literature on spillovers and returns to R & D.

3. Sometimes the term *social returns* embraces total benefits to society—the private returns as well as the value of spillovers. Here, we use the term in a more limited sense, to refer only to the benefits that are not appropriated by the innovator.

4. For discussions of these issues, see Stiglitz and Sah (1989) and Barzel (1995).

5. For a discussion of the R & D tax credit, see Hall (1993).

6. See Masahiko, Murdock, and Okuno-Fujihara (1997) for a general discussion.

7. See Wallsten (1998b) for a more in-depth discussion of this issue.

8. Initially, a Phase I award was worth up to $50,000 and a Phase II award was worth up to $500,000. Congress increased these amounts when it renewed the SBIR Program in 1992.

9. Although ATP has rules mandating small-firm participation, ATP competitions are open to firms of any size.

10. See Irwin and Klenow (1996) and Sematech (1998) for more information on Sematech.

11. Most of the information in this paragraph comes from Cohen and Noll (1995).

12. For example, Adam Jaffe (1998) notes that perhaps the best way to evaluate programs that solicit proposals is to randomize awards. Some percentage of selected projects would randomly not be funded and some percentage of rejected projects would be funded (with preliminary screening to ensure that truly ridiculous proposals were not funded). This randomization approach would generate control groups and help identify whether government funding was actually necessary in undertaking the research project.

REFERENCES

Advanced Technology Program, National Institute of Science and Technology. (1998). [On-line]. Available: http://www.atp.nist.gov/atp/overview.htm.

Barzel, Y. (1995). Productivity change, public goods and transaction costs: Essays at the boundaries of microeconomics. In M. Perlman & M. Blaug (Eds.), *Economists of the twentieth century series*. Aldershot, U.K.: Edward Elgar Publishing, Limited.

Branscomb, L., & Keller, J. (1998). Towards a research and innovation policy. In L. Branscomb & J. Keller (Eds.), *Investing in innovation* (pp. 462-496). Cambridge, MA: MIT Press.

Brody, R. (1996). *Effective partnering: A report to Congress on federal technology partnerships*. Washington, DC: U.S. Department of Commerce, Office of Technology Policy.

Clinton, W., & Gore, A. (1993). *Technology for America's economic growth, a new direction to build economic strength*. Washington, DC: Executive Office of the President.

Cohen, L., & Noll, R. (1991). *The technology pork barrel*. Washington, DC: The Brookings Institution.

Cohen, L., & Noll, R. (1995). Feasibility of effective public-private R & D collaboration: The case of cooperative R & D agreements. *International Journal of the Economics of Business, 2*, 223-240.

Council of Economic Advisers, Executive Office of the President. (1995). *Supporting research and development: The federal government's role* [On-line]. Available: http://www.white-house.gov/WH/EOP/CEA/econ/html/econ-rpt.html.

Executive Office of the President. (1996). *Technology in the national interest*. Washington, DC: Author.

General Accounting Office. (1989). *Federal research: Assessment of Small Business Innovation Research Programs* (GAO/RCED-89-39). Washington, DC: Government Printing Office.

General Accounting Office. (1992). *Federal research: Small business innovation research shows success but can be strengthened* (GAO/RCED-92-37). Washington, DC: Government Printing Office.

General Accounting Office. (1995). *Federal research: Interim report on the Small Business Innovation Research Program* (GAO/RCED-95-59). Washington, DC: Government Printing Office.

General Accounting Office. (1996). *Measuring performance: The Advanced Technology Program and private-sector funding* (GAO/RCED-96-47). Washington, DC: Government Printing Office.

Greenwald, B., Salinger, M., & Stiglitz, J. (1990, April). *Imperfect capital markets and productivity growth* (Rev. 1991, March). Paper presented at the NBER Conference, Vail, CO.

Griliches, Z. (1992). The search for R & D spillovers. *Scandinavian Journal of Economics, 94*, 29-47.

Hall, B. (1992). *Investment and research and development at the firm level: Does the source of financing matter?* (National Bureau of Economic Research Working Paper No. 4096). Cambridge, MA: National Bureau of Economic Research.

Hall, B. (1993). R & D tax policy during the 1980s: Success or failure? In J. Poterba (Ed.), *Tax policy and the economy* (Vol. 7). Cambridge, MA: MIT Press.

Hill, C. (1995, June 19). *Private funds are unlikely to replace cuts in public funds for R & D in the U.S.* (Available from the Institute of Public Policy, George Mason University, Fairfax, VA).

Hill, C. (1998). The Advanced Technology Program: Opportunities for enhancement. In L. Branscomb & J. Keller (Eds.), *Investing in innovation* (pp. 143-173). Cambridge, MA: MIT Press.

Himmelberg, C., & Petersen, B. (1994). R & D and internal finance: A panel study of small firms in high-tech industries. *Review of Economics and Statistics, 76*, 38-51.

Irwin, D., & Klenow, P. (1996). High-tech R & D subsidies: Estimating the effects of Sematech. *Journal of International Economics, 40*, 323-344.

Jaffe, A. (1998). Measurement issues. In L. Branscomb & J. Keller (Eds.), *Investing in innovation* (pp. 64-84). Cambridge, MA: MIT Press.

Jones, C., & Williams, J. (1997). *Measuring the social return to R & D* (Finance and economics discussion series). Washington, DC: Federal Reserve Board.

Lerner, J. (1996). *The government as venture capitalist: The long-run impact of the SBIR Program.* (National Bureau of Economic Research Working Paper No. 5753). Cambridge, MA: National Bureau of Economic Research.

Levy, D., & Terleckyj, N. (1983). Effects of government R & D on private R & D investment and productivity: A macroeconomic analysis. *The Bell Journal of Economics, 14*, 551-561.

Manufacturing Extension Partnership. (1998). [On-line]. Available: http://www.mep.nist.gov.

Masahiko, A., Murdock, K., & Okuno-Fujihara, M. (1997). Beyond the East Asian miracle: Introducing the market enhancing view. In A. Masahiko, H. Kim, & M. Okuno-Fujiwara (Eds.), *The role of government in East Asian economic development: Comparative institutional analysis* (pp. 1-40). New York: Oxford University Press.

Nadiri, I. (1993). *Innovations and technological spillovers.* (National Bureau of Economic Research Working Paper No. 4423). Cambridge, MA: National Bureau of Economic Research.

National Academy of Sciences, National Research Council. (1998). *Review of the research program of the Partnership for a New Generation of Vehicles: Fourth report.* Washington, DC: National Academy Press.

National Institute of Science and Technology. (1996). *Guidelines for economic evaluation of the Advanced Technology Program.* Washington, DC: Government Printing Office.

National Science Foundation. (1998). *Science and engineering indicators.* Washington, DC: Government Printing Office.

Office of Management and Budget, Executive Office of the President. (1996). *Budget of the United States government.* Washington, DC: Government Printing Office.

Office of Management and Budget, Executive Office of the President. (1997). *Budget of the United States government.* Washington, DC: Government Printing Office.

Office of Management and Budget, Executive Office of the President. (1998). *Budget of the United States government.* Washington, DC: Government Printing Office.

Partnership for a New Generation of Vehicles. (1998). [On-line]. Available: http://www.ta.doc.gov/pngv/introduction/intro.htm.

Reinganum, J. (1989). The timing of innovation: Research, development, and diffusion. In R. Schmalensee & R. Willig (Eds.), *Handbook of industrial organization* (pp. 850-908). New York: Elsevier Science Publishers.

Robson, M. (1993). Federal funding and the level of private expenditure on basic research. *Southern Economic Journal, 60*, 63-71.

Romer, P. (1993). Implementing a national technology strategy with self-organizing industry investment boards. *Brookings Papers: Microeconomics, 2*, 345-399.

Schumpeter, J. A. (1939). *Business cycles: A theoretical, historical, and statistical analysis of the capitalist process.* New York: McGraw-Hill.

Sematech. (1998). [On-line]. Available: http://www.sematech.org.

Stiglitz, J. (1988). *Economics of the public sector* (2nd ed.). New York: Norton.

Stiglitz, J., & Sah, R. (1989). Technological learning, social learning and technological change. In S. Chakravarty (Ed.), *The balance between industry and agriculture in economic development* (pp. 285-298). New York: Macmillan.

Wallsten, S. (1998a). Rethinking the Small Business Innovation Research Program. In L. Branscomb & J. Keller (Eds.), *Investing in innovation.* Cambridge, MA: MIT Press.

Wallsten, S. (1998b). *Can government-industry R & D programs increase private R & D: The case of the Small Business Innovation Research Program.* Unpublished doctoral dissertation, Stanford University.

Yager, L., & Schmidt, R. (1997). *The Advanced Technology Program: A case study in federal technology policy.* Washington, DC: AEI Press.

4

The Good Lessons of Bad Experience

Rethinking the Future of Commercial Nuclear Power

WALTER A. ROSENBAUM

Early in 1998, Senator Pete Domenici (R-NM) revived a once ferocious domestic policy debate that seemed destined for extinction. Speaking at Harvard University, Domenici sought to rekindle America's failing zeal for commercial nuclear power with a vigorous call for the industry's renaissance. Other nations, he warned, were racing ahead of the United States in nuclear technology. He predicted a 21st-century global struggle, led by developing nations, for new energy resources for which the United States without nuclear power was unprepared. Finally, he invoked the nuclear power industry's last, best hope for resurrection. "Nuclear energy," he observed, "which in 1996 reduced U.S. greenhouse gas emissions from electric utilities by 25% should be expanded to enable the United States to meet greenhouse-gas emissions goals without imposing taxes or other costly limitations on the use of carbon based energy forms" (Domenici, 1998, p. 40).

And so, implausibly, despite Three Mile Island and Chernobyl, the nuclear option redux. The Domenici challenge has already provoked considerable discussion within the nation's nuclear policy community and among a larger audience of policy practitioners and advocates concerned with America's energy future. Domenici's exhortation is an attempt to revive a failing energy technology that evolved from a unique, but misconceived, industrial-governmental partnership once prophesied to lead America into an era of unending, cheap electric power (Bupp & Derian, 1981). We need this renewed debate because we need to protect this energy option, although, like many environmentalists, I contemplate a domestic revival of commercial nuclear power with misgiving. However, there should be no intellectual quarantine on discussing alternatives. If alternatives are discussed, we had best look for lessons from past U.S. experience to inform the debate about appropriate relationships between public and private institutions in the management of a future nuclear power industry. Those who are familiar with the industry's well-documented and dismal history may well wonder why such retrospection is useful. The answer, I believe, is that current domestic and international energy realities confronting the United States make it improvident, even reckless, to abandon wholly the nuclear option however problematic it may seem in light of its past environmental, economic, or political history.

REFRAMING THE NUCLEAR POWER DEBATE

Senator Domenici is not proselytizing entirely among the unconverted. Support for a revitalized U.S. nuclear option has recently arisen from a surprising diversity of sources unaffiliated with the commercial nuclear industry itself. In 1996, the influential Trilateral Commission, for example, devoted several chapters of its evaluation of U.S. energy security to the argument that nuclear energy could contribute to long-term U.S. sustainable development and become the country's best hope for solving its future energy dilemmas (Bartin, Imai, & Steeg, 1996). More significantly, the Clinton administration, despite its apparent disaffection with nuclear power, has repeatedly associated a domestic nuclear power option with the implementation of the Kyoto Climate Agreement. Ambassador Stuart Eizenstadt recently assured the Senate Foreign Relations Committee that "nuclear power will have to play an increasingly important role because it does not emit greenhouse gases" and suggested that the United States "ought to be doing more" to promote it (Kriz, 1998, p. 2496). Part of the Clinton administration's Climate Change Initiative intended to address critical technology needs associated with future climate warming includes spending on R & D to safely extend the operating life of currently operating U.S. commercial nuclear power facilities by another 10 to 20 years (Geller & McGaraghan, 1998); in addition, the fiscal year 1999 budget includes a very modest $19 million for the Department of Energy's (DOE) Nuclear Energy Research Initiative to promote advanced nuclear technology research (Holt & Behrens, 1998, p. 2).

Despite assertions by many nuclear critics, the current discussion is not recycled history. The issues are now framed in significantly different terms than they were during the initial debate over the development of the U.S. commercial nuclear power industry in the 1950s and early 1960s; this change exemplifies a broad transformation in the scientific, economic, and political context of nuclear technology in the last three decades. The globalization of environmental science, especially the rapid evolution of international climate research, has profoundly altered this context. Still, the present debate is grounded in the industry's troubled institutional history, which demands brief consideration, together with the new domestic and global energy realities facing the United States, if a reappraisal of commercial nuclear power is to appear sensible.

AN HISTORICALLY UNIQUE PARTNERSHIP

American commercial nuclear power began in the 1950s with the federal government's Power Reactor Development Program, promoted by the Atomic Energy Commission (AEC), the Congressional Joint Committee on Atomic Energy, National Laboratory scientists, other nuclear energy specialists, and the White House as an initiative of the Eisenhower administration's Atoms for Peace Program (Del Sesto, 1979). It became a private-public partnership, which was unique at the time, created to develop and to market nuclear technologies for electric power generation. Directed by the AEC, it intended to "promote and encourage free competition and private investment in the development work, while at the same time accepting on the part of the government certain responsibilities for such development" (Del Sesto, 1979, p. 52).

During the crucial start-up decades between 1950 and 1970, the "certain responsibilities" undertaken by the federal government embraced a multitude of strategies. In the beginning, the AEC waived all charges for the use of fissionable materials (controlled by Washington at the time), conducted essential commercialization research at public cost through the National Laboratories, obtained technical and economic data for potential collaborators, and shared patents freely with reactor manufacturers. The federal government subsequently assumed the responsibility for developing a reprocessing technology to reduce and recycle the industry's radioactive wastes and for creating secure disposal sites for the remaining waste. Later, Congress created, by statute, the necessary limits on the new industry's insurance liability and mandated that the AEC both regulate and promote commercial nuclear power domestically. In reality, the federal government alternately seduced and coerced the initially wavering utilities and reactor manufacturers into creating a commercial nuclear power capability (Bupp & Derian, 1981). By the end of the 1970s, this cajoling, among other things, had amounted to more than $12 billion in federal subsidies to the emerging industry (General Accounting Office, 1979, p. ii).

In addition, the federal government used its authority to impose restrictions on public access to information about the technology and its commercial development and severely limited opportunity for consultation or participation with citizen organizations outside the nuclear science-utility governmental subgovernment managing nuclear power during its boom period (Hilgartner, Bell, & O'Conner, 1983, chap. 5).

In retrospect, it was a huge mistake for the utilities to enter this relationship with Washington without providing an opportunity for a broad scientific and public debate on the technical and economic merits of nuclear power. It was equally unwise for the utilities to order turnkey installations, which were built by the reactor manufacturers and their subcontractors to government specifications, without fully preparing their own staff for the responsibilities entailed in the subsequent facility management. We are reminded by economists Irvin Bupp and Jean-Claude Derian that the manufacturers committed themselves to deliver complete nuclear power generating systems. "They would assume responsibility for the cost of materials and equipment.... All the electric companies had to do was 'open the door' for its complete plant at a specific date in the future and start the generating equipment" (Bupp & Derian, 1981, p. 48). Furthermore, the utilities discovered a community of interest with governmental promoters, National Laboratory scientists, and reactor manufacturers and their subsidiaries who wanted to keep commercial nuclear power quarantined from public criticism as much as possible.

This well-documented history has been carefully culled to provide items for the industry's obituaries. It is now virtually the 21st century. New domestic and global realities exist that put commercial nuclear power in a new context and counsel thoughtful consideration about the industry's resuscitation.

THE NEAR FUTURE OF GLOBAL ENERGY

The first reality is that without a major change in current U.S. public policy, commercial nuclear power in the United States will become an orphan technology in less than a generation. Today, the nation's 101 commercial nuclear facilities are producing about 20% of the nation's electric power. No new reactor has been ordered by a domestic utility since 1976. Half the existing facilities are scheduled to retire by the year 2015; all of them will complete their presently scheduled production by 2026—well within the lifetime of today's younger generation. Several utilities, including Duke Energy and Baltimore Gas & Electric, have applied for 10- to 20-year extensions of their operating permits. It is uncertain whether these permits will be extended, and how many more utilities might also apply for extensions if these are granted.

The second reality is that global energy demand, particularly among developing nations in Asia and Africa, is predicted to expand rapidly in the next few decades and, with it, the volume of global greenhouse gas emissions. Most expert predictions suggest that global energy demand will rise 54% to 98% in the next 30 years (Schriesheim, 1997). Most of this new demand will be concentrated in Asia and Latin America, even with the recent Asian economic recession. More significantly, this new demand is most likely to be met by a major increase in the number of fossil-fuel–fired facilities, most of which are expected to burn coal

(Matsui, 1998). This prospective, massive increase in global electric power generation, even with a concurrent growth of nuclear electric power capacity among the major developing nations, is expected to create a significant increase in the global emission of greenhouse gases. Presently, the new renewables—hydroelectric, solar, and thermal energy—are anticipated to represent only about 2% to 4% of the global energy supply from now to the year 2020 (Livernash & Rodenburg, 1998).

THE IMPACT OF INDUSTRY DEREGULATION

A third reality is the imminence of domestic electric utility deregulation. If this soon occurs, as widely predicted, one plausible environmental impact would have significant implications for nuclear power. A recent analysis by the Congressional Research Service (CRS) notes that "the environmental concern with respect to restructuring is that the new economic signals being given by a competitive generation market could result in increased emissions of undesirable pollutants" (Parker & Blodgett, 1998, p. 5). The reason, they explain, is that (a) lower baseload prices resulting from restructuring would increase electricity demand and, thus, increase generation and emissions; and (b) the restructured market would encourage the rehabilitation and full utilization of older, more polluting (i.e., coal-fired) generating facilities (Parker & Blodgett, 1998, p. 5). This could have severe consequences for U.S. climate policy because increased coal-fired generation would greatly increase domestic CO_2 emissions and complicate further efforts to mitigate climate warming. The CRS concludes that these rising CO_2 emissions are possibly "the clearest and most quantifiable risk to the environment from restructuring" (Parker & Blodgett, 1998, p. 5).

Any rise in fossil-fuel emissions under these circumstances is likely to provoke an intensified search of mitigating strategies. The extension of permits for existing nuclear power generating facilities and reinvigorated federal R & D funding for the development of newer, more economically and environmentally attractive technologies, are two possible choices. Thus, if only providentially, it is in the interest of the United States to consider what institutional reforms might be undertaken if nuclear power reappears in the long-term U.S. future.

TECHNOLOGICAL ENCIRCLEMENT?

The fourth reality is that the United States faces the prospect of a technological encirclement by foreign nuclear electric facilities where R & D on nuclear-generated electricity continues even as it declines rapidly domestically. The Energy Information Administration reported in early 1998 that 31 other nations were generating electricity with nuclear power and 45 additional plants were under construction (EIA, 1998). U.S. nuclear reactor manufacturers are aggressively marketing their products abroad, particularly in China, India, Japan, South Korea, and Taiwan, which together will be expected to account for about

70% of new nuclear capacity worldwide; General Electric has now completed two of its advanced design reactors in Japan, and another two-unit plant has been ordered by Taiwan (Kido, 1998). In addition, implementation of the U.S.–China nuclear cooperation agreement in March 1998 now permits U.S. reactor sales in China (Holt & Behrens, 1998). Asia's recent economic recession may reduce these projections, but the trend seems clear and probably irreversible for the next few decades at least.

In any case, history is emphatic; no technological genie, once liberated, has ever been recaptured. Nuclear technology will continue to develop commercially somewhere else, if not here. The elimination of commercial nuclear power in the United States would inevitably mean an exodus abroad of nuclear scientists, technicians, planners, and related vocations and a decline in the domestic scientific infrastructure to support them. Recent warnings about the economic and security implications of an aggressive nuclear technology development program abroad have unfortunately been the most insistent from the most suspect sources, such as the DOE, the Department of Defense, and the nuclear power industry itself. Yet it seems prudent to keep U.S. nuclear technology sufficiently progressive to preclude a technological surprise originating from somewhere else.

THE KYOTO ISSUE

Finally, it is difficult to imagine a realistic policy scenario for reducing domestic and global greenhouse gas emissions to comply with the Kyoto Agreement on Climate Change without further R & D in nuclear-generated electric power. The Kyoto Agreement assumes that the United States and the rest of the world will meet its first critical emission reduction targets within 20 years. Today, the primary global energy produced by hydroelectric, geothermal, nuclear, wind, or solar sources accounts for only 10% of all commercial energy produced in the 1990s; almost 70% of this comes from nuclear reactors (Livernash & Rodenburg, 1998).

It is possible to contrive various energy forecasts that will account for required global greenhouse gas emission reductions through rapidly accelerated energy conservation and nonnuclear renewable energy sources domestically and internationally, but actually achieving these goals in the next 20 years seems politically and economically implausible. In the United States, for example, 85% of U.S. primary energy comes from fossil fuels, and this, in turn, accounts for 88% of all U.S. greenhouse gas emissions. More than one third of all domestic greenhouse gas emissions originate from electric utilities (Livernash & Rodenburg, 1998). Somehow, if not in the next decade, then in the next several decades, the United States will have to find a technological path to reducing these electric utility emissions, and nuclear power seems at least plausible. Whatever else it may do, nuclear electric power unquestionably reduces greenhouse gas emissions. The 109 existing U.S. nuclear facilities are estimated to reduce domestic emission of CO_2 by 20% below what it would have been had these plants been coal-fired. In short, if the United States means to decarbonize its energy resources to meet the Kyoto standards, no other energy source has the potential to produce the magnitude of required change as quickly (White, 1998).

I have not mentioned the possibility of technological innovation or the refinement of existing reactor technology that might be more attractive domestically than the existing light-water technologies used currently in the United States. Even if such a breakthrough technology is not imminent—and the debate about a technology breakthrough also proceeds—the realities already mentioned seem compelling enough to persuade a reasonable person that it is prudent, at the very least, for the United States to continue an aggressive program of R & D for commercial nuclear power in all its significant social aspects. And that should involve what I believe to be the most crucial aspect, rethinking and redesigning the institutional management of future commercial nuclear power.

RETHINKING INSTITUTIONAL DESIGN

The presently insecure edifice of U.S. commercial nuclear power has been erected over a period of 50 years on three tenuous foundations. Two of these, the technological and the economic, have been thoroughly examined and their flaws meticulously documented (Wood, 1983; Kemeny, 1979). The third foundation, the industry's institutional design—by which I mean the complex legal and political structures through which the federal government, electric utilities, and the scientific community created and managed this enterprise—deserves more consideration.

THE INSTITUTIONAL CHALLENGE

The future domestic redevelopment of commercial nuclear power has been debated for the last decade primarily in terms of technology and economics. Yet many of the economic and technological problems experienced by the U.S. nuclear power industry, many of which have never been considered as institutional problems, originated directly from the character of the industry's institutional misdesign. The institutional management style involved extreme secrecy, public disclosures of technological decisions as fait accompli, distrust of public involvement in the technology planning, an exuberant confidence in the technology's economic viability, and reliance upon regulatory models derived from experience with military nuclear weapons development during World War II. Remedies for such institutional problems are the sine qua non on any agenda of further strategies for commercial nuclear power in the United States because public trust and governmental willingness to invest political capital in nuclear energy depends as much upon restored confidence in the management of the technology as it does upon proof of its technical or economic viability. This is not news. For instance, almost 20 years ago, a high-level workshop among domestic energy experts at Harvard's Kennedy School of Government finished their rigorous review of American energy options in the gathering twilight of commercial nuclear power and concluded that the industry could remain viable only if there were "fundamental changes in the governance of nuclear power" (Allison & Carnesale, 1983, p. 151). That emphasis needs to be reaffirmed.

THE POVERTY OF CLOISTERED INCREMENTALISM

Commercial nuclear power was initiated by the federal government, and later embraced by the nation's electric utilities, with an astonishing lack of reflective planning. Its developmental history was, in fact, unique. Its economic and technical merits were declared without any operating history, and without any open and prolonged public debate. "The Atomic Energy Commission and the [Congressional] Joint Committee [on Atomic Energy]," explains Stephen L. Del Sesto, "actually represented only one part of a broad attempt to set policy and rationally evaluate the costs and benefits of a major technology before rather than after substantial amounts of experience had been accumulated" (1979, p. 29). The technical planning was equally myopic. The failure to consider how high-level radioactive waste (HLRW) from the commercial reactors would eventually be disposed of safely became an embarrassment to the government agencies responsible for the industry's safety (Bupp & Derian, 1981). The private utilities that eventually collaborated with the federal government in developing the industry chose to accept Washington's extremely benign technical and economic predictions for the new technology to the point that an intoxication with nuclear power seemed evident (Bupp & Derian, 1981). The few early, outspoken critics of this strategic planning charade within the community of nuclear scientists were abrasively silenced.

In retrospect, it is obvious that the early public designing and management of the emergent nuclear power industry was, in fact, the epitome of the incremental planning style so deeply embedded in the institutional structure of American government—with an added twist. In typical incremental fashion, the planning style rejected a deliberative, comprehensive exploration of developmental alternatives and a careful weighing of the consequences from alternative development strategies; problems of policy implementation were left to be resolved serially, "at the margins" as policy evolved (Hayes, 1992, chap. 2). Heavy reliance was placed on experience with the management of wartime nuclear weapons to provide guidelines for the management and regulation of the newly emerging industry. The twist was that this planning was extraordinarily cloistered, even by the standard of public involvement in government during the 1950s. The public, the media, large segments of the scientific community, and governmental entities (including most of the congress) were rigorously excluded; there was virtually no public debate on any aspect of the government's planning for the nuclear future.

THE EVOLUTION OF FAUSTIAN TECHNOLOGIES

The government's cloistered approach might have made some sense if nuclear power was essentially akin to other technologies with which the government had prior experience. Commercial nuclear power represents, in fact, the earliest federal experience in big-scale technology development and their first creation, development, and regulation of a historically unique class of technologies that emerged in the mid-20th century. These technologies, which now include genetic engineering; new resource extraction methods; and numerous others derived from scientific, commercial, and industrial applications of nuclear energy, have several distinguishing characteristics: (a) a certain capability to alter profoundly, if not to destroy wholly, the biochemical and physical basis of human life in less than a generation; (b) an entailed risk of lesser but still catastrophic consequences when improperly managed; and (c) an ability to displace the potentially enormous human and ecological risks, or costs, of their utilization to future generations while conferring immediate benefits on the generation creating them. I call them Faustian technologies, using a metaphor suggested by the physicist Alvin Weinberg, because these technologies involve an implicit social bargain in which society embraces the technology's benefits, which often may be relatively short-lived, in return for a pledge that succeeding generations will be wise and constant guardians against the technology's potentially catastrophic failures (Weinberg, 1972).

These technologies require what Todd R. LaPorte and Ann Keller call the quality of institutional constancy in their management that traditional, incremental policy-making styles cannot achieve (1996). It is not the technology itself, but the need for long-range planning implicit in the technology's prudent management that is the most important social problem. It is a problem inherent to incrementalism, which "can provide neither the rationale nor the structure to support areas of public policy that require long-term planning and commitment" (Heineman, Bluhm, Peterson, & Kearny, 1990, p. 5).

THE TRUST PROBLEM

An insidious consequence of the culture of secrecy surrounding military and commercial nuclear power management from 1945 to the mid-1970s is a profound public distrust of the institutions associated with nuclear power, a mistrust apparently evoking and magnifying public perceptions about the human risks entailed with commercial nuclear technology. Research into public risk perceptions suggests that perceptions about the hazards associated with particular technologies are often tightly interlaced with beliefs about the institutions that manage them. "We know," summarized the National Research Council in its exhaustive 1994 study of risk assessment, "that public perceptions of the need for regulation are influenced by . . . people's trust in government, their experience with experts' reassurances and their views about social justice" (p. 263).

Public distrust of these institutions, in particular, tends to incite, or amplify, public apprehension about the risks associated with the technology. "Today," argues Daniel Fiorino, "the challenge to effective risk management may not be so much technical or economic as political. By political, I mean the ways people view their relationship to institutions making collective decisions about environmental risk and their capacities for influencing these decisions" (1989, p. 503).

This public intermingling of institutional and technological attitudes is particularly relevant to nuclear waste, the commercial nuclear power industry's greatest political liability and deterrent to future development. For example, studies of public attitudes across the United States suggest that public distrust of the DOE and its contractors, as much as public beliefs about the risks involved with the waste or its repositories, incites opposition to nuclear waste siting proposals and promotes beliefs in the riskiness of the waste facilities (Dunlap, Rosa, Baxter, & Mitchell, 1993). Indeed, lack of public trust in the institutions associated with commercial nuclear power appears to be the single greatest political obstacle the industry must overcome and, therefore, its most important strategic objective for any revival. "In order to make a comeback," Alan Nogee, the program director of the Union of Concerned Scientists, recently remarked, "the nuclear industry needs to rebuild public trust." Unfortunately, he adds, "I don't see a lot of signs that they have done a good job" (Kriz, 1998, p. 2495). It is important to note that both public and private institutional managers bear the stigma of public suspicion in commercial nuclear management.

THE IMPERATIVE OF INSTITUTIONAL CONSTANCY

Todd R. LaPorte and Ann Keller are among a growing number of social scientists currently investigating how organizational structures and styles are related to the capability of public and private institutions to manage extremely risky or dangerous technologies. Their research about the management of long-lived hazards, such as nuclear waste, suggests highly useful criteria for evaluating past management of the nation's commercial nuclear power program and for creating more appropriate managerial strategies in the future.

LaPorte and Keller assert that the management of long-term hazards such as nuclear waste—and I would add nuclear energy technologies—requires the development of new public organizations capable of an institutional constancy, which institutions grounded upon incrementalism are unlikely to attain. This institutional constancy involves

> faithfulness, unchanging commitment to, and repeated attainment of performance, effects, or outcomes in accord with agreements by agents of an institution made at one time and carried out or experienced in a future time. . . . An institution exhibits constancy when, year after year, it achieves outcomes it agreed in the past to pursue. (LaPorte & Keller, 1996, p. 538)

LaPorte and Keller assert that institutions of this sort are necessary, specifically for a class of hazards such as nuclear waste, which is widely recognized to pose potentially severe negative effects distributed over a potentially vast time period. These types of hazards require an assurance of long-term, dependable, and damage-limiting and mitigating capabilities in the institutions responsible for the hazard management. Stated differently, this management requires institutions capable of creating and justifying public trust in their technical capabilities and commitment to manage responsibly over centuries rather than decades.

Unfortunately, the authors argue that management organizations, whether public or private, embodying incremental decision-making styles are probably incapable of this institutional constancy for several reasons. First, incrementalism emphasizes relatively short time frames for decision-making and short-term incentives for action—a style especially characteristic of American governmental institutions and epitomized by customary congressional policy making. (Consider, as an especially egregious example of policy inconstancy, the wildly mutable congressional policies over the last two decades regarding the method of selecting and constructing a permanent nuclear waste repository.) Second, incrementalism favors continual policy innovation and policy adjustments at the margin as a strategy for policy implementation. Moreover, incrementalism favors bargaining and compromises as a means of policy formulation rather than an unwavering agenda of policy objectives. For these and other reasons, the argument concludes, existing models of institutional management for hazards such as nuclear waste have not, and cannot, inspire public trust in their technical competence or policy commitments over long periods.

THE PROBLEM OF CROSS-GENERATIONAL COSTS

Nuclear technologies and their wastes have vividly dramatized to the public, as well as to its political representatives, the special problem of intergenerational equity created by Faustian technologies developed in the latter half of the 20th century. One example of this problem involves the decommissioning and decontamination (D & D) of existing commercial nuclear power facilities. After domestic commercial facilities complete their licensed lifetime, typically 40 to 50 years, they must be D & D. This extremely costly process is meant to assure that each facility, including all its technology and associated structures and equipment, is no longer dangerous to humans or to the environment. This, in turn, requires a variety of strategies, including the physical disassembly of the facility along with the removal of all equipment and waste to another location, or sequestering the existing facility in situ from human contact, perhaps by permanent entombment in huge concrete shells.

Unfortunately, almost no domestic utility with commercial nuclear facilities anticipated the cost of D & D in designing its initial rate structures or its subsequent economic operations. Now, facing the prospect of D & D within a few years, nuclear utilities are belatedly attempting to finance the job with income from current and future ratepayers (General Accounting Office, 1990). Current utility customers have vigorously opposed this strategy in many states, arguing that it is inequitable to impose the whole cost of D & D upon a single generation of customers and that stockholders should bear the costs as well. Here, the equity in cross-generational distributions of costs and benefits was apparently never considered a serious problem, and solutions were never thoroughly considered in the institutional strategies during the industry's initial planning.

A MILLENNIAL PROPOSAL

The one thing that virtually all sides of the commercial nuclear power controversy recognize is that reviving the industry will be arduous and problematic. Not the least problem is that regulatory institutions capable of the institutional constancy that is seemingly required for future commercial nuclear facilities do not exist anywhere. The strategy I am suggesting emphasizes the primacy in redesigning, and then implementing, institutional management structures in the most publicly visible manner as the initial phase in a new commercial nuclear power program. This redesign must be imaginative enough to make earlier reforms seem comparatively homeopathic by aiming for the elusive goal of institutional constancy. The industry today can afford no small plans, but the planning should begin with comparatively small generating facilities and only with start-up or scale-up technologies. This can reduce risk—political, fiscal, human, and ecological—to acceptable magnitudes. If successful, a very potent psychological advantage could also be obtained by creating a badly needed, new developmental narrative for the technology.

A PUBLIC-PRIVATE CITIZEN CONSORTIUM

I believe that the next generation of commercial nuclear facilities, if built in the United States, should initially involve only public-private partnerships. This future development must constitute not only a collaboration among government regulators and promoters, private (or public) utilities, and technology manufacturers as in the past, it should include, from the outset, the active involvement of environmental, public interest, and other citizen-based organizations in some sort of public-private consortium embracing both planning and financing; it should aim first at a few pilot projects. Moreover, the public institutional role should be assumed by an entity created for this purpose and divorced from, as much as possible in public and official association, the DOE, the public credibility of which is, perhaps, the single greatest political stigma that commercial nuclear power must contend with in the future (Flynn et al., 1995, chap. 5). The nuclear power industry and, especially, the environmental community may regard such collaboration as having the devil to dinner, but conspicuous citizen participation is, I believe, the sine qua non for reestablishing the industry's public credibility. In this respect, it is worth noting that important segments of the mainstream environmental movement are reluctantly rethinking their adamant aversion to commercial nuclear power in light of global climate warming and the Kyoto negotiations (Schriesheim, 1997, p. 563).

It may be necessary to create a special public entity for these purposes, but the participation of federal government entities in this consortium would have several attractions. It will assure a relatively open planning process governed by several federal statutes, including the National Environmental Policy Act, enforceable by the judiciary; moreover, the federal entities would be liable to citizen lawsuits if significant public involvement were absent. The active, high-profile involvement of citizen groups, environmental or otherwise, is conducive to public trust in the process—there are no guaranties, however. The planners could take advantage of past mistakes, using the lessons learned as public principles for planning the next generation of reactor facilities.

The purpose of this consortium, in any event, is to both plan and finance one or more small pilot projects that would involve relatively limited capital investment for all parties, including at least some investment by the public interests.

CROSS-GENERATIONAL EQUITY

The problem of cross-generational equity has to be recognized explicitly and publicly at the beginning of planning, and institutional strategies beyond a symbolic response must be discovered for a new generation of planned nuclear facilities. This strategy directly addresses one previously mentioned requirement for institutional constancy. Based upon past experience, two types of cross-generational equity issues are likely to arise at the outset of planning: (a) How do we assure that the economic costs associated with waste disposal and the decommissioning of nuclear facilities will be equitably distributed over the project's lifetime, and (b) how do we assure that the human and ecological risks entailed in the development and operation of the facility are acceptable and fairly distributed both temporally and spatially? In the latter case, temporal distribution of risk refers to the disaggregation of risk over the lifetime of the facilities and their waste products, whereas spatial distribution involves the initial social and geographic distribution of risk around facilities at start-up.

Solutions to the economic issue are easier to imagine because they would involve variations on familiar, existing fiscal instruments or institutions. All would involve some equivalence to a surety bond underwritten by the consortium, involving significant capital set aside for the estimated lifetime of the facility as a demonstration of good faith and subject to forfeiture by the consortium's failure to meet stated standards of operation during the facility's lifetime. In addition, or in some combination with a surety bond, a sinking fund could be established in which a sufficient portion of existing income would be allocated over the project's lifetime to fund the facility's D & D. This, in fact, should be one of the easier aspects of the facility planning because much more information will be available about the costs associated with future facility D & D, and considerably more candor about the problem can be expected than in the first era of the commercial reactor program.

The risk aspect of equity involves the most formidable political problem. It is important to emphasize that waste and waste disposal, not the safety of the existing commercial facilities themselves, incite the greatest and most consistent public fear associated with domestic commercial nuclear power (Flynn et al., 1995, chap. 5). It is this aspect of the risk equity problem that needs to be addressed first. During the developmental euphoria for commercial nuclear power in the 1960s, it was assumed, and never seriously debated between the governmental or private planners, that commercial fuel reprocessing (the back end of the fuel cycle) would substantially eliminate the waste disposal problem. Clearly, it was a fundamental mistake to neither plan seriously for the contingency of reprocessing failure nor to publicly recognize its possibility during the early stages of planning. Many of the political problems now associated with commercial radioactive waste disposal grew from the inevitable surprise, political ineptness, and unpreparedness associated with this failure to display and discuss all realistic contingencies at the outset. There must be an assured disposal site for any waste associated with newer commercial reactor technologies before pilot facilities are constructed.

Despite current federal government efforts to establish a permanent high-level nuclear waste (HLNW) facility at Yucca Mountain, Nevada, a truly permanent, operational repository seems increasingly unlikely for many decades (General Accounting Office, 1993). Technically acceptable, temporary federal storage sites exist, and several constituencies likely to meet technical requirements have indicated a willingness to accept nuclear waste, at least temporarily. In fact, insisting upon the existence of a permanent HLNW repository as a condition for the further development of commercial reactor technology will assure its failure. In this respect, the experience of other nuclear nations with HLNW is worth considering. Although the siting of a permanent HLNW repository for commercial nuclear waste has been politically controversial in virtually all of these countries, it appears that the disposal of HLNW from electric power facilities has been considerably easier because these nations have not established a firm, ambitious date for the creation of a permanent repository; the date was left floating in order to allow time to work through the complex technical and political obstacles to public acceptance of a permanent waste site (General Accounting Office, 1994).

Whatever else it may be, the currently proposed permanent repository at Yucca Mountain, Nevada, is a political failure that, in the opinion of a growing community of experts, will eventually be abandoned or converted to an interim storage facility. A resolution to the ongoing conflict over a permanent federal nuclear waste site must occur in the near future, given the currently fierce political and judicial pressure upon Washington to redeem its failed commitment to creating a permanent repository before the year 2000. There are no guarantees that a permanent repository will ever become available for the waste from a new generation of commercial reactors. Yet, given the political realities just mentioned, there is also reason to initiate discussions or negotiations about the relatively small waste volume associated with the pilot phase of new commercial reactors.

If the waste issue can be initially resolved, at least to the point that a pilot reactor program can proceed on the basis of a designated (if temporary) waste disposal site, the risks associated with commercial nuclear facilities themselves must be addressed next. Here the temporal aspect of the risk issue arises. It will be necessary to find facility sites invulnerable to legal or political indictments of environmental injustice because they expose minorities in their proximity to disproportionate risk from their operation. It ought to be possible, in a pilot program, to sidestep this issue by locating a new reactor facility at one of the existing federal National Laboratories or nuclear reservations.

Neither approach to equity transfers comes with a guarantee of success. However, the value of this approach lies in its open and early commitment to confronting the waste problem, not as a contingency but as an inevitability, and in its recognition of the cross-generational equities as an inherent strategic and political issue in facility planning. Furthermore, other nations with HLNW have been able to confront the repository problem with greater success (General Accounting Office, 1994).

PREPARING PLANNERS AND MANAGERS

The management of utilities buying the turnkey commercial facilities that initiated the industry's operational phase were unprepared, due to the lack of experience, education, and federal initiative, for the political complexities they encountered in dealing with the public, especially after the mid-1970s when the industry confronted an increasingly well-organized, scientifically sophisticated and critical citizen opposition. "Both the [reactor manufacturers] and their customers overlooked the fact that development of commercially competitive nuclear technology . . . required the establishment of a new and intricately interrelated industrial process and services. And it required public acceptance" (Bupp & Derian, 1981, p. 186). In particular, the utility managers and their staff had to learn—if learn they did—about risk communication by experience. Many of the important, difficult lessons about risk communication with the public were acquired through the experience of this generation of facility managers. Even so, at least two issues—cross-generational equity and environmental justice—have so recently climbed to political salience that their implications for the future management of nuclear technologies are still poorly understood, and the implications for management itself only tentatively explored.

It is not obvious that the industry's prior history will prepare the next generation of nuclear facility managers to deal with the new political implications of their technology without a substantial, sustained socialization to this responsibility. This socialization will have to embrace not only relatively new issues, like generational equity and environmental justice, but also a rigorous education in risk communication. Even today, most MBA programs include few courses in any aspect of environmental management, let alone risk communication (World Resources Institute, 1998). Even executives trained in risk management are likely to need additional education about the importance of process as well as substance in risk communication.

CONCLUSION

Toward the end of World War II, a high-ranking British Air Force officer accounted for his country's successful strategic bombing campaign against the Axis with the statement, "It is the enemy who in the end designs our planes." Why do we not apply this logic of exploiting adversity to good effect in the future development of nuclear power and craft adversity into a weapon against itself? This essay has argued that the nation's deeply flawed historical experience with its initial promotion of commercial nuclear power, and the criticism spawned in its aftermath, can be the adversary that informs, and ultimately crafts, a strategy to defeat a repetition in the future. In this perspective, past experience should be considered less a trajectory toward technological failure than the upward arc of a learning curve to some new inflection point where commercial nuclear power assumes new viability.

The lessons to be learned from this past experience, I have argued, are clear in principle. First, the political problems associated with the new developmental phase should be fully articulated and attacked first. Only when a constructive political context has been created should the planning of the new technology itself be implemented. Second, the institutional problems are the most important of all the political problems that need to be addressed, for it is here, as much as anywhere else in nuclear power's domestic past, that the seeds of failure were sown. The institutional design must achieve at least some of the innovative, requisite qualities for institutional constancy. Third, any future technology planning must be relentlessly public and must involve the environmental community and other habitual critics of commercial nuclear power. Fourth, the new technological initiative must be modest in scale and economic scope; no more grand designs. Fifth, the new institutional arrangements must address the issues of intergenerational equity implicit in nuclear technology. Finally, the private management for the new technology must be prepared by training to deal with the political and social dimensions of the technology.

These are, at best, seminal ideas—a basis for discussion. They could, I believe, at least move us beyond the rapidly approaching time when, if nothing changes, our only nuclear option will be dependence upon the existing generation of reactors with all their obvious problems or no commercial nuclear power at all.

REFERENCES

Allison, G., & Carnesale, A. (1983). The utility director's dilemma: The governance of nuclear power. In D. S. Zinberg (Ed.), *Uncertain power: The struggle for a national energy policy* (pp. 134-156). New York: Pergamon Press.

Bartin, W. F., Imai, R., & Steeg, H. (1996). *Maintaining energy security in a global context*. New York: Trilateral Commission.

Bupp, I. C., & Derian, J.-C. (1981). *The failed promise of nuclear power*. New York: Basic Books.

Del Sesto, S. L. (1979). *Science, politics, and controversy: Civilian nuclear power in the United States, 1946-1974*. Boulder, CO: Westview Press.

Domenici, P. (1998). The Domenici challenge. *Bulletin of the Atomic Scientists, 54*, 40-44.

Dunlap, R. E., Rosa, E. A., Baxter, R. K., & Mitchell, R. M. (1993). Local attitudes toward siting a high-level nuclear waste repository at Hanford, Washington. In R. E. Dunlap, M. E. Kraft, & E. A. Rosa (Eds.), *Public reactions to nuclear waste: Citizens' views of repository siting* (pp. 136-172). Durham, NC: Duke University Press.

Energy Information Administration. (1998). Nuclear energy gaining market share. *Power Engineering, 102*, 8.

Fiorino, D. J. (1989). Environmental risk and democratic process: A critical review. *Columbia Journal of Environmental Law, 14*, 2.

Flynn, J., Chalmers, J., Easterling, D., Kasperson, R., Kunreuther, H., Mertz, C. K., Mushkatel, A., Pijawka, K. D., Slovic, P., & Dotto, L. (1995). *One hundred centuries of solitude: Redirecting America's high-level waste policy*. Boulder, CO: Westview Press.

Geller, H., & McGarahgan, S. (1998). Successful government partnership: The U.S. Department of Energy's role in advancing nuclear-efficient technologies. *Energy Policy, 26*, 167-177.

General Accounting Office. (1979). *Nuclear power costs and subsidies* (Rep. No. EMD 79-52). Washington, DC: Government Printing Office.

General Accounting Office. (1990). *Nuclear research and development: Shippingport decommissioning—how applicable are the lessons?* (Rep. No. RCED 90-208). Washington, DC: Government Printing Office.

General Accounting Office. (1993). *Nuclear waste: Yucca Mountain Project behind schedule and facing major scientific uncertainties* (Rep. No. RCED 93-124). Washington, DC: Government Printing Office.

General Accounting Office. (1994). *Nuclear waste: Foreign countries' approaches to high-level waste storage and disposal* (Rep. No. RCED 94-172). Washington, DC: Government Printing Office.

Hayes, M. T. (1992). *Incrementalism and public policy*. New York: Longman.

Heineman, R. A., Bluhm, W. T., Peterson, S. A., & Kearny, E. N. (1990). *The world of the policy analyst*. Chatham, NJ: Chatham House Press.

Hilgartner, S., Bell, R. C., & O'Conner, R. (1983). *Nukespeak: The selling of nuclear technology in America*. New York: Penguin Books.

Holt, M., & Behrens, C. (1998). *Nuclear energy policy* (Rep. No. 88090). Washington, DC: Congressional Research Service.

Kemeny, J. G. (1979). *The need for a change: The legacy of TMI*. Washington, DC: President's Commission on the Accident at Three Mile Island.

Kido, A. (1998). Trends of nuclear power development in Asia. *Energy Policy, 26*, 577-582.

Kriz, M. (1998). A comeback for nukes? *National Journal, 28*, 2492-2496.

LaPorte, T. R., & Keller, A. (1996). Assuring institutional constancy: Requirements for managing long-lived hazards. *Public Administration Review, 56*, 535-544.

Livernash, R., & Rodenburg, E. (1998). Population change, resources, and the environment. *Population Bulletin, 53*, 2-39.

Matsui, K. (1998). Global demand growth of power generation, input choices and supply security. *The Energy Journal, 19*, 93-107.

National Research Council, Committee on Risk Assessment of Hazardous Air Pollutants. (1994). *Science and Judgment in Risk Assessment*. Washington, DC: National Academy Press.

Parker, P., & Blodgett, J. (1998). *Electricity restructuring: The implications for air quality* (Rep. No. 98-615 ENR). Washington, DC: Congressional Research Service.

Schriesheim, A. (1997). Power to grow: An expanding world considers its power options. *Vital Speeches, 63*, 561-565.

Wood, W. C. (1983). *Nuclear safety: Risks and regulation*. Washington, DC: American Enterprise Institute.

World Resources Institute. (1998). *Grey pinstripes with green ties: MBA programs where the environment matters*. Washington, DC: World Resources Institute.

Weinberg, A. M. (1972, July 7). The many dimensions of scientific responsibility. *Science, 177*, 33.

White, R. W. (1998). Kyoto and beyond. *Issues in Science and Technology, 14*, 5965.

5

Transportation

Policy-Level Partnerships and Project-Based Partnerships

JAMES A. DUNN, JR.

Transportation policy operates on the frontier between politics and markets. Because transportation is so important, so obtrusive, and so expensive, governments inevitably intervene to influence transportation markets. Because transportation is closely linked to so many private investments, employment, and residential choices, it is impossible, in a capitalist country, for government alone to control all the key aspects of the transportation system. The challenge of transportation policy is to discover the most economically efficient and politically acceptable arrangements for coordinating public and private efforts to improve mobility and to apportion costs and benefits among the many stakeholders.

Thus, public-private partnerships are very common in transportation, but they are not always recognized as such. We can identify two broad categories of public-private partnerships in transportation. First, there are *policy-level partnerships*, which lay down a set of general rules for public and private investment, operation, and dispute resolution in a given transport mode, such as railroads, urban transit, highways, inland waterways, and others. Because transportation policy making has historically been fragmented along modal lines, I call the

TABLE 1: Types of Transportation Policies and Examples of Partnerships

Type of Policy	Policy-Level Partnership	Project-Based Partnership
Promotion	Federal highway assistance program	Private toll roads
Regulation	CAFE standards	PNGV
Protection	Urban mass transit assistance program	Contracting out bus service
Rationalization	ISTEA—intermodalism	Employer trip reduction program, TMAs

institutional framework of these broad policy partnerships "modal benefits regimes" (Dunn, 1998, pp. 24-25). Such regimes are always the product of elaborate political compromises that allocate costs and benefits between public and private sectors. Under the Interstate Commerce Commission (ICC) railroad regulatory regime, for example, private rail companies had the right to earn a fair return on capital, but a public regulatory commission had the right to approve the prices charged to the customers. Second, there are project-based partnerships, which focus on a specific site or circumstance. Often local political leaders will promote particular project-based partnerships to achieve a goal that can not be accomplished following the normal rules of an established modal benefits regime. For example, if a new transit terminal would be an asset to a downtown revitalization plan, but there are not enough public funds available, city officials will try to find ways to entice private capital into the project.

The types of public-private partnerships that are formed are related to the stages of growth of particular transport modes. Different transportation technologies are often at different stages of their cycle of growth, stability, decline, and renewal, and they need very different types of policy support. Generally speaking, policy making in a mode will be dominated successively by promotion, regulation, protection, and rationalization. Table 1 illustrates the typical sequence of policy types in a mode and shows how the examples discussed in this article fit into the framework.

PROMOTION AND PUBLIC-PRIVATE PARTNERSHIPS

In the early stages of a mode's growth, public policy focuses on promotion. Public officials seek to attract as much investment in the new means of transport to their territory as they can. In the 19th century, it was state and, even more often, local officials who led efforts to promote, successively, turnpikes, canals, and railroads, in what a distinguished transport historian called "metropolitan mercantilism" (Taylor, 1951, p. 98). They scrambled to stay ahead of their neighbors and were willing to offer as many inducements as necessary (direct stock ownership, subsidies, loans, monopoly charters and franchises, land grants, tax incentives, dedicated streams of public revenue, etc.) to make sure that their community was not bypassed by the new mode. Thus, each new mode began as a diverse series of decentralized project-based partnerships. Turnpikes and canals never got beyond this decentralized stage before being overtaken by railroads as the rising technology on which promotional incentives were lavished. After the civil war and the completion of the transcontinental rail links, public capital and land grants were no longer needed to promote investment to the rail sector, but the privileged position of private capital and management were firmly embedded in an implicit laissez-faire rail benefits regime.

Highways offer a 20th-century example of the federal government leading the first truly nationwide policy-level partnership for promoting a new transport mode. After decades of sporadic efforts (initially by bicyclists, then by motorists) to get local governments to fund good roads, the Federal Aid Road Act of 1916 and the Federal Aid Highway Act of 1921 laid the foundations of a remarkable policy-level partnership that explicitly linked federal and state governments and implicitly included important sections of the business community as well as millions of individuals (Seely, 1987, pp. 46-66). The federal and state governments agreed to cooperate to provide a growing, well-planned network of roads. Public financing would come not from taxes on adjacent property owners, but from motor fuel taxes dedicated exclusively to state and federal highway trust funds.[1] In addition to this explicitly intergovernmental partnership, the highway promotion regime also included an implicit partnership with private individuals and groups. Private motorists and truckers agreed to invest their own money to provide vehicles, fuel, insurance, and other operating expenses. Over many decades, this highway promotion regime based on public funding of infrastructure and private funding of rolling stock created a supremely successful mobility partnership that transformed American lifestyles and land-use patterns.

Today, the promotion era for highways is drawing to a close amid controversy and confusion. Environmentalists, anti-auto activists, opponents of sprawl, and not-in-my-backyard (NIMBY) groups make building any new highway segments a drawn-out ordeal. Escalating road construction costs and political resistance to increased government spending have limited highway departments' ability to provide publicly funded new road capacity, even in severely congested areas. One option that is coming increasingly into play in the construction of new highway capacity is private finance and operation of new roads (Lockwood, 1995).

There are a number of such public-private road-building partnerships around the nation. One of the best known examples is the Route 91 express lanes project in California's Orange County. The partners are the California Department of Transportation (Caltrans) and the California Private Transportation Company (CPTC), a consortium of American companies and the French firm, Compagnie Financière et Industrielle des Autoroutes (Cofiroute), said to be the world's largest private toll-road operator. CPTC built the project, transferred ownership of the improvements to the State of California, and received in return a 35-year lease to operate the facility, charge tolls, and make a maximum of 17% to 23% annual rate of return after taxes. Caltrans saved the $130 million construction cost, which was financed by debt instruments provided by commercial banks such as Citicorp, Banque Nationale de Paris, and Deutsche Bank. In addition, Caltrans estimates that it will save another $120 million in operations and maintenance expenses over the 35-year lease (California Department of Transportation, 1998).

Opened in December 1995, the express lanes project is a 10-mile, 4-lane, fully automated toll road running in the median of the existing 8-lane expressway between State Route 55 in Orange County and the Riverside County line. It uses the Fastrak electronic transponder system to collect the tolls, which vary according to the time of day and the days of the week. Motorists pay a one-way toll that ranges from $0.60 in the late night and early morning hours to $3.20 at peak periods, thus embodying congestion pricing principles long recommended by economists. Discounts are offered for disabled persons and zero-emission vehicles (ZEVs). A specially marked 3+ lane is toll free for car pools with three or more passengers (California Private Transportation Corporation, 1998). Since the opening, tolls have already had to be increased because traffic was backing up at rush hours and because the CPTC had a deficit of about $3.7 million in 1997. Some analysts blamed the revenue lost to the 3+ carpool lane as contributing to the cash shortfall (Gorell, 1997).

It is easy to see why a growing number of private toll roads are being built or planned in other states, for example, the Dulles Green Way in Virginia (Conrad, 1995). Technically, improvements in electronic toll and vehicle identification technology lower the cost of collecting revenue, speed the flow of traffic, and reduce the emissions generated by congested toll plazas. Financially, the partnerships improve access to private long-term capital markets without requiring states to raise their debt ceilings or pay tax-free interest on general obligation bonds. Organizationally, the projects can draw on the global expertise of international companies such as Cofiroute, which may help lower development and operating costs. Politically, having private companies levy the tolls gives state transportation departments and elected officials some political cover, makes toll increases somewhat easier to justify to the public, and enables them to proclaim that they are stretching their limited road construction budgets and saving the general taxpayers money.

There is also opposition to such project-based partnerships. Environmentalists object to any new highway construction, no matter how it is financed. They would prefer to see tolls levied on existing highways to encourage drivers to carpool or take public transit. Liberals, such as California state senator Tom Haydon, denounce new toll expressways as "Lexus lanes" that enable the wealthy to speed past the traffic jams that ensnare the working classes. Unions representing current tollbooth workers fear job losses. Truckers fear that successful new toll roads might encourage the spread of tolls to existing freeways and that trucks may face discriminatory tolls based on axle weight.

These opponents can slow but not stop the growth of public-private toll facilities. Although it seems a safe bet that most freeways will continue to be free for the foreseeable future, public-private partnerships and electronic tolls will likely play a larger role in financing and managing highways than they did in the heyday of the interstate era from 1956 to 1991.

REGULATION: PARTNERSHIPS INSTEAD OF ADVERSARIALISM?

At some point in the growth of any mode, the focus of politics and policy making shifts from promotion to regulation. Groups that had been excluded from most of the benefits of promotion realize that they have important interests at stake. They cry foul, and organize a countermovement to correct the injustices of the powerful new mode. Classic instances of the shift from promotion to regulation were seen in the late 19th- and early 20th-century movements to restrain the power of giant railroads and urban electric traction companies with new regulatory institutions such as the ICC and state public utility commissions.

In the 1960s, the "new social regulation" emerged from "an uneasy marriage between the New Deal and the New Left" and aimed some of its most successful efforts at the U.S. auto industry (Harris & Milkis, 1989, p. 55). Unlike classic economic regulation, the new social regulation's goal was not competitive fairness in market transactions. Its aim was to protect the general public from the dangers of unsafe automotive design, worsening air quality caused by auto emissions, and energy problems caused by gas-guzzling vehicles. It extended public power into the previously sacrosanct private domains of product design and marketing strategies. The National Highway Traffic Safety Administration, the Environmental Protection Agency (EPA), and the federal Corporate Average Fuel Economy (CAFE) standards are institutional legacies of this period, as are the federal mandates for public hearings, advisory committees, environmental impact statements, and also the spate of lawsuits that virtually every major highway project must now face.

In the decade and a half between the dramatic eruption of Ralph Nader on the scene and the election of Ronald Reagan as president, relations between Detroit and Washington were often bitterly adversarial. The Reagan administration sought a restoration of more supportive relations with the auto industry by means of its voluntary auto export restraint agreement with Japan and executive orders to push regulatory rollback as far as legally possible (Dunn, 1998). With Bill Clinton's election to the presidency in 1992, and Democrats controlling both the executive and legislative branches for the first time in 12 years, and with Vice President Gore's well-publicized views on the environment, expectations were high that the new administration would renew the regulatory push toward cleaner, more fuel-efficient automobiles. However, as was often his pattern,

Clinton confounded his opponents and disappointed his supporters. Instead of submitting bills to congress calling for stricter regulation, Clinton and Gore invited the heads of the Big Three auto companies to the White House in 1993 to announce the Partnership for a New Generation of Vehicles (PNGV). The goal of the partnership was a joint research program to develop a passenger vehicle that was three times more fuel efficient than a 1994 intermediate size car by the year 2004.

The announcement was designed to signal the arrival of a new era in Washington's relations with Detroit, one of cooperation rather than confrontation. The administration described it as "a model for the new partnership between government and industry envisioned by President Clinton" (White House, 1993). It would provide a "peace dividend" by making available the resources and expertise of the Defense Department and the Energy Department's national labs. The industry stressed that the partnership "allows American business to set a path . . . and define areas where government support can be most helpful. . . . Success in this venture means practical vehicles sold by U.S. auto companies in competitive markets" (White House, 1993). The new partnership "replaces controversy with cooperation, breaking decades of gridlock between industry and government" (White House, 1993). The industry participates in PNGV through the U.S. Council for Automotive Research (USCAR), an organization formed in 1992 by Chrysler, Ford, and General Motors (GM) to carry out and monitor precompetitive research on energy and environmental matters.

The government and industry agreed to survey potential new technologies and select the most promising ones. Auto companies would then fabricate concept vehicles embodying the selected innovations by 2000, and prepare preproduction prototype vehicles by 2004. Technologies that received prominent mention in the early PNGV literature were compression ignition direct injection (CIDI) engines; four-stroke direct injection spark-ignited (4DISI) engines, gas turbines, Stirling engines, fuel cells, ultracapacitors, lithium-ion batteries, flywheels, and sophisticated electric power converters and electronic controllers (National Research Council, 1997).

In regulatory policy, the partnership approach has important political advantages for both sides. It enables the administration to tell environmentalists that something is being done about auto-related energy and pollution problems. It finesses a confrontation with Congress over whether to impose new federal regulations on the auto industry. It gives the executive-branch scientists and engineers a valuable observation point from which to assess the progress of automotive research and development and judge what is technically feasible. For Detroit, the PNGV promised a 10-year breathing spell during which it could continue to market its profitable lines of sport utility vehicles without having to worry about their impact on the auto manufacturers' CAFE conformance. The era of good feelings fostered by PNGV has led the administration to launch several other more modest partnerships, including the Intelligent Vehicle Initiative and the National Intelligent Transportation Infrastructure project to explore how the latest developments in electronics and communications can improve vehicle safety and smooth the flow of highway traffic.

The PNGV does not require the new types of cars developed to be actually mass-produced. Federal officials hope that Detroit will voluntarily incorporate enough new technology into cars coming off future assembly lines to make substantial improvements in overall energy consumption and emissions levels. However, it is possible that after 2004, the partnership will have to be supplemented or supplanted by a return to stricter regulatory standards in order to get the new generation of vehicles off the drawing boards and into the showrooms.

PROTECTION: PUBLIC TRANSIT AND PRIVATE MARKETS

With the passage of the Urban Mass Transportation Act of 1964, policy making for public transportation shifted from local and state regulation to a federally driven regime for protection. Prompted by big-city mayors and certain commuter railroads, the Democratic Kennedy and Johnson administrations and the Republican Nixon and Ford administrations led the congress to provide federal funds to rehabilitate the capital plant of public transit enterprises and then to provide money to cover operating deficits. However, the political dynamics of protecting transit tended to push the public sector involvement onto a slippery slope. If the benefits of the old transit system are worth preserving, and if the competition—the private automobile—is constantly improving, one cannot protect transit very long unless something significant is done to improve its competitiveness. Why increase subsidies to a decrepit old system when, with some more money, a newer, faster, and more high tech system can be had that will have a better chance of luring back the riders?

Once serious federal money was on the table, all the stakeholders (unions, equipment manufacturers, urban and suburban politicians, downtown businesses, etc.) wanted to make sure that they got their fair share. Following the Urban Mass Transportation Assistance Act of 1964, hundreds of privately owned bus and rail operations were acquired by public sector authorities. Between 1970 and 1980, federal aid to transit increased 1,600% (from $230 million to $3.9 billion), but ridership increased only 18% (American Public Transit Association, 1987, p. 30, 57-58). The overall financial deficit of the transit sector had been $90 million in 1968. By 1980, it had grown to $7.8 billion. The average transit operation in that year could only cover 41% of its operating expenses to say nothing of its capital expenditures (Pucher, Markstedt, & Hirschman, 1983, p. 73). Transit operating expenses, driven by generous wage settlements, rose by 319% compared to the overall consumer price index increase of 147%. Fares, on the other hand, only rose by 67% (Lave, 1985, p. 11). Transit had been protected, but the sector was again perceived to be in a fiscal crisis.

In the face of figures like these, thoughtful transit analysts had to acknowledge that the protection regime for transit had serious financial flaws and that the limits of subsidy would soon be reached (Altshuler, Womack, & Pucher, 1979). The Carter administration sought to slow transit spending without abandoning the goal of the system. One of its strategies was to encourage local authorities to identify innovative sources of funds for transit, including public-private partnerships. Federal urban transit administrators sponsored conferences, research reports, and pilot projects on innovations such as joint development around rail stations, special benefits assessment districts, development of transit malls, employer-paid transit passes, and the like (Public Technology, Inc., 1980; Kirby & Ernst, 1981).

When Ronald Reagan took office, executive branch skepticism on transit spending increased by an order of magnitude. For Reagan, federal transit aid was one of those Great Society, big government programs that was the problem and not the solution. "There is no reason for someone in Sioux Falls to pay federal taxes so that someone in Los Angeles can get to work on time by public transportation" (Smerk, 1991, pp. 191-192) was the President's most quoted line about transit. If cities wanted to subsidize their transit systems, let them do it with their own money. With Democrats still in control of the House of Representatives, the administration was unable to make the drastic cuts in transit spending that would have abolished the post-1964 protection regime outright. Instead, it turned to a conservative version of public-private partnerships, administratively pushing for privatization of the actual provision of public transit service through contracting out and competitive bidding.

Drawing on accumulated economic and organizational studies of the transit industry, Reagan's privatizers argued that the typical transit enterprise was a local monopoly in which organizational form and operating procedures dated from 1890 to 1920. Transit's radial structure depended on compact cities that were centered on downtown. Transit worked best in an era when few people had cars, and they used buses, subways, and streetcars for both peak-hour work trips and off-peak shopping and recreational travel. However, by the 1960s, the old compact city was already being restructured into a much more decentralized metropolitan area that was ill suited to efficient transit operations. The protectionist regime based on federal subsidies simply rescued a fading anachronistic style of operation and prevented Schumpeter's "winds of creative destruction" from doing their necessary work (Hilton, 1974; Lave, 1985).

The solution was to use publicly guided privatization to restore competition and efficiency to the sector. First, local officials should give the power to decide how much transit service is needed to an institution such as a Regional Transportation Commission, which is separate and distinct from the monopolistic public agency that actually operates the existing system. Once this separation is clearly established, the political authorities can begin to reintroduce competition into the urban transport service provision sector. They can put more and more services out for competitive bidding. Weekend and evening bus services can be contracted out to independent bus or taxi companies. Elderly and handicapped paratransit services can be privatized. Even some peak-hour fixed-route bus service can be contracted out. This kind of strategic privatization, far from "skimming the cream" of the most profitable traffic, would actually be skimming the deficit because it would enable the main public transit enterprise to buy fewer buses and hire fewer drivers (Cervero, 1988). Instead of its costs being inflated by the need to have a very large fleet and work force to handle peak-hour demand, they could be sized closer to average demand and hence significantly lower costs. Privatization would also put pressure on transit worker unions to be more willing to accept productivity-enhancing work rule changes, such as part-time drivers and cross training in multiple job categories. Likewise, transit managers would have to be more cost conscious, more customer driven, and better able to tailor service to individual market niches (Lave, 1985; Weicher, 1988).

Whatever the theoretical merits of this privatization paradigm, there were and are practical and political limits on how much change can actually be achieved through privatization. The highly capital-intensive parts of urban transit systems (the subways, the commuter rail lines, etc.) are very difficult to privatize. Even if the public authorities took over responsibility for providing the infrastructure of tunnels, bridges, tracks, signals, and stations, while putting the management of the rolling stock under private enterprise, the amount of true competitive pressure introduced would be minimal (Gomez-Ibanez & Meyer, 1993). In addition, there will be stiff political resistance to privatization of other operations (bus service, maintenance, accounting, etc.). Unions are obvious candidates to lead the fight. But public sector managers, who know that salaries, perks, pensions, and expense accounts tend to rise in proportion to the size of the operation being managed, can also expect to be very reluctant privatizers. Passenger groups fear fare hikes and service cuts. Some politicians would be glad to raise a variety of objections to privatization, from the union busting issue to the impact on minorities (Blacks and Hispanics are well represented among both the passengers and the workers in large urban transit enterprises).

The Reagan era privatization push did not achieve its ambitious goal of making far-reaching changes in the protection regime for transit. Federal transportation policies are essentially incentive systems. When a federal initiative is perceived as bringing new resources to the table, state and local officials tend to accept the initiative and redirect their own programs toward its goals. However, when a controversial federal policy provides no new resources, and many stakeholders perceive it as undermining an established benefits regime, resistance is inevitable.

If the privatization push was unable to contract out most transit service to private partners, the Reagan-Bush era freeze on federal transit spending did stimulate transit's state and local governmental partners to increase their own transit subsidies substantially. Federal transit spending slipped from $3.9 billion in

1982 to $3.6 billion in 1992. The combined total of state and local government spending on transit rose from $7.4 billion to $18.7 billion in the same period (U.S. Department of Transportation, Bureau of Transportation Statistics, 1997). The taxpayers of Sioux Falls are paying a much smaller portion of a bureaucrat's Washington subway ride today than they were before the Gipper took office.

RATIONALIZATION: SEARCHING
FOR AN ALTERNATIVE TO SPRAWL

Rationalization policy is an emergent type of transportation policy in the American system. Not as fully developed as the other types, it differs from them in two other important respects. First, it is not tied to a single mode. It is self-consciously intermodal and seeks to develop the institutional capability to shift the balance between modes to maximize social benefits and minimize external costs. Second, its aim is not to expand the transportation system. It assumes that we already have all the transportation we need. Indeed, in the case of the automobile-highway mode, we have too much. Rationalization focuses on reducing the need for so much (auto)mobility. Its proponents are primarily urban and regional planners, environmentalists, transit supporters, and anti-auto activists.

The main target of rationalization policy is sprawl—low-density suburban development that is "poorly planned, land-consumptive, automobile dependent," dominated by the "sellscape" of roadside fast food franchises, shopping strips, discount outlets, and car dealerships, and expanded by the "leapfrog" development of single-family homes into previously undeveloped areas (Young, 1995). Rationalizers argue that the sprawl pattern of land development is more costly, in almost every respect, than a rationally planned pattern of development would be. They want to redesign the links between land use and transportation so that people can travel less but still have access to everything they need from their community.

A mild form of rationalization policy is *intermodalism*, which stresses improved planning and coordination of investments among different modes (e.g., more park-and-ride locations for commuters, more rail links to airports, etc.). Intermodalism has had a certain amount of success in freight transportation, especially when a single private company can integrate road and rail shipments (General Accounting Office, 1992). In passenger transportation, it runs into the difficulty of having to get people out of their cars in the current auto-dominated environment. However, the Intermodal Surface Transportation Efficiency Act of 1991 (ISTEA) was widely perceived as the harbinger of a trend toward giving state and local officials more flexibility to spend their federal transportation dollars on nonautomotive modes and enhancements, and toward requiring planners to pay more attention to "air quality, intermodal issues, long range planning, and intergovernmental coordination" (Gage & McDowell, 1995, p. 133).

A stronger version of rationalization seeks to change the template for how growth is spatially distributed in metropolitan areas. It calls for the creation of new metropolitan institutions with broad new powers over land development. These powers include urban growth boundaries, in-fill development mandates, mixed-use development permitting and zoning, and subsidies for innovative community designs. Regional transportation authorities might even be granted powers to restrict auto use directly by such means as congestion pricing of highways, taxes on free parking for employees, and mandatory employer-based ride-sharing programs. The goal of strong rationalization is to reduce the total amount of mobility required by American cities and towns.

Rationalizers are much enamored of the "new urbanist" neotraditional neighborhoods championed by Andres Duany and Elizabeth Plater-Zyberk (1992), and the "pedestrian pocket" and "transit-oriented developments" associated with Peter Calthorpe (1993). These community designs look back to preautomobile pedestrian and streetcar land use patterns that fostered intense social interaction among neighbors and built a fabric of community that puts people, not automobiles, first. With smaller-scaled communities, more trips can be made on foot and on bicycles. Modern electronics will enable people to substitute communication for transportation by telecommuting and electronic shopping. Public transportation will provide convenient links to the larger city. Community-based car-sharing services will attenuate the average person's psychological dependence on the auto and reduce their proclivity to make the car the first, and often only, mode of travel (Carlson, Wormser, & Ulberg, 1995).

However, until most U.S. metropolitan areas can build an antisprawl land use and transportation regime, rationalizers offer various kinds of public-private partnerships to help fill the gap. One relatively new but increasingly widespread partnership is the transportation management association (TMA). These are nonprofit organizations that give employers, developers, and property owners in high growth areas an opportunity to discuss their transportation and planning needs with each other and with representatives of local governments and transit agencies. TMAs typically have a board of directors to set general policy, and a full-time executive director with one to five staff members. They are financed by a combination of dues levied on the corporate members, in-kind contributions such as office space or staff support from members or public agencies, and public grants for start-up costs and for specific projects. New Jersey's Meadowlink TMA received financial aid from the state's Department of Transportation, the Meadowlands Development Corporation, the New Jersey Turnpike Authority, and the Port Authority of New York and New Jersey. TMAs carry out a wide range of traffic mitigation activities. These include surveys of employee travel patterns, developing transportation management plans, promoting and operating ride-sharing services, assisting members in leasing vans and subscription bus services, arranging flex-time and staggered work hours, and being an informed advocate for expanded public transit services (Dunphy & Lin, 1990).

A more controversial type of activity in which public authorities work through private employers to mitigate traffic congestion and automotive air pollution is the mandatory employer trip reduction program. The Southern California Air Quality Management District's Regulation XV established such a mandatory program for employers with more than 100 workers in 1987. The U.S. EPA mandated a similar program for firms in severe nonattainment areas, which was scheduled to take effect in the later half of the 1990s. Because the public requirement was backed by the threat of fines on employers who failed to comply, it was hardly a true partnership. An outside evaluation of the Southern California program concluded that the evidence "tends to cast doubt on the feasibility and cost effectiveness of regulatory, employer-based trip reduction programs as a tool of regional air pollution and traffic congestion mitigation" (Orski, 1993, p. 341). Around the nation, the EPA-mandated program proved so unpopular that, after the Republican victory in the 1994 congressional elections, it was shelved.

CONCLUSION: THE POLITICS OF MOBILITY

Negotiating the terms under which the public and private sectors cooperate to provide transportation for the growing country has been the essence of America's politics of mobility for more than 200 years. The negotiation process will become even more complex and contentious in the 21st century. More groups will participate in the process than ever before. And there will be pressures to pursue a broader and more diverse set of goals—from reducing traffic noise to combating global warming—than ever before.

In most American communities, there is no system of transport technology and land use planning that offers more convenience, comfort, and security than the automobile. In the past, railroads and urban electric transit had the power to shape dense, centralized cities. That power is now gone. As long as Americans are wealthy enough and free enough to own automobiles, no economically feasible amount of public investment in transit or politically feasible public-private traffic management projects can stop sprawl and recentralize our cities. In very large cities like New York, transit will continue to play an important role. However, in most U.S. cities and towns, it is the automobile that is the true means of mass transportation, whereas public transit serves a very small minority of passenger trips—about 1% of total surface passenger miles nationwide (Department of Transportation, Bureau of Transportation Statistics, 1995, p. 64).

The new urbanists remind us that there are many modest ways to improve the spatial layout and accessibility of our communities. Bike paths, pedestrian zones, clustering of homes and shops, and the like are useful ideas that deserve to be given a chance. However, political realism should temper excessive optimism. Such innovations can improve access in local neighborhoods. For access to the wider metropolitan community, the automobile will remain the means that most people will use.

Thus, if continued reduction of the transportation system's negative environmental impact is a goal that most stakeholders can broadly agree on, policies and partnerships aimed at inducing auto manufacturers to design and market cleaner, more fuel-efficient vehicles promise the biggest improvement for the amount of private financial and public political capital invested. Whether the technology developed by the PNGV is or is not incorporated into automobiles and light trucks after 2004 will set the tone for one of the most important transportation and environmental policy discussions of the new century. Will it require a second coming of Ralph Nader and a return to contentious adversarialism to wean Detroit (and Tokyo and Stuttgart) from their dependence on sport utility vehicles that are getting 14 miles per gallon? Alternatively, can the government and the automakers extend the cooperative spirit of the PNGV beyond the research lab and into the policy arena?

If Washington and Detroit can maintain enough mutual trust, they can work together to develop innovative regulations and incentives to actually help create markets for the super clean, super efficient cars that many auto writers and energy analysts have been promising (Riley, 1994; Lovins, 1995). Instead of a bitter fight over simply increasing the current CAFE standards, the industry and the government might work together on a more flexible regime. One approach might be to give automakers carry-over credits; if they improve the efficiency of their auto fleet, they could carry over credits to their light truck fleet. Another possibility might be carry-over between emissions standards and fuel economy. Perhaps companies could get credit for selling a certain number of ZEVs. This could be used to offset any shortfalls in their car or light truck fleets. Alternatively, a trading system might be instituted whereby a small new company that makes electric ZEVs would receive a credit for each vehicle that it sells to a full-line manufacturer to be counted toward its ZEV quota. GM might find it cheaper initially to buy such credits than to incur the cost of building electric cars. In addition, small start-up electric vehicle manufacturers would be encouraged by the extra source of income that the scheme would offer them. Later, GM could simply buy a successful electric vehicle company and use its established sales to meet its own quota.

Many more possibilities for innovative mixes of regulations and incentives exist. The key to developing a new policy-level partnership for the automobile will be for Washington and Detroit to work together in the spirit of the PNGV to achieve what the American people manifestly want—cars that meet people's individual need for mobility while protecting their collective need for a clean and safe environment.

NOTES

1. There were certain other complexities in the intergovernmental highway promotion regime that space does not permit me to cover here. The most important was the issue of how toll roads fit into a regime based predominantly on free roads. The 1956 legislation on the interstate highway system stopped the toll-road movement in its tracks for 35 years. See Seely, 1987, pp. 166-177, 204-213.

REFERENCES

Altshuler, A., Womack, J., & Pucher, J. (1979). *The urban transportation system: Politics and policy innovation.* Cambridge, MA: MIT Press.

American Public Transit Association. (1987). *Transit fact book, 1987.* Washington, DC: Author.

California Department of Transportation. (1998). *Private investment, public infrastructure* [On-line]. Available: http://www.dot.ca.gov/hq/paffairs/about/toll/rt91.htm.

California Private Transportation Corporation. (1998). *Frequently asked questions* [On-line]. Available: http:/www.91expresslanes.com/faqs.htm.

Calthorpe, P. (1993). *The next American metropolis: Ecology, community, and the American dream.* New York: Princeton Architectural Press.

Carlson, D., Wormser, L., & Ulberg, C. (1995). *At road's end: Transportation and land use choices for communities.* Washington, DC: Island Press.

Cervero, R. (1988). *Transit service contracting: Cream skimming or deficit skimming?* Washington, DC: U.S. Urban Mass Transit Administration.

Conrad, S. H. (1995). Dulles Green Way—breaking the old paradigms. *Transportation Quarterly, 49,* 15-22.

Department of Transportation, Bureau of Transportation Statistics. (1997). *Federal, state, and local transportation statistics, fiscal years 1982-1992* (BTS97-E-02). Washington, DC: Department of Transportation.

Department of Transportation, Bureau of Transportation Statistics. (1995). *National transportation statistics, 1995* (DOT-VNTSC-BTS-94-3). Washington, DC: Department of Transportation.

Duany, A., & Plater-Zyberk, E. (1992). The second coming of the American small town. *Wilson Quarterly, 16,* 19-50.

Dunn, J. A. (1998). *Driving forces: The automobile, its enemies, and the politics of mobility.* Washington, DC: The Brookings Institution Press.

Dunphy, R. T., & Lin, B. C. (1990). *Transportation management through partnerships.* Washington, DC: The Urban Land Institute.

Gage, R. W., & McDowell, B. D. (1995). ISTEA and the role of MPOs in the new transportation environment: A midterm assessment. *Publius, 25,* 133-154.

General Accounting Office. (1992). *Intermodal freight transportation: Combined rail truck service offers public benefits, but challenges remain.* Washington, DC: Author.

Gomez-Ibanez, J. A., & Meyer, J. R. (1993). *Going private: The international experience with transport privatization.* Washington, DC: The Brookings Institution Press.

Gorell, J. (1997, Fall). Building bridges without taxes. *California Manufacturer* [On-line]. Available: http://www.camfg.com/members/pubs/.

Harris, R. A., & Milkis, S. M. (1989). *The politics of regulatory change: A tale of two agencies.* New York: Oxford University Press.

Hilton, G. W. (1974). *Federal transit subsidies: The urban mass transportation assistance program.* Washington, DC: American Enterprise Institute.

Kirby, R. F., & Ernst, U.F.W. (1981). *Involving private providers in public transportation programs: Administrative options* (DOT-82-44). Washington, DC: U.S. Urban Mass Transportation Administration.

Lave, C. A. (1985). *Urban transit: The private challenge to public transportation*. San Francisco: Pacific Institute for Public Policy Research.

Lockwood, S. C. (1995). Public-private partnerships in U.S. highway finance: ISTEA and beyond. *Transportation Quarterly, 49*, 5-26.

Lovins, A. B. (1995, January). Reinventing the wheels. *Atlantic Monthy, 275*, 75-93.

National Research Council. (1997). *Review of the research program of the Partnership for a New Generation of Vehicles*. Washington, DC: National Academy Press.

Orski, C. K. (1993). Employee trip reduction programs—an evaluation. *Transportation Quarterly, 47*, 327-341.

Public Technology, Inc. (1980). *Proceedings of the joint development marketplace '80*. Washington, DC: U.S. Urban Mass Transportation Administration.

Pucher, J., Markstedt, A., & Hirschman, I. (1983). Impacts of subsidies on the costs of urban public transit. *Journal of Transport Economics and Public Policy, 17*, 155-176.

Riley, R. Q. (1994). *Alternative cars in the 21st century: A new personal transportation paradigm*. Warrendale, PA: Society of Automotive Engineers.

Seely, B. E. (1987). *Building the American highway system: Engineers as policy makers*. Philadelphia: Temple University Press.

Smerk, G. M. (1991). *The federal role in urban mass transportation*. Bloomington, IN: Indiana University Press.

Taylor, G. R. (1951). *The transportation revolution, 1815-1860*. New York: Rinehart & Co.

Weicher, J. C. (1988). *Private innovations in public transit*. Washington, DC: American Enterprise Institute for Public Policy Research.

White House, Office of the Press Secretary. (1993). *Historic partnership forged with auto makers aims for threefold increase in fuel efficiency in as soon as ten years* (Press release). Washington, DC: Author.

Young, D. (1995). *Alternatives to sprawl*. Cambridge, MA: Lincoln Institute of Land Policy.

6

An Organizational Analysis of the Public-Private Partnership in the Provision of Public Infrastructure

RONALD J. DANIELS
MICHAEL J. TREBILCOCK

INTRODUCTION

Recently, fiscal constraints have prompted policymakers to endorse government "reinvention," a term that contemplates for-profit and third-sector provision of goods and services.[1] The claim is that the for-profit and third sectors have greater incentives for lower-cost, innovative production. We focus on the claim in the context of government's role in supplying physical infrastructure.

Physical infrastructure is useful in evaluating the scope for government reinvention because of concern with existing levels of infrastructure investment.[2] This concern is traceable to studies that assert linkages between infrastructure investment and productivity. This relationship, as well as the welfare gain from the reallocation of public and private investment toward infrastructure,[3] is well documented although the degree of correlation varies among studies.[4] A second reason for focusing on physical infrastructure is the

Authors' Note: *This article is based on R. Daniels and M. Trebilcock, "Private Provision of Public Infrastructure: An Organizational Analysis of the Next Privatization Frontier" (1996) 46* U. Toronto L.J. *375.*

challenge of reconciling private-sector involvement with the state's role, especially where efficiency and distributional arguments support state intervention.
The final reason to examine infrastructure is its distinct properties including:
large, up-front investments (given asset lumpiness and high minimum-efficient
scales); longevity of assets (life spans often exceed the term of the project
contract); sunk investment (since these assets are use-specific, redeployment
to next-best uses is impossible); its anticipatory character; and the difficulties
in devising contracts against ex post government opportunism.

We canvass private-sector involvement in public infrastructure by focusing
on the lessons from three major Canadian physical infrastructure projects:
Terminal 3 and the aborted redevelopment of Terminals 1 and 2 at Pearson
International Airport in Toronto, the 407 Express Toll Route (407 ETR) in
Toronto, and Confederation Bridge on Prince Edward Island (PEI). These
projects rely on an allegedly innovative form of organization: the so-called
public/private-sector partnership.

We develop two themes in this chapter. First, the efficiency gains from
private-sector infrastructure development can be offset by faulty selection
processes or contractual arrangements. Second, severe contracting problems
are posed by government being a party to the infrastructure arrangement. We
conclude that insufficient attention to the challenges of highly integrated pub-
lic/private-sector infrastructure partnerships has led to uncritical enthusiasm
for them.

THREE CANADIAN PUBLIC-PRIVATE PARTNERSHIPS[5]

INTRODUCTION

The public/private-sector infrastructure partnerships that are proliferating
internationally vary widely in both scale and nature. According to the World
Bank, the average size of projects in low-income countries' has been $440
million. In middle-income countries' average project size is more than 25%
smaller.[6] However, even in developed economies, some projects (such as the
following case studies) are of a very large scale. In this part, we discuss three
Canadian public-private infrastructure partnerships that form the basis of the
organizational analysis in this chapter.

THE 407 EXPRESS TOLL ROUTE (407 ETR)

The 407 ETR is a $929.8 million toll highway in the northern Greater
Toronto Area.[7] Selecting a project developer was the responsibility of a Crown
corporation, the Ontario Transportation Capital Corporation (OTCC), which
used a multistage selection process involving an initial request for expressions

of interest and qualifications, a value engineering exercise,[8] and a closed-bid request for proposals. Three consortia participated in the first round, with two submitting final bids. Concerns by the remaining bidders with traffic volumes led to demands for government financial guarantees. The government concluded that guarantees were not justified, and the project was financed by an OTCC debt issue. Canadian Highways International Corporation was ultimately selected as the developer for the project. In February 1998, the Ontario government announced that it intended to privatize the 407 ETR. After multistage competitive bidding, the highway was sold to 407 ETR International Inc.[9] for $3.107 billion.

CONFEDERATION BRIDGE

Confederation Bridge is a 13.5 km fixed link between PEI and New Brunswick built as a substitute for ferry service, which the federal government was constitutionally obligated to subsidize. The bridge was designed to enhance the region's competitiveness and increase tourism[10] while reducing the federal government's financial obligation. Concerns with the social impact of the project led to a six-and-a-half-year public review before a contract was executed. The government used a multistage selection process: a request for expressions of interest and qualifications, a request for proposals, and a request for more complete proposals (including a financial plan). Twelve consortia expressed interest in the project; however, by the final stage, only three remained. The winner, Strait Crossing Inc. (SCI),[11] was selected because, inter alia, it required the least federal financial assistance.[12] Sixteen months of negotiations were required to conclude the contract.[13] The contract limited the government's ability to compete with the project. Since this created a monopoly, CPI-linked limits on toll increases were imposed.

THE PEARSON INTERNATIONAL AIRPORT (PIA) REDEVELOPMENT

PIA was a multistage private-public project to redevelop Toronto's international airport.[14] The first stage, Terminal 3 (T3), involved the construction of a new terminal building, parking garage, and adjacent hotel and office complex, while the second involved the replacement of the two existing terminals (T1T2) with a single terminal. T3 used a two-stage selection process: a request for expressions of interest and qualifications, followed by a request for proposals. The criteria for the first round were broadly defined: provide a "world-class" terminal in the shortest time; provide a financial return to the Crown; and maintain safety and security. Bidder requests for the weighting of these factors were refused. Eight bids were submitted, with five qualifying for the second stage. Only four consortia submitted final proposals, and the project was awarded to Airport Development Corporation (ADC). Within five months, the government was able to contract for a 40-year lease (with a 20-year period of renewal) with annual payments that varied with gross revenues and time since completion. Although the expected cost was $350 million, an expansion in capacity increased costs to $550 million. The project was completed in 32 months.

Whereas T3 was viewed as a model for public/private partnerships, T1T2 was less so. The project was controversial because of the federal government's departure from its policy of vesting responsibility in local airport authorities (not-for-profit organizations accountable to local groups),[15] and the use of a single-stage selection process. Concerns were compounded by the 125- (originally 90-) day period for the submission of proposals. Three bids were submitted, of which two were acceptable. Of these, Paxport Inc. was the winner. However, Paxport merged with the losing bidder, Air Terminal Development Group, to exploit business synergies that the two shared.

Within eight months, an agreement was concluded with the merged consortium, Pearson Development Corporation (PDC), involving a 57-year lease with sliding-scale payments. The contract limited the government's ability to undertake actions that would debase the operator's franchise, and in return retail concession prices and parking fees were limited. Anticompetitive activities by occupant airlines were also constrained. In both project stages, a scaled rental formula was used that resulted in de facto risk sharing. This was supplemented in T3 by a $70 million loan guarantee contingent on low passenger volumes.

Given concerns expressed during the 1993 federal election campaign with T1T2, the new Liberal government requested a review (the Nixon report). The relatively brief review found that the contract should be cancelled, subject only to minimal compensation (for expenditures already made).[16] In December 1993, the government cancelled the contract and, in April 1994, introduced legislation that imposed a settlement of approximately $30 million, but without the safeguards that normally accompany a public confiscation.[17] The legislation passed the House of Commons in June 1994 but was subsequently defeated by the Progressive Conservative majority in the Senate in 1996. In the meantime, PDC had brought suit against the federal government seeking $662 million in damages. In April 1997, the federal government settled with PDC for $60 million (covering out-of-pocket costs, legal costs, and interest). As part of the settlement, T3 was sold to the Greater Toronto Airports Authority, the local airport authority that had assumed control of T1T2 after the cancellation of the contract with PDC.

SUMMARY: CHARACTERISTICS OF PUBLIC-PRIVATE PARTNERSHIPS

All the case studies contained common characteristics. First, each entailed large, up-front, investments by bidders that were not directly compensated for by government. Second, each implicated policy concerns that could not be sidestepped through a public-private partnership. As illustrated by Confederation Bridge, heightened public concern resulted in considerable delay. In some cases, contractual limitations were placed on monopoly pricing. Given developer concerns over up-front investments in specific assets, sensitivity to policy concerns conflicted with the need to ensure that the franchise would not be debased ex post by governmental action. Third, with the exception of T1T2, the selection process involved multiple stages, typically an initial design tournament and a final competition.[18] One notable feature was the small number of bidders who progressed. A fourth common characteristic was the lengthy delay between the formal award of the franchise and the contract. Fifth, as with most long-term contracts, the project contracts relied on elaborate adjustment formulae and governance structures, based on standard private-sector arbitration models, to deal with incompleteness.[19]

THE STRUCTURE OF PUBLIC-PRIVATE INFRASTRUCTURE PARTNERSHIPS

INTRODUCTION

In order to appreciate the distinctiveness of public-private partnerships, the dichotomy between the public and private sectors should not be overstated. Governments have traditionally contracted out many infrastructure functions, including construction, through competitive bidding against specifications developed either internally or through external specialists. The distinctive feature of current public-private sector infrastructure partnerships is the bundling of finance, design, construction, operations, and maintenance. Because these functions are extremely specialized, private-sector providers tend to be consortia consisting of engineering and project management firms, construction firms, financial underwriters, and operating firms that form to develop a particular facility. While these consortia typically incorporate themselves, they are more transitory than conventional firms. However, there are reputational and learning curve advantages in preserving stability where opportunities exist for similar projects, and consortia may therefore evolve permanent corporate structures.

In this section, we explore the efficiency gains from bundling. Simultaneously, we examine problems in bidding, contract negotiation, monitoring, and enforcement in these arrangements, which may attenuate efficiency gains. Challenges also arise from creating and preserving competitive bidding and rebidding, writing long-term contracts, large sunk costs, and financial sensitivity to policy changes. We also consider distributional and political factors in these arrangements. We then analyze the problems of credibility raised by contracting with the government.

POTENTIAL EFFICIENCY GAINS FROM VERTICALLY INTEGRATED PRIVATE-SECTOR INFRASTRUCTURE PROVISION (CONSORTIA PROVISION)

In assessing gains from consortia provision, we must evaluate them against the traditional model. Governments traditionally have identified the need for infrastructure internally, with the decision to proceed dependant on fiscal capacity and prospects for revenue generation (which depend on efficiency and distributional considerations that determine pricing structure). If the project proceeds, the government will devise technical specifications for construction and advertise for construction tenders through competitive bidding. To qualify, firms must demonstrate relevant credentials such as performance records on similar projects. The contract with the winner will specify completion date, security, and penalties for defaults in performance and a payment schedule based on satisfactory completion of sequential stages. Contracts could be cost-plus, fixed-price, or incentive contracts.[20] Cost-plus contracts lack cost minimization incentives and entail greater public-sector risk, which necessitates costly government monitoring of costs. Under a fixed-price contract, the contractor's costs will not concern the government, leading to decreased monitoring of costs. If costs are uncertain, this risk, borne by the contractor, will be reflected in a premium embodied in the fixed price. Under incentive contracts, shared risks will lead to risk-incentive trade-offs. Incentives to minimize costs may be reduced, although the risk premium charged will decrease. With respect to exogenous risks, the government may be the more efficient risk bearer, given its capacity to spread risk. Upon completion, the government may either operate the facility or contract out various operations.

a. Project identification. The consortia provision model differs from the traditional in important respects. First, the government may invite firms to identify projects. However, complete government detachment from the question of which projects should proceed is impossible. The private sector, in identifying projects, will be driven primarily by expected private rates of return, while the government is responsive to political pressures and social costs and benefits. However, since the government's evaluation will necessarily implicate political and social dimensions, proposers will heed these considerations. Unless indications are provided as to the range of likely projects, proposers are unlikely to invest in developing proposals that may be of no interest to the government. Proposals are likely to be conceptual, leaving details for the next stage. Under the consortia model, once a project has been identified, the government would call for integrated bids on the project.

b. Design. The argument for privatizing the design function is that efficiency gains are generated from stimulating a competition for ideas. Implicit is the notion that governments should shift from specifying inputs to specifying desired outcomes, which allows the private sector to determine the most cost-efficient and technologically effective method for achieving the specified outcome. Specifying outcomes may prove nearly impossible in projects where the policy objective involves the aggregation and reconciliation of many preferences.[21] In these cases, private-sector providers face difficulties in determining how their designs will be evaluated, and government will have difficulty evaluating sharply different designs.[22] The less clear the selection criteria, the greater the latitude in selecting projects; hence the greater the investment by bidders in socially unproductive influence activities.[23]

The government could hold a separate competition just for designs. Here again, the problem of stipulating the outcome criteria would arise. Indeed, government traditionally has often contracted out the design of public facilities. In so doing, the government is able to utilize the technical expertise of the private sector. In the past, government has approached several design firms and sought preliminary ideas and then committed itself to further development of only the chosen design. It is not clear that this generates an optimal supply of designs, particularly where the optimal design combines features from various proposals. In this case, losing bidders realize that the government may use part of their design without any compensation (the problem of appropriability). Thus an expected return that reflects an appropriate risk premium is required to attract sufficient losing bidders to develop a set of design specifications. However, bidders still face incentives to develop proposals dependent on their firm-specific advantages. In this way, bidders limit government's ability to transfer their designs to others.[24]

Similar problems exist with the consortia model. Bidders are unlikely to have equal strengths across all functions, yet the winner must be chosen on the basis of some balance of strengths and weaknesses. Even if bidders have equivalent strengths in design, it is unlikely that one design is superior in all respects. Thus, ideally, the government would combine the best features of the proposals. However, this combination creates complications in the bidding and contracting process.[25] In this respect, the consortia model exhibits tied sales properties. One option is to decouple design from the other functions by requiring all consortia first to submit designs, on the assumption that it remains in their interests to bid on the winning design (which may be a combination of competing designs). The consortium with the winning or predominant design may have advantages in bidding on the remaining functions, which is an incentive to prepare the most appealing design. Here again the cost of preparing a detailed design is substantial, but unlike an unbundled design competition there may be no direct compensation for the winning design. By restricting the design to consortia capable of bidding on the remaining functions, proposers in the design competition face the risk that a consortium with an inferior design but superior construction capability may win the integrated bidding competition. These risks are likely to generate premiums in consortia bids, given the costs of comprehensive bids and appropriability problems.

Bundling also reduces the risks that designers will be insensitive to "constructability" problems that tend to arise where construction and design are performed by distinct teams. Since 80% of the costs of many construction projects are estimated to be determined by the design, dissonances may prove costly.[26] In the consortia model, the design and construction teams form part of a larger team, which tends to reduces coordination problems. However, design and construction expertise reside in different groups so the coordination problems are not entirely eliminated through this integration.

   c. *Financing, design, and construction.* Construction of public facilities has traditionally been contracted out, and so the consortia model represents no change. However, it does affect interdependencies between financing, design, and construction by altering incentives. If the private-sector provider is to finance construction from facility operations, the government is unconcerned with capital costs, provided the design is acceptable. Alternatively, where government subsidies finance the project, the government will constrain design and construction options. The government is vulnerable to opportunism in this context, given the "essential" nature of infrastructure facilities and the political inability of a government to let a facility fail. The operator may coerce the government into relaxing constraints on user fees so as to permit monopoly pricing or to raise subsidies. Thus, design and construction are sensitive to incentives created by financing.

   Interdependencies are key to understanding private-sector finance. Private-sector financing costs more than government financing because it reflects project-specific risks and limited liability. The reason that government does not finance all infrastructure is that while the cost of capital to the private sector is higher, there are offsetting efficiency gains from having the project monitored and disciplined by "at risk" investors. Lenders improve performance by screening consortia carefully, by insisting on adequate security and financial penalties against default, and by monitoring performance closely through covenants.[27]

   Private-sector financing also serves a verification function, by allowing only positive net present value projects to proceed. This argument has only qualified force because private-sector providers are influenced only by private costs and benefits and may proceed even though a project's social value may be negative (as with monopolies). Thus, a private-sector provider's judgment is a check on government only if issues relating to externalities and pricing are resolved at the outset. A private-sector firm's willingness to finance a project may reflect a disregard for negative externalities or be a function of monopolistic pricing (or alternately oversubsidization), and thus be incongruent with a social welfare calculus.

   d. *Operation and maintenance.* Operations could also be unbundled through a discrete management contract with a private-sector provider chosen through competitive bidding. Several problems exist with this option.[28] First, if the facility has monopoly features, the government faces a choice between maximizing the sale price or soliciting bids based on the lowest contractually permitted pricing. The latter is the social ideal, although it imposes a substantial burden on the government in reviewing bids and monitoring prices.

Under either scenario, the winner has incentives to minimize costs during the operating contract. However, a divergence between private and social calculi in this respect relates to maintenance. Where the assets are long-lived but the operating contract is shorter, there are incentives to skimp on maintenance costs that have little impact on revenues during the contract. This problem is eliminated by matching the length of the operating contract and the expected life of the assets. However, this raises problems related to long-term contracting. Integrating operations also motivates the provider to minimize life-cycle costs. Initial investments and maintenance are substitutes; thus, an optimal combination is more likely through integrated provision. However, uncertainties affecting costs or revenues make long-term contracts riskier to the private-sector operator, while the government will find it difficult to specify all obligations ex ante and must resort to costly monitoring. Short-term contracts reduce these problems but exacerbate the incentive to degrade the assets. Moreover, while the contract may be re-tendered, asset specificity creates advantages for the incumbent that militate against competitive contracting.[29]

More generally, the case for vertical integration in the provision of infrastructure is that firms coordinate at a lower cost than the government. Evidence suggests that consortia providers complete infrastructure construction more quickly than traditional models do by reducing transaction and coordination costs through a more simultaneous construction process and greater freedom from budget allocation and procurement regulations.[30] An offsetting feature of integration is reduced competition, since few consortia are able to assemble all the relevant inputs[31] leading to fewer bidders than traditional discrete contracting. Empirical evidence with respect to government procurement suggests that increasing the bidders from three to four results in savings of up to 18%; from seven to eight, up to 4%; and from ten to eleven, up to 2%.[32] Nevertheless, if new designs impact on the value of a project, if ideas cannot be easily specified, and if innovative designs cannot be explicitly rewarded without controversy, then restrictions on entrants elicits increased research effort.[33]

DISTRIBUTIONAL/POLITICAL CONSIDERATIONS

Distributional considerations relating to privatization depend upon the service in question. For instance, cross-subsidization is unlikely under unconstrained, consortia provision,[34] resulting in adverse distributional effects especially where there is an absence of choices, thus permitting monopoly pricing. Providers may be required to maintain cross-subsidies; however, this makes the project less attractive and reduces the advantages of privatization.

Constituencies whose interests may be jeopardized by privatization include public-sector labor unions (who face an erosion of compensation and job security), consumers (who risk monopolistic pricing), and environmental groups (who fear private-sector developers will ignore negative environmental externalities). A more amorphous constituency that may oppose privatization of existing infrastructure (and consequent user charges) are present users who believe they have already paid for the facility through taxation.

These constituencies translate the distributional impacts from privatization into political resistance. Some of these constituencies (labor or users) are less resistant to the privatization of new infrastructure facilities, particularly where the facilities are unlikely to be built without privatization. However, opportunities for profitable private new infrastructure in developed economies are limited and may generate negative environmental impacts.

However, privatization also offers some political attraction to government by moving expenditures off-budget or capitalizing existing infrastructure by sell-off. However, two caveats are warranted. First, governments can borrow more cheaply so the case for privatizing infrastructure from a social perspective turns on the efficiency benefits that flow from integrating financing within the consortium. Second, government technically is as capable as the private sector of charging for services. Thus, if an infrastructure project has a positive net present value, the net worth of the public sector may not be enhanced by privatizing existing infrastructure.[35] Unfortunately, because of the use of cash rather than accrual methods in public accounting, moving the investment off-budget or capitalizing existing infrastructure, while not reporting foregone revenues, encourages a fiscal illusion that may fool taxpayers.[36]

Another political attraction of infrastructure privatization is that it enables credible commitments with respect to policy-related risks that relate to the financial viability and social benefits of a project.[37] By privatizing a project and then developing it on a vertically integrated basis, a commitment to maintain the assets is built into the arrangement. Similarly, pricing and subsidies can become more predictable by embodying them in contractual commitments with private-sector providers.[38] The government, by tying its hands, can reduce the political costs of pursuing these policies itself. Privatizing infrastructure provision also creates employment without consuming additional public resources. However, since consortia draw on existing capital, these projects simply divert capital from one activity to another with a higher expected private return and the net job creation effect is ambiguous.

GOVERNMENT AS A CONTRACTING PARTY

Because of its legislative power, government involvement presents vexing contracting problems.[39] First, particularly in countries that lack constitutionally entrenched property rights, governments can legislatively abrogate contractual commitments. Consequently, the value of even a contractual commitment to fairly compensate for a "taking" is doubtful. Second, even where governments face constitutional constraints on their power to confiscate, contracting problems emanating from the breadth of governmental powers remain. Here, it is difficult to anticipate the ways in which governments can infringe franchise value and to differentiate legitimate governmental actions from those that are intended to force investors to tender their interests on exploitative terms.

As demonstrated by the government's abrogation of its contractual commitments in respect of T1T2, it is clear that governmental abrogation of state franchise contracts is more than a speculative concern. This problem is, however, by no means novel in Canada. A study of long-term franchise contracts governing natural monopolies from the mid-1800s to the 1930s in Canada demonstrated that infirmities in the institutional environment enabled governments to exploit the sunk investments of franchise operators.[40] The failure of these franchise contracts is attributable to weak judicial traditions (specifically, a failure to regard governmental action other than an outright expropriation of title as a taking) and the absence of constitutional protection for property rights.[41]

Interestingly, many of the franchise contracts studied had properties similar to current public-private partnerships. The contracts were long term, involved durable assets in changing or uncertain environments, and often contemplated government participation in project revenues. Further, the contracts specified obligations in vague terms, which ultimately forced detailed specification of terms and arbitral governance mechanisms to deal with changing conditions.[42] The question then arises as to whether the current environment renders the problem moot. The role of the judiciary in constraining governmental opportunism remains debatable in the Canadian context and international obligations impose only weak constraints on ex post governmental action.[43]

Given the dearth of formal constraints on governmental opportunism, what constraints operate to ensure governmental fidelity in public-private partnerships? To the extent that public-private partnerships are not isolated affairs, then the reputational costs of government opportunism should be correspondingly increased. In this respect, the current costs to government of impairing its obligations to public-private partnership debtholders are greater since impairment of public-private partnership debt could have severe effects on government's ability to borrow.

Yet reputational mechanisms are insufficient to constrain governmental opportunism[44] without institutions that augment the restraint of reputational markets. Government could commission arm's-length review of the contract to certify the selection process, congruence with the proposal submitted by the winner, and compatibility with public goals. If we assume that a project has been vindicated through such a review, the costs of government abrogating the contract due to alleged frailties should increase. Another option is to limit independent review to only where government reneges on its contractual undertakings. While such review might economize on the certification costs, savings would come at the cost of uncertainty regarding the contracts. It is essential that ex post constraints on government conduct exist only for stark governmental opportunism. For more subtle impairment, the case for conferring protection on parties making infrastructural investments is the same as that for investments in other industries whose value is subject to policy changes. Kaplow has argued that compensation for losses from regulatory change is undesirable, since it would distort incentives for market-based risk management.[45] Additionally, so long as government owns infrastructure assets similar to those in public-private partnerships, then the incentive for opportunistic expropriation through generalized initiatives is reduced. This is because government will suffer losses on its investments similar to those of private investors.

Nevertheless, for stark takings, protection through expectation damages or injunction is required. To the extent that sanctions are inadequate, investors will use pricing to protect their interests. Expected opportunism costs are reflected back onto government as a lowered rate of return from project or a higher risk premium. Another pricing-related strategy is to compress the payback period, which may have distortionary effects on risk taking. Even for a government that keeps its promises, the inability to commit credibly will be costly.[46]

CONCLUSION

This study has focused on the complexity of public-private partnerships in realizing efficiency gains in physical infrastructure. In the case studies, the details determined whether the projects generated excess welfare gains. Examination of the incentive effects of the selection processes and the contracts involved provides a foundation upon which conclusions can be drawn about the broader implications for policymakers.

The first lesson is responsible project selection through cost-benefit analysis. While some have advocated public-private partnerships as a means of certifying the alleged welfare properties of projects, the arrangements governing the case studies demonstrate that this has limited value. Each project revealed important levels of public financial assistance. Once the state insinuates itself into these projects through subsidization, the market's capacity to independantly value the project is compromised. The problem with relying on private markets to make public choices was illustrated by Confederation Bridge, where policymakers misleadingly touted private-sector interest as evidence of societal value.

Assuming that the most valuable projects are selected for development in descending order of their social value, and further that public-private partnerships constitute the best means of organization, then the next challenge is to devise a process that identifies the most deserving projects while recognizing legitimate political concerns. The role that auctions play in reducing endemic information problems when valuing highly idiosyncratic assets must be stressed. In the case studies, there were no obvious benchmarks that policy-makers could invoke to determine the minimum return required for private developers; hence, the auction.

Nevertheless, the information revelation function of auctions operates best when the allocated good is stable and well defined. But the bundled character of public-private partnerships poses competitive bidding design problems. Nebulous project standards allow bidders the latitude to propose novel solutions. However, the less crystallized the project, the more out-of-pocket costs incurred in creative designs and the increased risk that the project will be evaluated on factors unrelated to the merits of the proposal. As these ex ante expenses increase, so too does the need for ex ante compensation to entice bidders to participate. In other words, ideas matter, but the government will have to pay for them, and the question becomes how best to pay. Given the public funding typically involved, auctions also implicate political legitimacy values. The intense public sentiment surrounding the Pearson terminals demonstrates the centrality of these values. Even if there are efficiency gains realized through multidimensional bidding, the public's inability to monitor the selection process becomes salient.

Assuming that projects are allocated to the most deserving bidder through auctions, the next problem relates to the contractual design used to eliminate opportunism. The major problem with these partnerships relates to asset degradation, due to the fact that infrastructure projects typically have expected lives beyond the term of the lease, which creates incentives for chiseling on maintenance. The costs of devising contracts to temper these problems must be balanced against the efficiency gains sought.

The bundling of functions (the principal source of efficiency gains) also raises issues. The most significant problem stems from de facto unbundling of the bundled partnership. A striking feature of the public-private partnership is the high degree of government financial assistance. The simplest explanation for this is the need to subsidize public goods or to compensate for positive externalities. Yet, if this was the motivation for government assistance, we would expect one-time subsidies instead of the financial risk-sharing contracts documented in this study. Why, given the loss of integration benefits entailed, do governments intervene in this way?

The persistence of public financing is explained by the risk of governmental opportunism faced by private developers. In a first-best world, private developers would be responsible for endogenous production risks and the government responsible for policy-related risks, each being the least-cost avoider of the risks that it has been assigned. Exogenous risks should be transferred to the least-cost insurer—in this case, the government—owing to its superior risk-bearing capacity.[47] Unfortunately this allocation of risks is not possible, given problems of contractual design. Put simply, a fully contingent contract cannot be specified owing to foreseeability problems. But even if such a contract were possible, government's legislative and regulatory jurisdiction makes the contract susceptible to unilateral ex post opportunism by government. This problem is particularly acute in the case of physical infrastructure because of its sunk costs, anticipatory nature, and asset lumpiness properties.

Government's inability to commit credibly to nonconfiscation and high probabilities of such intervention remit the parties to the second-best world. Here the financial arrangements in the case studies become understandable. In the absence of contractual risk-allocation mechanisms, governmental supply of financial capital will attenuate the apprehensions of private developers. This will also ensure that projects that might otherwise be negative net present value decisions will be undertaken. In terms of the optimal balance between incentives and insurance, these arrangements must be structured so as not to dampen developer incentives for cost containment while providing some insurance. The case studies all contain hybrid levels of financial risk sharing, whether achieved through subsidies or performance-based payments.

Contractual equilibria are conditioned on external factors including the institutional framework for contractual enforcement. In Canada, the events surrounding the abrogation of T1T2 have contributed to concerns over government motivations, creating an environment that is less congenial to these projects. To remedy this situation, supplemental institutions that will support durable government commitments are required. In the case of public-private partnerships, the sui generis nature of the projects, the difficulty of specifying clear outputs, the capacity of governments to confer gains on ratepayers through price restrictions, the need for project flexibility, all combine to subvert the capacity and cost effectiveness of domestic remedies aimed at constraining governmental opportunism. In this setting, greater reliance may need to be placed on supranational institutions. Alternatively, international lenders could agree to condition the provision of investment on governmental adherence to independent arbitral decisions concerning takings.

If the public-private partnership is to realize the expectations of its proponents, an objective means of reconciling government's need for policy flexibility with the market's need for certainty must be devised. The ad hoc and politically motivated inquiry will simply not suffice. Nor are conventional forms of judicial review likely to possess the institutional expertise to evaluate the integrity of the decision-making process in complex projects.[48] In the absence of such innovation, it may be that the enthusiasm for private development of public infrastructure may turn out to be a form of political "cycling" that will replay the demise of the municipal franchise contract in Canada and the United States early in this century. Let us hope that we will not be condemned to repeat the errors of history by neglecting that history.

NOTES

1. See David Osborne and Ted Gaebler, *Reinventing Government* (New York: Plume, 1993); *The National Performance Review* (Gore Report on Reinventing Government) (New York: Random House, Times Books, 1993); Michael Trebilcock, *The Prospects for Reinventing Government* (Toronto: C.D. Howe Institute, 1994).

2. The World Bank has studied infrastructure investment in the developing world: *The World Bank Report Infrastructure for Development* (New York: Oxford University Press, 1994) notes developing countries invested 4% of national output in infrastructure, which was expected to increase to 7% by 2000. While private investment in infrastructure constituted 15% of total investment, it was expected that fiscal pressures would raise this figure.

3. See, for instance, Douglas Holtz-Eakin, "Public Sector Capital and the Productivity Puzzle" National Bureau of Economic Research, Working Paper No. 4122, July 1992.

4. David Aschauer "Is Public Expenditure Productive?" (1989), 24 *J. of Monetary Econ.* 177; "Does Public Capital Crowd Out Private Capital?" (1989) 24 *J. of Monetary Econ.* 171; and "Public Investment and Productivity Growth in the Group of Seven" (1989) 13 *Econ. Perspectives.* Aschauer attributes 100% of the productivity slowdown in the United States over the last several decades to declining infrastructure investment. In contrast, Catherine Morrison finds that only 20% of productivity growth in the United States could be attributed to infrastructure investment. (Catherine J. Morrison, *A Microeconomic Approach to the Measurement of Economic Performance: Productivity Growth, Capacity Utilization, and Related Performance Indicators* (Springer-Verlag Press, 1992); "Macroeconomic Relationships between Public Spending on Infrastructure and Private Sector Productivity in the U.S.," in J. Mintz (ed.), *Infrastructure and Competitiveness* (Ontario: Queen's University, 1995).

5. A detailed description of the case studies is on file with the authors.

6. World Bank, supra note 2.

7. jobsOntario: Capital, news release, 8 April and 11 May 1994.

8. See note 25, infra.

9. 407 ETR International Inc. is a consortium composed of CINTRA (a subsidiary of Grupo Ferrovial), SNC-Lavalin and Capital d'Amerique CPDQ (a subsidiary of the Caisse de depot et placement du Quebec).

10. The economic value of the reduced travel time was estimated to be $398.4 million (1993$) (A Benefit-Cost Analysis of the Northumberland Strait Crossing Project, prepared by Gardner Pinfold Consulting Economists Limited, September 1993 at p. 4).

11. SCI is a joint venture of four firms: Strait Crossing Inc. of Calgary (15%); Northern Construction Co. (35%); GTMI (Canada) Inc. (30%); and Ballast Nedam (20%). Consultation with Strait Crossing office, Charlottetown, 26 August 1994.

12. The federal government's $41.9 million (indexed) annual obligation supported a $661 million debt issue by the developers. After 35 years, the subsidy would end and maintenance costs would be covered from tolls.

13. This delay was due to two environmental challenges.

14. The stated purposes of T3 were to provide a world-class air terminal facility, reduce government investment in airport facilities, increase private-sector participation, and provide a financial return to the federal government. See LBPIA-General Distribution, p. 6.

15. Privatization was motivated by a desire for rapid development and by infighting among local politicians over the composition of the Toronto airport authority. Patronage was also alleged (see, for instance, Robert F. Nixon, "Pearson Airport, Review" [Ottawa: Office of the Prime Minister, 1993]). The government's preference for local airport authorities was set out in *Guiding Principles* (Ottawa: Ministry of Transport, 1987) and elaborated upon in *Supplementary Principles for the Creation and Operation of Local Airport Authorities* (Ottawa: Ministry of Transport, 1989).

16. The review concluded that the project "fell far short of maximizing the public interest" (Nixon, supra note 15). The recommendation to cancel the deal was based on perceived infirmities in the selection process and the implementation contracts.

17. Bill C-22 (reintroduced as Bill C-28): An Act respecting certain agreements concerning the redevelopment and operation of Terminals 1 and 2 at Lester B. Pearson International Airport (First Session, Thirty-Fifth Parliament, 42–3 Elizabeth II, 1994).

18. Information respecting these projects was derived from interviews conducted with public- and private-sector experts involved in the projects, from inspection of the project contracts, and from disclosure documents filed with securities regulators by the project developers.

19. For instance, concerns over asset degradation through chiseling on maintenance were alleviated through exhortatory duties to maintain assets, stipulated expenditures on asset mainte- nance, annual reserve fund contributions, monitoring by third parties, and binding arbitration for asset maintenance disputes.

20. See R. Preston McAfee and John McMillan, *Incentives in Government Contracting* (Toronto: University of Toronto Press, 1988).

21. See David Sappington and Joseph Stiglitz, "Privatization, Information and Incentives" (1987) 6 *J. of Policy Analysis & Management* 567, 575.

22. See Curtis Taylor, "Digging for Golden Carrots: An Analysis of Research Tournaments" (1995) 85 *Amer. Econ. Rev.* 4.

23. The problem of influence activities in the context of a multistage auction process is briefly alluded to in Paul Milgrom, "Auctions and Bidding: A Primer" (1989) 3 *J. of Econ. Perspectives* 3, 20.

24. Investment in these firm-specific features bears analytical similarity to the entrenchment problem related to excessive investment by managers in manager-specific investments. See Andrei Shleifer and Robert W. Vishny, "Management Entrenchment: The Case of Manager-Specific Investments" (1989) 25 *J. of Fin. Econ.* 123.

25. These problems are revealed by the value engineering exercise in the 407 ETR selection process. After the first stage, the government pooled the best designs into a baseline description for subsequent proposals. By increasing the information available in a common values auction, uncertainty over value was diminished, which enhanced competitiveness.

26. See Issaka Ndekugri and Adrian Turner, "Building Procurement by Design and Build Approach" (1994) 120 *J. of Construction Engineering and Management* 243.

27. See George Triantis and Ronald Daniels, "The Role of Debt in Interactive Corporate Governance" (July 1995) 83 *Calif. L. Rev.* 1073; William Pearson, President, Agra Engineering Group, Toronto, interview with the authors, 1 September 1994.

28. For a review of these problems, see Keith Crocker and Scott Masten, "Regulation and Administered Contracts Revisited: Lessons from Transaction-Cost Economics for Public Utility Regulation" (January 1996) 9(1) *J. of Reg. Econ.* 5.

29. Oliver Williamson *The Economic Institutions of Capitalism* (New York: Free Press, 1985) chapter 13 ("Franchise Bidding for Natural Monopoly"); see also Crocker and Masters, supra.

30. Ndekugri and Turner, supra note 26, 250.

31. See Sappington and Stiglitz, supra note 21, 571, 572.

32. McAfee and McMillan, supra note 20, 151.

33. Curtis Taylor, supra note 22: "Because equilibrium research effort by each firm increases with the size of the prize and decreases with the number of contestants, there is a one-to-one correspondence between choosing the optimal prize and entry fee and choosing the optimal number of contestants and equilibrium effort level."

34. See John Vickers and George Yarrow, "Economic Perspectives on Privatization" (1991) 5 *J. of Econ. Perspectives* 111, 114.

35. See Oliver Williamson, "Credible Commitments: Using Hostages to Support Exchange" (1983) 73 *Am. Econ. Rev.* 519.

36. See Jack Mintz and Ross Preston (eds.), *Capital Budgeting in the Public Sector* (Kingston, Ont.: John Deutsch Institute for Study of Economic Policy, 1993).

37. World Bank, supra note 2, 27, 29.

38. See Pablo Spiller, "Institutions and Regulatory Commitment in Utilities Privatization" (1993) 2 *Industrial & Corporate Change* 387.

39. The lack of institutional safeguards against government takings is a constraint on national economic development. See Douglass C. North Institutions, *Institutional Change and Economic Growth* (Cambridge: Cambridge University Press 1990); and Douglass C. North and Barry R. Weingast, "Constitutions and Commitment: The Evolution of Institutions Governing Public Choice in Seventeenth-Century England" (1989) 49 *J. of Econ. Hist.* 803. See also Spiller, supra note 38, 387; Brian Levy and Pablo Spiller, "Regulation, Institutions, and Commitment in Telecommunications," in *Proceedings of the World Bank Conference on Development Economics* (Washington, DC: The World Bank, 1994); and Pablo Spiller and Ingo Vogelsang, "The Institutional Foundations of Regulatory Commitment in the UK" draft paper dated 16 June 1994, on file with the authors.

40. John Baldwin, *Regulatory Failure and Renewal: The Evolution of the Natural Monopoly Contract* (Ottawa: Economic Council of Canada 1989); see also Christopher Armstrong and H. V. Nelles, *Monopoly's Moment: The Organization and Regulation of Canadian Utilities 1830–1930* (Toronto: University of Toronto Press, 1986).

41. Many of these same themes are developed by George Priest, "The Origins of Utility Regulation and the Theories of Regulation Debate" (1993) 36 *J. of Law & Econ.* 289.

42. The same point is made by Priest, supra note 41, who argues that the theories of regulation in natural monopolies ignore the similarity between regulation by public commission and contractual innovations found in long-term franchise contracts.

43. See Evan Atwood and Michael Trebilcock, "Public Accountability in an Age of Contracting Out" 27 *Can. Bus. L.J.* 1.

44. Jeremy Bullow and Kenneth Rogoff, "A Constant Recontracting Model of Sovereign Debt" (1989) 97 *J. of Pol. Econ.* 155 (more complex institutional arrangements necessary to support state opportunism than reputation alone).

45. Lewis Kaplow, "An Economic Analysis of Legal Transitions" (1986) 99 *Harv. LR* 509.

46. See Spiller, supra note 38.

47. The claim that government constitutes the best risk bearer of exogenous risks is criticized by George Priest in the context of losses from catastrophes: see "The Government, the Market, and the Problem of Catastrophic Loss" (paper presented at the Conference on Social Treatment of Catastrophic Risk, Stanford University, Lucas Conference Center, draft dated 21 October 1994).

48. See Atwood and Trebilcock, supra note 43.

7

Forming Partnerships
in Environmental Policy

The Business of Emissions Trading in Clean Air Management

SHELDON KAMIENIECKI
DAVID SHAFIE
JULIE SILVERS

Several states and the federal government have implemented emissions trading programs; however, the most ambitious plan—the RECLAIM—was initiated in 1994 by the South Coast Air Quality Management District (SCAQMD; Bryner, 1997). The goals of RECLAIM are to reduce significantly sulfur oxides (SO_x) and nitrogen oxides (NO_x) emissions. The latter are precursors of ozone and controlling them will help bring the region into compliance with the national and state ambient air quality standards for ozone. The 1990 Clean Air Act lists the four county areas (i.e., Orange, Los Angeles, Riverside, and San Bernardino) comprising the South Coast Air Basin as a severe nonattainment area for ozone. Under RECLAIM, oil refineries and other large industrial polluters must reduce their emissions of certain pollutants by a fixed percentage each year. Firms that

Authors' Note: *The authors would like to thank Helen Ingram, Michael E. Kraft, and Nancy Pfeffer for their insightful comments on a previous draft of this article.*

reduce emissions by more than the required amount can sell pollution credits to other firms that exceed their limits.

A major objective of RECLAIM is the reduction of 80 tons of NO_x emissions per day and 14 tons of SO_x emissions per day by 2004. The command-and-control approach, initially required under the 1991 South Coast Air Quality Management Plan (SCAQMP), had outlined the same goal (SCAQMD, 1991, 1994).[1] The RECLAIM program regulates stationary sources that produce NO_x and SO_x in excess of 4 tons per year. In 1994, each facility received an annual emissions cap, an annual rate of reduction, and the right to trade credits for every ton of emissions with other firms regulated under RECLAIM. In all, 92% of the region's SO_x emissions and 53% of its NO_x emissions are regulated under RECLAIM. By setting an emissions cap and allowing the regulated companies to decide how to meet those levels on their own, the program should cut emissions by at least the same amount as outlined in the 1991 SCAQMP.

In an attempt to ensure that ambient air quality standards are met in the basin, the SCAQMD established restricted zones between which trade of RECLAIM trading credits (RTCs) is limited, based on the potential for emissions concentration. For regulatory purposes, the Basin is divided into two zones, a Coastal Zone and an Inland Zone, referred to as Zone One and Zone Two, respectively. New facilities within the Coastal Zone can only buy credits that originate in that same zone. Old sources of pollution can buy some credits from the Inland Zone as long as they do not violate California health and safety code restrictions and do not exceed their initial 1994 allocations. Facilities in the Inland Zone, considered the more sensitive area due to pollution blown in from the coast, may purchase credits from either zone (Fromm & Hansjürgens, 1996; Polesetsky, 1995; SCAQMD, 1994). The intended purpose of this arrangement is to protect the sensitive inner basin region as a whole from emissions blown inland from the coast.

Title IV of the 1990 Clean Air Act addresses SO_2 emissions by establishing a market-based incentive system to reduce emissions from coal-fired power plants that contribute to acid rain. The goal of the program is to reduce SO_2 emissions by 50%, or approximately 8 million tons, from 1980 levels by 2010 in two phases. Phase I contains new emissions limitations on 263 electric-generating plants at the 110 dirtiest coal-fired units in 21 Eastern and Midwestern states (Ringquist, 1998). Beginning in 1995, each of these units was required to meet increasingly stringent emissions requirements. Phase I power plants can satisfy these new emissions requirements by installing more effective pollution control equipment, switching to a less polluting fuel or to a different electrical generation process, or purchasing pollution allowances from other sources (Ringquist, 1998).

Utilities are given allowances (i.e., permits or credits), each one permitting them to release 1 ton of SO_2, and they must obtain permits designating their allowances. The total level of emissions is prohibited from exceeding a 10 million ton limit. Allowances can be banked for future use, traded, bought, or sold. If utilities exceed their emissions allowances, they are charged an excess emissions fee and must offset the additional emissions the following year. Utilities that are able to reduce their emissions below levels permitted can trade their surplus emissions allowances so that reductions can be made at the lowest possible cost. A few states with high-polluting units have been awarded extra allowances that can be sold to generate revenues to help pay for cleanup costs, whereas clean states have been awarded additional allowances to promote economic growth (Ringquist, 1998). Phase II begins in 2000 when all fossil-fuel–fired power plants and other industrial electrical generating stations become part of the acid rain emissions trading program. Enforcement in both the RECLAIM and SO_2 trading systems is simple and is similar to that of other environmental regulatory programs (Rosenbaum, 1998).[2]

This paper considers the advent of the RECLAIM emissions trading system a movement away from direct government intervention and toward the formation of a partnership between government and the private sector. In this vein, government and industry have formed a novel collaborative relationship to improve air quality. Rather than government being entirely responsible for air pollution control, private industry is assigned the duty of maintaining and improving air quality by reducing emissions. Government still sets the parameters for these market-based systems, establishes national standards, and determines annual benchmarks for standards; however, the mechanism for controlling air pollution, along with the economic incentives, now rests in the hands of the market and the private sector. This approach represents a different conception of privatization, one that signifies the devolution of total government control over policy implementation.

Among other things, the SO_2 emissions trading program is different from that of the RECLAIM program because the former primarily involves public electric utilities that pollute, whereas the latter targets mainly private industries that pollute. In this sense, the SO_2 emissions trading program is not as private; instead, it represents a new partnership between the national government and local government agencies that operate electric power plants.[3] Economic incentives are, of course, at the heart of both trading schemes through the buying and selling of emissions credits on the open market. Neither program depends on direct government intervention to control air pollution and reach present and future air quality goals.

THEORETICAL CONTEXT

Those who support greater private sector involvement in the delivery of government services nearly always cite the need for increasing effectiveness and efficiency in policy implementation (e.g., Portney, 1990; Savas, 1987). Government, due to its large size, lack of incentives, and vulnerability to the influence of outside forces, is not in a position to provide services at the least cost and greatest benefit on its own. Because of the demands and incentives inherent in the free market system, private and nongovernment organizations are in a better position to perform at the lowest cost possible and achieve the greatest gains. In addition, economic incentive approaches can be administered simply and economically, and they are likely to result in the development of new and effective pollution control technologies. A commonly held assumption is that market incentive approaches are easier for the public (and business) to understand and therefore easier to legislate (Rosenbaum, 1998).

The underlying rationale for market-based air pollution control programs resides in the policy science and public choice literature. According to Schneider and Ingram, "from a policy science perspective, the purposes of policy analysis are to provide scientifically reliable, useful information that will enable decision makers to make better decisions. Better decisions are those that result in rational, efficient, effective public policy that will solve important problems and improve societal conditions" (1997, p. 31). Quade's (1991) explanation of the aims of policy analysis epitomizes this point of view. From the perspective of Schneider (1986) and Schneider and Ingram (1997), this process can be described as a series of analyses that accompany each step in rational decision making, namely, to "determine goals and objectives, create or identify policy alternatives, assess the probable effects of each alternative on each goal, adopt the most efficient or effective policy, implement the policy, and evaluate the results. The central concepts within this paradigm are rational decision making, efficiency, and effectiveness" (Schneider & Ingram, 1997, pp. 31-32). The main goal is to maximize utility, and a good public policy is one that achieves a specific, beneficial goal (i.e., is effective) at the lowest possible cost (i.e., is efficient).

Public choice is the application of economic rules and principles to politics and public policy and has both a positive theory that is axiomatic and deductive, and a normative theory of value (Schneider & Ingram, 1997). This approach is pursued in works by Mueller (1981), Ostrom (1991), Sproule-Jones (1984), and others. Public choice theorists accept the microeconomic assumption that humans are self-interest utility maximizers and will behave as such in nearly every setting, including natural resource conservation and environmental protection. The main objectives of human (and group) behavior are efficiency and effectiveness.

A distinct cynicism toward government runs through much of the public choice literature. As Schneider and Ingram (1997) explain,

> Most public choice theorists do not view government positively and prescribe only a limited role for it in society, namely, to correct for market failure and provide goods that are not likely to be produced at all by the market. Democratic governments are viewed as excessively inefficient and as growing inevitably until they are seeking to provide far more than people want. The movement to privatization is one of the major impacts of public choice theory in the United States. (pp. 38-39)

Clearly, central concepts and principles found in policy science and public choice approaches have been used to justify a movement away from command-and-control regulation of air pollution to the adoption of market-based systems and the creation of partnerships between government and industry and between different levels and agencies of government.

Some scholars (e.g., Cahn, 1995; Ingersoll & Brockbank, 1986) and many environmentalists, however, argue that economic incentive approaches such as RECLAIM and SO_2 emissions trading are undemocratic. Such approaches, once put into place, tend to circumvent traditional mechanisms for public participation and public input by placing decision making in the hands of a few individuals and corporations. Only those with substantial wealth can participate in emissions trading schemes, and most citizens have little choice but to stand by and be spectators in the process. As a consequence, this type of regulatory program does not encourage policy learning, an essential element for the functioning of democratic societies, within the public, but instead, it creates a separate class of elite experts, technicians, and financial advisors.

Bobrow and Dryzek (1987) believe it is wrong to equate efficiency with equity, and they argue how public choice theory, when used in policymaking, can negatively impact equity. Okun (1974) maintains that policies that focus on efficiency frequently ignore equity principles in the process. In Ringquist's (1998) comprehensive analysis of SO_2 emissions trading, he raises the possibility that transferable discharge permit systems can have serious distributional consequences. By allowing some facilities to sell pollution credits while permitting other facilities to purchase pollution credits, significant inequities in exposure to pollution may result. Because pollution control costs are normally lowest for newer facilities and highest for older facilities (Ringquist, 1998), and because older facilities are located in the industrial sections of inner cities where poor and minority citizens often live, poor and minority people can be exposed to higher concentrations of pollution even though the total amount of emissions for the region declines. The following sections examine whether and, if so, in what way emissions trading—as a movement toward developing partnerships in clean air policy—impacts effectiveness, efficiency, equity, and democracy.

EFFECTIVENESS

Effectiveness is the extent to which a policy accomplishes its intended goals (Hamilton & Wells, 1996). In order to satisfy its overseers, an agency must have a clearly defined purpose for its program, and the means to demonstrate success. Inasmuch as democratic institutions demand accountability from administrative agencies, the question of effectiveness is an important one. To be judged effective, a program must be compared to its chief alternative.[4] In the case of RECLAIM, the proper baseline for comparison is the 1991 SCAQMP, the

TABLE 1:   Emissions From RECLAIM Sources, 1993-1996

	1993		1994		1995		1996	
	NO_x	SO_x	NO_x	SO_x	NO_x	SO_x	NO_x	SO_x
Emissions (tons)	24,982	7,167	25,314	7,732	25,764	8,064	24,200	6,484
Total RTCs (tons)			40,017	10,363	35,395	9,610	31,935	8,892
Unused RTCs (tons)			14,813	3,133	10,267	1,548	7,735	2,410
Percentage unused			37	30	28	16	24	27
Percentage change from 1993			1.3	0.9	3.1	12.5	−3.1	−9.5

SOURCE: SCAQMD, 1998a.

command-and-control regulatory framework that it replaced. The RECLAIM program is designed to meet the same overall emissions reductions as command-and-control regulation, however, it is not designed to reduce emissions as rapidly as nonmarket alternatives.

In fact, one early criticism of RECLAIM was that it might increase emissions in the short run, even in the process of achieving substantial reductions over the long haul. One reason for this fear was that the program was set to begin at a time when California was recovering from a recession and emissions were reduced due to a significant slow down in industrial activity. To allow for reasonable economic growth, companies were permitted to choose their peak year between 1989 and 1992 as the baseline for emissions, rather than 1991 or 1992 as some environmentalists had urged. Critics argued that the over allocation of credits would create a windfall for the largest polluters, mainly refineries and utilities, allowing them 15% to 18% more emissions than they generated in 1991 (Elliott, 1993).

Despite the concerns that emissions would increase as a result of the initial allocation, emissions remained fairly close to 1993 levels during the first 2 years of the program. Emissions data in Table 1 indicate that levels increased by only about 1% in 1994, with 37% of NO_x credits and 30% of SO_x credits going unused. By 1996, emissions of both pollutants had fallen below 1993 levels, despite a rebounding economy. A 3-year audit of RECLAIM indicates that actual emissions from 1994 to 1996 were far below the projected yearly average levels if command-and-control regulations had remained in place during the same period (SCAQMD, 1998a). These data suggest, therefore, that the RECLAIM program has been fairly effective in reducing certain air pollutants.

EFFICIENCY

Efficiency is generally defined in the public policy literature as the ratio between inputs and outputs. A policy's efficiency is determined by the extent to which waste is minimized. In the case of clean air policy, efficiency is the achievement of a set level of pollution reduction at the least cost (Hall & Walton, 1996). Tietenberg (1985) argues that a system of emissions trading is more desirable than command-and-control regulation because it can achieve the same level of reduction at a lower cost. Indeed, RECLAIM has been more cost-effective to implement than the command-and-control approach, primarily because the nature and the level of SCAQMD's involvement are transformed under the RECLAIM program. Despite the additional demands of maintaining a trading database and a strict monitoring of emissions, the agency is relieved of the responsibility of making implementation decisions. Rather, the regulated industries choose the best way to meet their emissions levels on their own. An efficient program is cost-effective for society and internally cost-effective for the agency. Both aspects of efficiency should be considered in justifying a change from command-and-control regulation to a market-based system (National Academy of Public Administration, 1994), along with the formation of partnerships between government and industry and different levels and agencies of government to control pollution.

Key to the concept of efficiency is the utilitarian principle of the greatest good for the greatest number. The policy tool of creating new marketable goods is generally assumed to increase efficiency because both the buyer and the seller are better off as a result of the transaction (Weimer & Vining, 1989). If this were not true, the two parties would not consent to their transaction in the first place. Because polluting firms can buy and sell RTCs, they have the flexibility to determine for themselves the best way to meet their emissions limit, which is determined by the number of RTCs they own. A firm may choose to pay for new equipment to reduce its pollution level or, if that option is too costly, it may purchase additional RTCs from another firm at market price. The marginal cost of pollution control, then, is equalized across all firms. It is in the interest of each polluter to cut emissions to the socially efficient level, where the price of an additional RTC equals the marginal cost of abatement. At that point, any increase in emissions would reduce the firm's profit. Firms that are able to reduce their emissions may sell their unused credits on the open market. Furthermore, the trading scheme encourages technological innovation by giving firms an additional financial incentive to find cheaper ways to reduce pollution. This incentive is absent under command-and-control regulation, which stipulates both the output level and the technology that must be used for compliance.

Trading is key to the efficiency of RECLAIM. The existence of a competitive market makes it possible for firms to meet specified emissions levels at a lower overall cost than is possible under direct command-and-control regulation. The following three conditions are required for an efficient, competitive market in emissions credits: (a) there must be an adequate number of participants in the market, (b) there must exist low transaction costs, and (c) government must provide sufficient monitoring and enforcement (Hahn & Noll, 1982). In the case of RECLAIM, all three conditions have been satisfied.

TABLE 2:   Dollar Values of Trades of RECLAIM Credits, 1994-1997

	1994		1995		1996		1997	
	NO_x	SO_x	NO_x	SO_x	NO_x	SO_x	NO_x	SO_x
Total trades (millions)	$1.5	$.008	$8.3	$1.6	$4.4	$5.5	$9.4	$11.7
RTCs traded for price	2,210	4	11,681	3,052	5,595	5,172	9,176	5,077
RTCs traded for $0	5,769	286	66,820	14,105	41,691	19,118	38,652	15,614

SOURCE: SCAQMD, 1998a.

The first condition for an efficient market is the existence of enough participants to ensure frequent trading. This increases the probability that credits will
be traded at a market-clearing price. If there are too few participants, they may
decide to monopolize the market and refuse to trade credits. The initial
RECLAIM NO_x market included 390 facilities, and the SO_x market included 41
facilities. By the end of 1997, more than 1,200 trades of RTCs were recorded.
The volume of RTC trading, broken down by year, appears in Table 2. More than
400 of these transactions were traded at a price totaling more than $42 million.
The rest were zero-price trades. In many of these transactions, RTCs are transferred within companies. In other cases, the RTCs are transferred to a broker to
sell, but are transferred back to the original owner if they are not sold. Still others
are transferred between brokers. As the data show, trading increased significantly after the first year. Only 4 tons of SO_x and 2,210 tons of NO_x were traded
for a price in 1994. By the end of 1997, 13,305 tons of SO_x and 28,662 tons of NO_x
had been traded at a price in volume of $18,886,000 and $23,649,000, respectively (SCAQMD, 1998a). During one active week in April 1997, 2.9 million
pounds of RTCs were traded for a total value of $2.2 million (Kraul, 1997).

A second condition for an efficient market requires that transaction costs be
not so high as to discourage trading. The RECLAIM program has avoided this
problem by keeping administrative costs down. Some earlier attempts at tradable permit programs included a requirement that participating firms secure the
permission of regulators before making a trade. Other programs have imposed
additional administrative costs by limiting the number of permits that a single
firm may own (Hahn & Hester, 1989). In contrast to these efforts, the SCAQMD
plays no active role in the market beyond recording transactions, monitoring
emissions, and imposing sanctions. Transaction costs have also been kept under
control with the aid of an electronic trading system, the Automated Credit
Exchange, which allows companies to buy and sell RTCs without the use of a
broker (Kraul, 1997). This reduces the time and effort spent searching for trading partners.

A final condition for an efficient tradable permit program requires the government to protect the market by strict enforcement, thereby guaranteeing its

longevity. Participation in such a market is based on an assumption of accurate monitoring. Thus, polluters are required to install electronic monitoring systems, most of which were operating after 2 years (SCAQMD, 1998a). In addition, the SCAQMD conducts extensive annual audits of the emissions records at each site. Like a consumer market, the market for RTCs is based on trust. If polluters have the opportunity to cheat, then the credits will lose their value and demand will plummet.[5] Furthermore, trading will collapse if the government fails to maintain the program, because tradable permits have no value outside a well-defined emissions market.

Due to the emergence of a competitive market under RECLAIM, emissions reductions were achieved at a lower total cost to the participants than those projected under direct command-and-control regulation. Average annual costs to participants for RECLAIM have been estimated at $80.8 million, compared to the projected average annual cost of $138.7 million over the same period for the command-and-control scheme it replaced (SCAQMD, 1994). The low cost has meant fewer job impacts than were projected under the 1991 SCAQMP. The impact of RECLAIM on employment has been minor, and most of the job losses occurred early. During the first compliance year, regulated businesses reported that 70 jobs were eliminated and only 3 jobs were created as a result of RECLAIM. During the 1995 compliance year, 49 jobs were lost and 10 were created because of the program, whereas only 2 job losses and 1 new job were attributed to RECLAIM in the 1996 compliance year (SCAQMD, 1998a). Altogether, the program was blamed for a net loss of 107 jobs during its first 3 years. This is a substantial improvement over the projected annual loss of 2,000 jobs for the same period under command-and-control regulation (SCAQMD, 1994).[6]

The RECLAIM program thus far has demonstrated that it is possible, given the necessary conditions, for a market-based system of regulation to achieve a reduction in air pollution comparable to traditional command-and-control approaches. As proponents of market-based solutions argue, such an arrangement can reduce emissions at lower cost. Appealing as they may be, innovative solutions such as RECLAIM must be evaluated on criteria other than effectiveness and efficiency. The effectiveness and efficiency standards merely require that policies be designed to achieve their goals at the lowest possible cost. In particular, there exists an implicit tension with other values seen as essential to general welfare, such as equity and democracy.

EQUITY

With significant discussions taking place within other aspects of environmental policy involving equity and justice, the establishment of the RECLAIM program in Southern California and the SO_2 market under the 1990 Clean Air Act also raises questions as to how the new partnerships between regulators and polluters affects equity. At first, some groups opposed the market system, fearing that leaving policy decisions up to the market would actually lead to worse environmental conditions (McLean, 1996) by giving utilities a "license to pollute" or by creating emissions "hot spots" in certain areas (Stavins, 1998). There was also concern that the market would unfairly shift the burden of pollution to poor and minority areas where citizens could not financially compete with utility companies in the purchase of emissions credits. This assumes that plants with the dirtiest emissions (and the most interested in purchasing allowances) are disproportionately located in poor or minority areas, thereby exposing area residents to greater risk (Ringquist, 1998).

The areas of southeast Los Angeles and the communities of El Segundo, San Pedro, and Wilmington, which include the marine terminals of the Los Angeles harbor, are two regions in the South Coast Air Basin where environmental equity concerns have been raised. These locations are characterized by their predominantly minority and low-income residents who are "already overburdened with high levels of pollution from refineries and industrial sources" (Bansal & Kuhn, 1998, p. 18). Southeast Los Angeles contains a large number of polluting industries, and residents are exposed to far more concentrated levels of toxic air emissions in comparison to other parts of Los Angeles County (Bansal & Davis, 1998). According to the California legislature, hot spots such as the ones in southeast Los Angeles are

> localized concentrations [of toxic air releases] . . . where emissions from specific sources may expose individuals and population groups to elevated risks of adverse health effects, including but not limited to cancer, and contribute to the cumulative health risk of emissions from other sources in the area. (Bansal & Davis, 1998, p. 26)

Hot spots occur when certain areas suffer from continued concentrated pollution emissions even though overall emissions for the region are reduced (McLean, 1996).

Despite preventative efforts by SCAQMD, hot spots have appeared within the basin. Environmental and community groups argue that this is the result of industries (e.g., oil refineries) along the Coastal Zone scrapping old vehicles under Rule 1610 for pollution credits, which in turn permits these industries to emit pollutants locally at relatively high levels. According to one group, Communities for a Better Environment (CBE), this swapping ignores the "cumulative impacts and therefore exacerbates environmental injustices" (Bansal & Kuhn, 1998, p. 16). In an effort to correct this situation, CBE successfully filed five federal lawsuits under the Clean Air Act. Four of the lawsuits are against Unocal, Chevron, GATX, and Ultramar, oil companies operating in the Coastal Zone. The fifth, against the SCAQMD directly, cites violation of the 1964 Civil Rights Act (Bansal & Kuhn, 1998). In attempting to reduce levels of certain problematic motor vehicle emissions (such as volatile organic compounds [VOCs], nitrogen oxide, carbon monoxide, and particulate matter) by providing transferable emissions credits for scrapped vehicles, SCAQMD inadvertently compounded emissions problems in poor and minority areas of the basin (SCAQMD, 1998b).

Responding to questions about equity and the creation of hot spots, the SCAQMD argues that although hot spots are a complex issue, there is no definite, visible shift in emissions from one area to another (D. Luong, personal communication, December 22, 1998). Therefore, because the number of credits allowed each year declines, emissions will never exceed 1994 levels. The problem, however, is that aspects of the RECLAIM program allow certain participants to evade compliance legally. Although the SCAQMD has divided the basin into two zones to prevent concentration of pollution in the Inland Zone, no mechanisms exist to prevent concentrations of pollution (i.e., hot spots) in particular areas within each of the zones. As a result, even though overall emissions levels have declined, certain sectors of the population are denied the benefit of having the same level of cleaner air or having it as quickly as residents in other parts of the basin. Hence, emissions trading programs such as RECLAIM have a negative impact on the equity of benefits received from the program. In contrast, Ringquist's (1998) study does not find such inequities in the SO_2 emissions trading program under the 1990 Clean Air Act. Ringquist is quick to point out, however, that "environmental equity is relative," and numerous other studies over the past several years have chronicled the ways in which poor and minority populations are confronted by disproportionately high levels of environmental risk (1998, p. 24). What remains more difficult to discern is whether the same level of inequity in the RECLAIM program is present in traditional command-and-control forms of regulation.

DEMOCRACY

The emergence of a new partnership between government and industry under the auspices of the RECLAIM program raises important questions about traditional conceptions of democratic participation in the policy process. A major concern is whether market-based approaches seriously restrict public input in the policy process, or whether they provide the public with a new means of involvement. On one hand, the privatization of the RECLAIM program reduces public involvement by placing decisions on the means of achieving emissions reductions solely in the hands of private industry. On the other hand, it also creates new possibilities for democratic participation through the purchase and trading of emissions credits.

Despite fears by some that "the AQMD [Air Quality Management District] has been taken over by the corporations it is legally mandated to regulate" (Mann, 1994, p. 22), the formation of a partnership between the public and private sector to improve environmental quality does not signify a complete elimination of government oversight, citizen participation, and accountability. The federal and state governments still set emissions limits, monitor the program, and impose penalties for noncompliance. Participation in the RECLAIM program does not excuse industries (and public utilities) from complying with other local, state, and federal environmental standards such as those under the California and U.S. Clean Air Acts. As far as government policy is a reflection of public choice, "the total level of emissions going into the Los Angeles Air Basin remains a public decision" (Polesetsky, 1995, pp. 396-397).

According to the SCAQMD, "anyone can participate in the RECLAIM trading markets, including RECLAIM facilities, brokers, non-RECLAIM facilities, and individuals interested in trading RTCs" (SCAQMD, 1994, p. EX-13). Nonetheless, the majority of trading activity involves industries and brokers. According to the SCAQMD, although there have been purchases from polluters by third-party traders or middlemen, there have been almost no purchases of pollution credits by environmental groups (for the purpose of retiring credits) or private citizens (D. Luong, personal communication, December 22, 1998). Financially, individuals and many public interest groups may not be able to act at the same level as many utilities. Therefore, although, in theory, these groups have the same access to the policy process, in practice, they do not.

Despite some initial fears, environmental and public interest groups are participating in the national SO_2 market. National Sulfur Dioxide Allowance auction records from 1994 to 1998 show that several environmental, public interest, and educational groups such as the Natural Resources Defense Council, the Adirondacks Council, the Clean Air Conservancy, Carolina Clean Skies, and the Acid Rain Retirement Fund, as well as individuals have bid for and purchased sulfur dioxide allowances (Environmental Protection Agency [EPA], 1994, 1995, 1996, 1997a, 1998). Although there has been more public participation in the SO_2 emissions trading system than in RECLAIM, the involvement of environmental and public interest groups and citizens in the national SO_2 market represents only a small fraction of the total number of allowances being traded.

Although there has been some public participation in the SO_2 emissions trading program, some still consider this participation "largely symbolic" (EPA, 1997b). Who has access to emissions credits, who is actually purchasing credits, and whether they are doing so in significant amounts are some of the different questions. Because of the much smaller scale of the RECLAIM program and the cost of purchasing credits, it is not clear as to what extent local citizens can actually participate in this program.

Along with financial resources, there is a certain amount of knowledge and effort required to participate in the emissions market. At the national level, all of the EPA's Allowance Tracking System information, along with emissions monitoring data, is available to the public over the Internet on the Acid Rain Program's homepage. Despite an interest in helping the environment, many individuals may not have the time nor the inclination to read through the substantial amount of information available on the EPA web site in order to prepare themselves for the allowance bidding process. For this reason, nonprofit groups such

as the Acid Rain Retirement Fund or the Clean Air Conservancy play an important role as brokers. These groups know how the system works, and they track
allowance market trends in order to facilitate bidding. Furthermore, by combining funds from different individuals, these groups can purchase allowances
when individuals would not have been able to do so alone (Carman, 1998). In the
RECLAIM program, organizations such as CBE or the Community Health
Foundation in East Los Angeles might fulfill this role of monitoring the market
and combining funds for allowance purchases at the local level.

Another criticism of the RECLAIM program has been aimed at the lack of
public access to market information. Groups such as CBE have suggested that
the SCAQMD facilitates public awareness by publishing emissions data on-line
(Bansal & Davis, 1998). In a 3-year program audit, advisory committee members found that "the data on the Bulletin Board has been perceived to be out-of-
date and difficult to access" (SCAQMD, 1998a, p. 10-4). RECLAIM could be
made more user friendly by posting improved trading data on the SCAQMD
Web site.

Thus far, attention has been focused on public participation in the actual
allowance-trading market. Public input and oversight in the RECLAIM program does take place in the form of working groups, advisory committees, and
steering committees that, among other responsibilities, oversee annual and
3-year program audits. To ensure that the views of different sectors of the community are represented, committee membership includes representatives from
industry; small business; environmental, labor, public health, and community
groups; financial organizations; and public agencies. Unlike the EPA's Acid
Rain Advisory Committee, which was brought together to discuss options and
potential problems with the initial implementation of the SO_2 program, but has
not met for several years since the initial design of the program (McLean, 1996),
RECLAIM continues to solicit feedback. Most recently, advisory committee
members commented on the Three-Year Audit and Progress Report. The views
of citizens, therefore, are not entirely excluded from clean air policy making in
the RECLAIM program (SCAQMD, 1998a).

CONCLUSION

This paper evaluated the effectiveness and efficiency of the RECLAIM program, and it investigated whether this market-based approach provides equitable benefits and is democratic. Evidence from the SO_2 emissions trading program was also cited at relevant points in the study. Overall, the findings show
that emissions trading programs are fairly effective and efficient at meeting their
goals (in this case, improved air quality), particularly when compared to traditional direct command-and-control regulatory efforts. Of course, RECLAIM is
still a relatively new program, and future researchers will want to take into
account variations in weather and economic conditions, as well as improve-

ments in technology, in their evaluations of the long-term effectiveness and efficiency of the program. Serious questions remain, however, as to whether market-based approaches can satisfy environmental justice concerns and involve the public in an open, ongoing, and meaningful way.

Whether similar measures can be successfully employed in other environmental policy spheres is uncertain. Clearly, not all environmental problems lend themselves to the use of market incentives. It is difficult to imagine, for example, how such strategies could be used to protect endangered species, regulate the disposal of hazardous and nuclear waste, or preserve scenery. Despite such limitations, these approaches, when employed in the proper policy context, tend to forge generally constructive partnerships between the public and private sector as well as between different government levels and agencies. Program success also depends on adequate funding and oversight, the presence of an institutional structure, the availability of scientific and technical expertise, and the existence of clearly defined policy goals. Future policymakers, however, must pay close attention to the equity and democratic aspects of these types of programs and partnerships.

As this study suggests, market-based approaches have been fairly successful in replacing traditional adversarial relationships between various stakeholders with constructive partnerships while limiting the emission of toxic pollutants. As a consequence, the adoption of an emissions trading system for CO_2 and other greenhouse gases is seriously being considered by global climate change negotiators and Congress. However, a number of problems must first be overcome before such a program can be implemented at the global level. Clearly, an international agency with the authority to set and revise standards, monitor compliance and enforce permits, and coordinate trading must be established. The existence of only a few well-organized, well-funded, and highly influential nongovernmental environmental organizations at the international level makes this an imperative. Those that do exist tend to be based in developed nations and tend to have a developed-nation bias. Moreover, international environmental policy makers must address critical equity and public involvement issues prior to the formation of emissions trading programs and the development of diverse partnerships if such strategies are to be successful. The greatest challenge lies in achieving equity and a reasonable level of public participation, especially in those nations that do not have democratic or quasi-democratic institutions in place. Otherwise, programs in nations that depend heavily on the modification of lifestyles of individuals to help reduce greenhouse gas emissions will be ineffective. The formation of different partnerships at the international level would be a welcome departure from the otherwise contentious relationships that now exist between developed and developing nations, between governments and large industries that emit enormous quantities of greenhouse gases, and between regulators and government-owned and -operated utilities and industries.

NOTES

1. See Kamieniecki and Ferrall (1991) for a comprehensive review of previous SCAQMPs and clean air policy making in California. The 1991 SCAQMP was the last plan before the adoption of RECLAIM. The projections in the 1994 and 1997 plans take RECLAIM into account and therefore do not offer appropriate baselines for comparison.

2. Note that RECLAIM requires monitoring equipment that transmits real-time emissions data from polluters to the SCAQMD every 24 hours. The costs related to the installation and maintenance of this equipment are borne by the polluter.

3. According to Ringquist (1998), a small percentage of trades in the SO_2 program do involve private parties, and this figure may increase in the future.

4. It is worth noting that policy analysts often disagree about which measurements of effectiveness are the most valid and accurate. Many methodological issues exist in this kind of research.

5. Due in part to doubts about effective monitoring, SCAQMD abandoned a plan to create an additional market for emissions of VOCs. In contrast to the nearly 400 sources in the NO_x and SO_x markets, the proposed VOC program would have regulated more than 1,000 sources. Many of these were light industries, such as print shops, furniture manufacturers, and automobile body shops (Cone, 1993).

6. Of course, air quality in the South Coast Air Basin is a complex function of meteorological and economic conditions and an array of different emissions sources. It is therefore impossible to know exactly how much of the reduction in emissions is due to the implementation of the RECLAIM program.

REFERENCES

Bansal, S., & Davis, S. (1998). *Holding our breath: Environmental injustice exposed in southeast Los Angeles, an assessment of cumulative health risk and local air policy*. Los Angeles: Communities for a Better Environment.

Bansal, S., & Kuhn, S. (1998). Stopping an unfair trade: Environmental justice, pollution trade, and cumulative impacts in Los Angeles. *Environmental Law News, 7*, 16-24.

Bobrow, D. B., & Dryzek, J. S. (1987). *Policy analysis by design*. Pittsburgh, PA: University of Pittsburgh Press.

Bryner, G. (1997). Market incentives in air pollution control. In S. Kamieniecki, G. A. Gonzalez, and R. O. Vos (Eds.), *Flashpoints in environmental policymaking: Controversies in achieving sustainability* (pp. 85-107). Albany, NY: SUNY Press.

Cahn, M. A. (1995). *Environmental deceptions: The tensions between liberalism and environmental policymaking in the United States*. Albany, NY: SUNY Press.

Carman, C. J. (1998, September). *Brokering interests: A theory of interest group policy maximization through regulatory market participation*. Paper presented at the Annual Meeting of the American Political Science Association, Boston, MA.

Cone, M. (1993, August 21). AQMD plan for blue skies turns hazy. *Los Angeles Times*, p. B1.

Elliott, W. (1993, October 2). *Letter to Representative Henry Waxman* (Submitted for the record by Group Against Smog Pollution, The Clean Air Act in California: The RECLAIM Program). Letter presented at the hearing before the Subcommittee on Health and the Environment of the House Committee on Energy and Commerce, 103rd Congress, Session 42.

Environmental Protection Agency. (1994). *1994 allowance auction results* [On-line]. Available: http://www.epa.gov/acidrain/auctions/94splob.html.

Environmental Protection Agency. (1995). *1995 allowance auction results* [On-line]. Available: http://www.epa.gov/acidrain/auctions/95splob.html.

Environmental Protection Agency. (1996). *1996 allowance auction results* [On-line]. Available: http://www.epa.gov/acidrain/auctions/96splob.html.

Environmental Protection Agency. (1997a). *1997 allowance auction results* [On-line]. Available: http://www.epa.gov/acidrain/auctions/97splob.html.

Environmental Protection Agency. (1997b). *Looking back on SO_2 trading: What's good for the environment is good for the market* [On-line]. Available: http://www.epa.gov/acidrain/pufartcl.html.

Environmental Protection Agency. (1998). *1998 EPA SO_2 allowance auction results* [On-line]. Available: http://www.epa.gov/acidrain/auctions/98results.htm.

Fromm, O., & Hansjürgens, B. (1996). Emissions trading in theory and practice: An analysis of RECLAIM in Southern California. *Environment and Planning C: Government and Policy, 14*, 367-384.

Hahn, R. W., & Hester, G. L. (1989). Where did all the markets go? An analysis of EPA's emissions trading program. *Yale Journal of Regulation, 6*, 109-153.

Hahn, R. W., & Noll, R. G. (1982). Designing a market for tradeable emissions permits. In W. A. Magat (Ed.), *Reform of environmental regulation* (pp. 119-146). Cambridge, MA: Ballinger Press.

Hall, J. V., & Walton, A. L. (1996). A case study in pollution markets: Dismal science versus dismal reality. *Contemporary Economic Policy, 14*, 67-78.

Hamilton, C. R., & Wells, D. T. (1996). *The policy puzzle*. Englewood Cliffs, NJ: Prentice Hall.

Ingersoll, T. G., & Brockbank, B. R. (1986). The role of economic incentives in environmental policy. In S. Kamieniecki, R. O'Brien, & M. Clarke (Eds.), *Controversies in environmental policy* (pp. 201-222). Albany, NY: SUNY Press.

Kamieniecki, S., & Ferrall, M. (1991). Intergovernmental relations and clean-air policy in Southern California. *Publius, 21*, 143-154.

Kraul, C. (1997, April 30). Companies trade smog credits on online exchange. *Los Angeles Times*, p. D1.

Mann, E. (1994, Winter). Trading delusions. *Environmental Action Magazine, 25*, 22-23.

McLean, B. J. (1996). The evolution of marketable permits: The U.S. experience with sulfur dioxide allowance trading. In D. Anderson & M. Grubb (Eds.), *Controlling carbon and sulfur: Joint implementation and trading initiatives*. London: The Royal Institute of International Affairs.

Mueller, D. (1981). *Public choice*. Cambridge, UK: Cambridge University Press.

National Academy of Public Administration. (1994). *The environment goes to the market*. Washington, DC: Author.

Okun, A. (1974). *Efficiency and equity: The big trade-off*. Washington, DC: Brookings.

Ostrom, E. (1991). Rational choice theory and institutional analysis: Toward complementarity. *American Political Science Review, 85*, 237-243.

Polesetsky, M. (1995). Will a market in air pollution clean the nation's dirtiest air? A study of the South Coast Air Quality Management District's regional clean air incentives market. *Ecology Law Quarterly, 22*, 359-411.

Portney, P. R. (1990). Air pollution policy. In P. R. Portney (Ed.), *Public policies for environmental protection* (pp. 27-96). Washington, DC: Resources for the Future.

Quade, E. S. (1991). *Analysis for public decisions*. New York: Elsevier Science.

Ringquist, E. J. (1998, September). *Efficiency versus equity in environmental protection: Trading SO_2 emissions under the 1990 Clean Air Act*. Paper presented at the Annual Meeting of the American Political Science Association, Boston, MA.

Rosenbaum, W. A. (1998). *Environmental politics and policy* (4th ed.). Washington, DC: CQ Press.

Savas, E. S. (1987). *Privatization: The key to better government*. Chatham, NJ: Chatham House.

Schneider, A. L. (1986). The evolution of a policy orientation for evaluation research: A guide to practice. *Public Administration Review, 46*, 356-364.

Schneider, A. L., & Ingram, H. (1997). *Policy design for democracy*. Lawrence, KS: University of Kansas Press.

South Coast Air Quality Management District. (1991). *Air quality management plan*. Diamond Bar, CA: Author.

South Coast Air Quality Management District. (1994). *Reclaim: Program summary*. Diamond Bar, CA: Author.

South Coast Air Quality Management District. (1998a). *RECLAIM program three-year audit and progress report*. Diamond Bar, CA: Author.

South Coast Air Quality Management District. (1998b). *Rule 1610: Old-vehicle scrapping* [Online]. Available: http://www.aqmd.gov/rules/html/r1610/html.

Sproule-Jones, M. (1984). Methodological individualism and public choice. *American Behavioral Scientist, 28*, 167-184.

Stavins, R. N. (1998). What can we learn from the grand policy experiment? Lessons from SO_2 allowance trading. *Journal of Economic Perspectives, 12*, 69-88.

Tietenberg, T. H. (1985). *Emissions trading*. Washington, DC: Resources for the Future.

Weimer, D. L., & Vining, A. R. (1989). *Policy analysis: Concepts and practice* (2nd ed.). Englewood Cliffs, NJ: Prentice Hall.

8

The Public-Private Nexus in Education

HENRY M. LEVIN

A partnership is generally viewed as a formal agreement between two or more parties that provides mutual benefits to those parties. It is rare that such partnerships exist between public and private elementary or secondary schools. Despite the fact that only about 10% of the students are enrolled in private schools, educational institutions in the two sectors are competing for many of the same students and do not find it to their advantage to work together. In higher education there exist a variety of agreements, such as consortia based upon joint sharing of libraries, course registrations, and cooperative programs; however, such partnerships are still modest in scope and are the exception rather than the rule.

At a broader level, there exist many intersections between the public sector in education and various private entities. Whether one would call them policy partnerships is less clear. It is probably fair to say that most formal partnerships between the two sectors are modest in scope. The most prominent of these are public assistance to private schools and business-education partnerships. In these cases, there are formal relations between government and private schools on one hand, and between private businesses and public schools on the other. In a broader context, it is clear that the education of each child must necessarily be a public-private undertaking to the degree that its success is premised on a parent-school partnership. What students learn depends on not only what happens in school, but also what happens in the home and the degree to which homes and schools are mutually supportive of each other's goals.

In this article, I will review a range of linkages between the public and private sectors in elementary and secondary education. I will begin by reviewing the peculiar nature of education in producing what is both a public and private good. This suggests that public-private collaboration should be central to education. I will follow with several existing interventions that link the public and private sectors. I will point out the necessity of public-private collaboration while also stressing the continuing sources of tension between the two sectors when it comes to education. Finally, I will present the most ambitious venture to link public and private sectors in education by providing publicly financed vouchers that could be used for private schools.

EDUCATION AS A PUBLIC AND PRIVATE GOOD

Education inherently serves both public and private interests (Levin, 1987). It addresses public interests by preparing the young to assume adult roles in which they can undertake civic responsibilities; embrace a common set of values; participate in a democratic polity with a given set of rules; and embrace the economic, political, and social life that constitute the foundation for the nation. All of this is necessary for an effectively functioning democracy, economy, and society. At the same time, education must address the private interests of students and their families by providing a variety of forms of development that will enhance individual economic, social, cultural, and political benefits for the individual. Embedded in the same educational experience are outcomes that can contribute to the overall society as well as those that can provide private gains to the individual.

To some degree, the public and private outcomes of schooling can overlap, because better educational results for the individual and her family may also contribute to social benefits. For example, if schooling makes the individual more productive (private benefits), the economy also receives a boost (social benefits). However, in other respects, there may be conflict between public and private benefits. For example, the public benefits of schooling require that students learn to consider different points of view that are presented and debated in the schooling experience. But, the private values of families may be in conflict with some of these viewpoints, and parents may not wish their children to be exposed to points of view that are at odds with those held by the family.

The problem is that schooling takes place at the intersection of two sets of rights, those of the family and those of society. The first is the right of parents to choose the experiences, influences, and values to which they expose their children, the right to rear their children in the manner that they see fit. The second is the right of a democratic society to use the educational system as a means to reproduce its most essential political, economic, and social institutions through a common schooling experience (Gutmann, 1987). In essence, the challenge is preserving the shared educational experience necessary for establishing a common foundation of knowledge and values that is crucial to reproducing the existing economic, political, and social order (public goals), while allowing some range of choice (private goals) within that experience. Because the schools represent the primary agency for preparing all students for the major institutions that constitute the bedrock of society, this requirement suggests a schooling process that comprises many common experiences for all students, even if some of these violate the choices that families might make independently for their children.

Both sets of rights are legitimate, and both are partially, but not completely, compatible. It is clear that public schools cannot be advocates for each and all of the many different and incompatible perspectives that parents have regarding culture, language, values, religion, and politics. As a concrete example, there are clearly very strong differences in viewpoint within the polity about the permissibility of allowing abortion. In the larger society, this very controversial matter must be resolved politically. However, emotions run very strongly on the perspectives. On one side of the issue, abortion is considered infanticide. On the other side of the issue, abortion is considered to be a matter of choice for determining the fate of a fetus that is not yet endowed with human properties. This conflict is embedded in deeply held philosophical, religious, and political ideologies.

One group of parents would like the young to see abortion as murder, and another group would like them to see it as family planning, and both sides would consider the contrary view to be illegitimate. This makes it difficult for the schools to present the issue in any form. The easiest route for the schools is to avoid the issue. However, the courts, legislatures, and Congress cannot avoid the issue, and it is one that all citizens should develop an informed understanding that can be communicated through the political process. This is an example of a public dimension of education that may be in conflict with the private goals of many families who want to keep the issue outside of public discourse or to inculcate the correctness of one particular view without debate. Many other public issues cry out for democratic resolution, but families find them objectionable for private reasons. This is often the situation when parents decry the teaching of inappropriate values in public schools because the schools did not inculcate the parents' values. In such a case, parents may put pressures on schools and school boards to make changes, or they may opt to send their children to other schools, public or private (Hirschman, 1970).

Any discussion on public and private issues in education must recognize the tension between public and private benefits and goals. As long as education has both public and private components, there must be a balance and blending. The solution will always be a compromise that will leave some parents dissatisfied. This dissatisfaction will lead parents to pressure schools for change or to escape from public schooling with private schools and home schooling as possible alternatives. In other cases, parents will move to other jurisdictions that sponsor public schools that are more compatible with their beliefs.

Much of the debate about the proper roles of public schools and the issue of public support for private schools can only be understood within this framework. Parents who believe that schools should be limited to meeting only their private objectives for their offspring will often object to many of the public goals of schooling. Even those parents who accept overall public goals may be at odds with specific activities and goals that are incompatible with their private educational values. Public policy toward education has been to steer a course that embraces the public interest while allowing as much of the private interest as can be accommodated without bringing the two into serious conflict. This is a difficult charge that always places schools under a tension that is not easily resolved. Indeed, Chubb and Moe (1990) have argued that democracy is the problem that besets public education.

Prior to the 1950s, parents and school districts were able to resolve these potential conflicts through what Michael Katz (1971) calls "democratic localism."[1] That is, within each local setting, communities were able to maintain public schools that reflected the predominant politics, values, culture, and wealth. Public schools in much of the nation were segregated by race, and school finance was largely a local matter based upon property taxes that raised more funding for students in wealthier districts, often considerably more, than for those in poorer enclaves. Many children with handicaps were excluded from schools or were provided with inadequate services, and those who were educationally at risk were given no special assistance and were often tracked into dead-end curricula. Inculcation of the religion of the dominant group at the local level was a common feature of school life. Although each of these policies might be incompatible with the public goals of schooling, they were based upon a tacit compromise premised on the view that those with power could influence policies and local practices in directions that would benefit their children over others. Children from groups that lacked powerful advocacy in their behalf, such as African Americans, the poor, and the handicapped were treated in a less enviable way.

But over the next 40 years, decisions and policies set out by courts, legislatures, and Congress reduced these prerogatives and inequalities so that schools became more and more alike, with fewer public alternatives for meeting private educational preferences. Laws were passed that provided special benefits to economically disadvantaged, bilingual, and handicapped students as well as pushed for racial and gender equality. School funding was more nearly equalized between school districts. Official policies of racial segregation were proscribed by law. The press for greater equity removed many of the privileges held traditionally by dominant groups in local communities.

By 1980, a general backlash emerged with the aim of regaining what was lost. If local political power could no longer be used to create schools that echoed the racial preferences, values, religious practices, and wealth of local residents, other alternatives had to be sought. Most of these alternatives revolved around ways to increase local choice within the public schools. Public choice alternatives refer to the ability of families to choose from public schools within a district or from different districts rather than having students assigned to schools (see the essays in Clune & Witte, 1990). Some districts even created magnet schools with special themes to attract families who were interested in those themes (e.g., science, the arts, technology, multiculturalism, business, health professions, and so on). However, even these forms of public choice have been superceded in the last decade of this century by more radical alternatives, such as charter schools and educational vouchers. Charter schools are schools established under public authority that are exempt from many state and local policies and laws as long as they meet the goals set out in their charter (Nathan, 1996). They can be initiated by parents or educators, and they can represent distinct educational philosophies within the broader public context for schooling. Educational vouchers represent the most complete response to the public-private dilemma by funding all schools that meet certain minimal requirements, whether publicly or privately sponsored, with public dollars.

EXISTING FORMS OF PUBLIC-PRIVATE COLLABORATION

Before addressing the educational voucher initiative, it is important to review briefly existing practices of public funding for private schools, business-school partnerships, and family-school connections.

PUBLIC FUNDING OF PRIVATE SCHOOLS

State and local governments provide considerable subsidies to private schools for nonsectarian purposes. The general view is that if state funding benefits the child rather than the religious institutions that sponsor most private schools, it is permissible under federal and state constitutions. Typical government subsidies to private schools are found in the following four areas: tax-free status, textbooks, transportation, and categorical programs.

Because almost all existing private schools are educational institutions that are not for profit, they are exempt from taxes even though they are eligible for all pertinent local and state services supported by tax revenues. Textbooks that are provided to public schools for the standard nonreligious courses are often provided free of charge to private schools. Many states also provide transportation of students to private schools on the same basis as public school students. Finally, federal and state programs for disadvantaged students are often offered at private schools in classrooms that are not adorned with religious symbols and staffed by employees from the local public school district. One early study (Sullivan, 1974) found that about one quarter of the cost of private schools is borne by government, but that study was done some two decades ago when the law was more restrictive, so the portion is likely to be much higher now.

BUSINESS PARTNERSHIPS

Businesses have had a long tradition of establishing partnerships with schools in a variety of ways. Usually these are based upon both self-interest and altruism. Such partnerships can improve the preparation of the labor force hired by businesses and provide good public relations, but they can also be forged in the spirit of community involvement. The forms of such partnerships are widely varied. At the local level, they include adopt-a-school programs that offer financial assistance to schools, expertise in particular subjects or managerial challenges, release time to employees for being volunteer tutors, and awards for student performance. At regional and national levels, they may include formation of private associations to provide political support for school reform as well as larger grant programs that assist schools to make major changes. For example, IBM sponsors grant competitions with awards in the millions of dollars to school systems that will make a significant commitment to new applications of computers and related technologies.

Schools have also had a long tradition of cooperative work arrangements with businesses for training and placing students in vocational studies (Steinberg, 1997). By providing part-time jobs for students that relate to their vocational preparation, these businesses offer both applied experiences and income. Such business arrangements may also include gifts of equipment and funds to support vocational programs. In addition, the same businesses will often hire the graduates of these programs if they have performed satisfactorily. This is an example of a mutually beneficial partnership activity because it supports both the learning and training of a local workforce.

SCHOOLS AND FAMILIES

At a less formal level, but even more consequential in terms of student outcomes, there is a tacit partnership between public entities (schools) and private ones (families). It is well known that student achievement in schools is heavily dependent upon family influences. In particular, children from families of higher socioeconomic origins, with higher income and parental education, tend to have better educational achievement than those from lower, more modest origins (Natriello, McDill, & Pallas, 1990). The former type of families is better able to provide the resources and experiences that support school learning.

It is useful to separate family influences on learning into two parts. The first part consists of the natural interactions that more educated and affluent families have with their children that lead to educational success. Such families use a standard version of the English language, an educated vocabulary, and styles of interaction that tend to be more oriented toward questioning and reasoning techniques (Heath, 1983). These are the types of interactions that lead to the knowledge and behavior that schools build upon and achievement tests measure. In addition, their higher incomes mean that students are exposed to a richer set of worldly experiences that contribute to their education. Examples of this range of experiences include travel, computers, summer camps, books, hobbies, and music lessons. Finally, they are more able to provide nutrition, health, counseling, tutoring, and other inputs that support school learning. However, in addition to these, there are specific practices that families can engage in, with respect to the schools their children attend, that will improve both their children's chances of success and the quality of the schools.

Joyce Epstein, the foremost scholar in the area of school, family, and community partnerships, has identified six types of family involvement (Epstein, Coates, Salinas, Sanders, & Simon, 1997).

1. Parenting—helping families establish home environments to support children as students.
2. Communicating—designing effective forms of school-to-home and home-to-school communication about school programs and student progress.
3. Volunteering—recruiting and organizing parental help and support for school.
4. Learning at home—assisting families to help students at home with homework and other school-related activities.
5. Decision making—including families in school decisions and developing parent leadership.
6. Collaboration with community—using community resources to support families, strengthen schools, and increase student learning.

It is noteworthy that these activities represent forms of school support for families and communities, and forms of community and family support for schools, both efforts focusing primarily on improving student success. An excellent handbook for action in all of these areas is found in Epstein et al. (1997).

EDUCATIONAL VOUCHERS

Although the concept of educational vouchers has been around for at least two centuries, the specific form that has been debated in recent years dates to an important publication by Milton Friedman on the role of the state in education (Friedman, 1962). In that work, Friedman argued that schools should be funded by the government because of their importance in producing the values required for democratic functioning. Although Friedman called these "neighborhood benefits," they are similar to what we have referred to as the public benefits of education, contributions to the larger society rather than just the individual. Friedman argued that just because government finances schools, it does not mean that government should operate them. Suggesting that the government was an unresponsive monopoly, he asserted that schools ought to be placed in the competitive marketplace that would promote a plethora of for-profit and not-for-profit schools. To accomplish this, the financing of schools would take place through government-issued vouchers that could be applied toward tuition at approved schools that met minimal requirements for assuring the public interest. These vouchers would be redeemed at the state treasury by schools, and parents could add on to the vouchers if they had the means and the commitment to do so.

According to Friedman, such a plan would assure efficiency, innovation, and responsiveness to parental concerns through the incentives of the competitive marketplace. Schools would emerge to serve particular market niches and compete between themselves, and parents could shift their patronage from schools that displeased them to ones that are more attractive. Furthermore, a much larger variety of schools would arise to serve the private interests of families, while protecting the public interest through minimal regulations on curriculum. Thus, the Friedman proposal acknowledged the existence of both the public and private benefits of education while creating a financial mechanism for the private marketplace that would presumably allow attention to both.

Whether the voucher plan that was proposed by Friedman would do all that he claimed has been a source of contention ever since. Friedman's initial voucher plan was shy on details with respect to the size of the voucher; regulations that would assure the production of public benefits; and provision of information to both schools and prospective producers, on one hand, and families, on the other, a prerequisite for a competitive market. Thus, a number of different voucher plans have arisen over the years that have made concrete provisions in each of these areas with somewhat different goals for each plan. Among the most notable are the plans proposed by the Center for the Study of Public Policy (1970) that were designed for a voucher experiment to be administered by the Office of Economic Opportunity as part of the Poverty Program; the proposal for transforming state school systems to vouchers by Coons and Sugarman (1978); and the plan by Chubb and Moe (1990), which caught the attention of many school reformers in recent years. In addition, publicly sponsored voucher demonstrations have been taking place in both Cleveland and Milwaukee, and privately financed voucher projects have been sponsored in San Antonio, New York, and Indianapolis (Moe, 1995).

Differences between voucher plans can be understood largely in terms of three dimensions: finance, regulation, and information (Levin, 1991).

Finance. Central to the potential impact of vouchers on equity is the size of the voucher and the issue of whether families can add their own resources to school payments. Friedman's original voucher plan would suggest a flat voucher of modest value with parental add-ons to that voucher if the parents had the means and desire. Later voucher plans typically limit parental add-ons and include compensatory vouchers, such as larger vouchers for the poor and the handicapped to compensate for the higher costs of meeting their educational needs (e.g., Center for the Study of Public Policy, 1970). In addition, school participation requires financial provision for transportation so that the many parents who cannot provide this for their children because of costs or work schedules can gain access to potential alternatives. The initial Friedman plan does not discuss transportation, but it is recognized as a requirement by later plans.

Regulation. Even Friedman suggests that voucher schools should be subject to some curriculum regulations to ensure that they produce public benefits, although such regulation would be minimal. However, subsequent voucher plans such as that of the Center for the Study of Public Policy (1970) or Coons and Sugarman (1978) would require a variety of other measures, including regular reporting of achievement test results of their students. In addition, they would require nondiscrimination in admissions and a lottery for some portion of their admissions if a school received more applications than it could enroll. Stringent curriculum and teacher licensing requirements have also been debated as requirements for schools to be approved to redeem vouchers.

Information. Efficiency in competitive markets requires that substantial information be available to both buyers and sellers. For example, families need to know the available alternatives and their educational consequences. Although the Friedman plan makes no provision for gathering and disseminating information on schools, other plans typically assume some responsibility for doing so.

In summary, there is no single voucher plan, but many different ones with different provisions that auger for different educational outcomes. Some tend to focus more fully on maximizing family choice, whereas others would sacrifice some choice through funding and regulations that would emphasize equity and a common core of learning.

FOUR MAJOR DIMENSIONS

In order to understand the arguments for and against educational vouchers and public dollars for private schools, it is important to identify four major criteria that emerge in the public debate. Each of these following criteria is highly important to particular policy makers and stakeholders: freedom to choose, efficiency, equity, and social cohesion.

Freedom to choose. For many advocates of vouchers, the freedom to choose the kind of school that emulates their values, educational philosophies, religious teachings, and political outlooks is the most important issue in calling for educational change. This criterion places a heavy emphasis on the private benefits of education and the liberty to choose schools that are consistent with the child-rearing practices of families.

Efficiency. Perhaps the most common claim for educational vouchers is that they will improve the efficiency of the schooling system by producing better educational results for any given outlay of resources. Numerous studies have been done that attempt to measure differences in student achievement between public and private schools or between students using vouchers in private schools and similar students in public schools in the few cases of voucher demonstrations (Levin, 1998; Metcalf et al., 1998; Peterson, Myers, & Howell, 1998).

Equity. A major claim of those who challenge vouchers is that they will create greater inequity in the distribution of educational resources and opportunities that may result from gender, social class, race, language origins, and geographical location of students. Voucher advocates argue that, to the contrary, the ability to choose schools will open up possibilities for students who are locked into inferior neighborhood schools, and the competitive marketplace will have great incentives to meet the needs of all students more fully than existing schools.

Social cohesion. As set out above, a major public purpose of schooling is to provide a common educational experience with respect to curriculum, values, goals, language, and political socialization so that students from many different backgrounds will accept and support a common set of social, political, and economic institutions. The challenge is whether a marketplace of schools competing primarily on the basis of meeting the private goals of parents and students will coalesce around a common set of social, political, and economic principles in the absence of extensive regulations or powerful social incentives.

EVIDENCE

The desirability of a voucher approach will depend upon how effective educational vouchers are relative to the existing alternatives on each of the four criteria as well as how much weight is attached to each criteria. It is important to note that if a particular dimension is not valued highly by a constituency, the evidence will not matter very much for that dimension. That is, preference for vouchers or a particular voucher plan is not completely dependent upon evidence on all of its dimensions, but only on what is deemed important by the observer. The fact that no full-fledged voucher program has been tested in the United States means that evidence is limited. However, in the 1990s there has been a considerable outpouring of empirical literature on some of the voucher demonstrations, differences in achievement between public and private schools, studies of choice patterns, and costs that can be used to partially examine these issues (a summary is found in Levin, 1998). On the basis of these literature, as well as the overall knowledge of how markets function, some conclusions might be drawn. However, even these conclusions will depend ultimately on the type of voucher plan that is being considered. For example, voucher plans with minimal regulations may have very different consequences from ones that are highly regulated.

With respect to the criterion of freedom of choice, the voucher alternative would seem to be superior in giving families a wider variety of possibilities that might match more closely their private goals in raising their children. The gap in favor of educational vouchers would be widest when compared with a traditional school system in which children must attend their neighborhood schools. The gap will narrow in those cases where public schools include intradistrict and interdistrict choices and magnet schools, and it will be narrowest when charter schools, with their quasi-independence, are allowed. Obviously, freedom of choice will depend heavily on the existence of and access to alternatives, factors that are dependent on the provision of transportation and good information.

With respect to the efficiency of schools under educational vouchers, we can divide the phenomenon into two types, micro and macro. Microefficiency refers to the ability to maximize educational results at the school site. Obviously, if different schools are producing different types of educational outcomes to please their clients, comparisons will be difficult. Indeed, market advocates would view the fact that parents could choose the kind of education that they want for their children as a major dimension of using resources more efficiently. Voucher detractors would argue that the absence of the public goods aspect of education in the market solution means that the voucher schools simply produce more of the private benefits at the expense of public ones.

When student achievement is used as the measure of educational result, it appears that private schools and those under voucher arrangements might have a small advantage over public schools with comparable students (Levin, 1998), possibly because they are able to more readily focus on a narrower range of outcomes than those under democratic control (Chubb & Moe, 1990). Studies examining differences in educational achievement between students in public and private schools or in voucher demonstration projects show a private school advantage, although the differences are small (Levin, 1998; Metcalf et al., 1998; Peterson et al., 1998). Typical differences are a few percentiles and are limited to one or two subjects out of four or five that have been measured. For example, after 2 years, the Cleveland voucher demonstration found advantages for voucher students over comparable public school students in language, but not in reading, science, mathematics, or social studies (Metcalf et al., 1998).

Macroefficiency includes not only results at school sites, but also the comparative costs of the overall infrastructure to maintain an educational voucher system relative to the overall costs for maintaining the existing system. Particular areas of such infrastructure include record keeping, school accreditation, transportation, information, and adjudication of disputes. Clearly, some of the costs of a voucher system will depend upon the provisions that are put in place. For example, if microefficiency benefits are to be obtained through competition, then a substantial investment in information and transportation may be required. If schools are to be accredited for vouchers on the basis of meeting the requirements for producing public benefits, a monitoring agency will be required. Even in the absence of these provisions, the cost of record keeping will rise as a central agency must keep track of student attendance, voucher eligibility, and redemption of vouchers on a statewide basis.[2] A study by Levin and Driver (1996, 1997) makes a first attempt at reviewing these measures of supportive infrastructure and finds that such costs for a system of educational vouchers would be considerably higher than for the existing system.

In summary, educational vouchers would promote higher efficiency at the school site, but the costs of infrastructure to support such a system would be considerably higher than that of the present system. On balance, it is difficult to say whether macroefficiency favors one system or the other in the absence of greater detail about the features of the voucher system and the setting where it would be emplaced. Furthermore, without taking account of the consumer gains from freedom of choice and the potential losses of public benefits, it is not clear which approach is more efficient in the use of resources.

Although the existing system of public schools is highly stratified by race and social class, as well as fiscal inequities, most analyses of educational vouchers suggest that they would increase inequities. There are three reasons for this conclusion. First, any voucher plan that allowed add-ons to the government-provided voucher would favor families with higher incomes and fewer children. A lack of investment in both transportation and an effective information system would also favor those who are better off because of their abilities to afford transportation and access information. Second, the evidence from many studies on educational choice finds that the poor are least likely to take advantage of choice, and that both family selection and school selection lead to "cream skimming" of students (Levin, 1998).

The first of these could be countered by specific provisions that favor the poor, such as compensatory vouchers that are larger, transportation solutions, and effective information strategies. Whether these would be adequate to reduce inequities relative to the existing schools is not clear, and the costs of infrastructure to support a more equitable system would be high.

Finally, the criterion of social cohesion is the one that would seem to be more conducive under public school systems than an educational marketplace. The very appeal of freedom of choice is to send children to schools that emulate the specific values and goals of individual families rather than the common goals of society. Schools would rise up to compete for specific market niches by religion, political orientations, national origin, language, culture, and other salient dimensions. The common values and institutions that are required for addressing public goals of education would be undermined by such market behavior. Only through heavy regulation—which inhibits freedom of choice—could attempts be made to coerce schools into producing these public benefits.

THE VOUCHER DEBATE

Those who believe that the issue of vouchers will be resolved by a spirited search for empirical evidence on some of these dimensions may be severely disappointed. Much of the support for or opposition to educational vouchers is premised on ideology and values rather than evidence. For those who believe strongly in freedom of choice in schooling and maximization of family preferences, the issues of equity and social cohesion may not be important, regardless of empirical findings in these domains. For those who believe strongly in social cohesion and equity, the issues of family preference and choice may not weigh heavily. Indeed, this seems to be why both sides have tended to limit the debate largely to efficiency and effectiveness comparisons of public schools with private and voucher schools, a matter that both sides agree has some importance. Ultimately, the matter will be decided more on the basis of values and political might than on evidence of which is superior. And the struggle between those who view schools predominantly for their private benefits and those who view schools predominantly for their public benefits will continue to challenge and modify whatever system is put into place (Carnoy & Levin, 1985).

NOTES

1. The argument in this section is developed more fully in Levin (1987).

2. For example, in California, a state agency would need to shift from keeping track of about 1,000 school districts to maintaining records on about 6,000,000 students and as many as 25,000 schools. See Levin, 1998.

REFERENCES

Carnoy, M., & Levin, H. M. (1985). *Schooling and work in the democratic state*. Stanford, CA: Stanford University Press.

Center for the Study of Public Policy. (1970). *Education vouchers, a report on financing elementary education by grants to parents*. Cambridge, MA: Author.

Chubb, J., & Moe, T. (1990). *Politics, markets, and America's schools*. Washington, DC: The Brookings Institution.

Clune, W., & Witte, J. (Eds.). (1990). *Choice and control in American education*. New York: Falmer Press.

Coons, J. E., & Sugarman, S. (1978). *Education by choice*. Berkeley, CA: University of California Press.

Epstein, J. L., Coates, L., Salinas, K. C., Sanders, M. G., Simon, B. S. (1997). *School, family, and community partnerships*. Thousand Oaks, CA: Corwin Press.

Friedman, M. (1962). The role of government in education. In M. Friedman (Ed.), *Capitalism and freedom* (chap. VI). Chicago: University of Chicago Press.

Gutmann, A. (1987). *Democratic education*. Princeton, NJ: Princeton University Press.

Heath, S. B. (1983). *Ways with words*. New York: Cambridge University Press.

Hirschman, A. (1970). *Exit, voice, and loyalty*. Cambridge, MA: Harvard University Press.

Katz, M. (1971). *Class, bureaucracy and schools: The American illusion of educational change*. New York: Praeger.

Levin, H. M. (1987). Education as a public and private good. *Journal of Policy Analysis and Management, 6*, 628-641.

Levin, H. M. (1991). The economics of educational choice. *Economics of Education Review, 10*, 137-158.

Levin, H. M. (1998). Educational vouchers: Effectiveness, choice, and costs. *Journal of Policy Analysis and Management, 17*, 373-392.

Levin, H. M., & Driver, C. E. (1996). Estimating the costs of an educational voucher system. In W. J. Fowler, Jr. (Ed.), *Selected papers in school finance* (NCES 96-068). Washington, DC: Department of Education, National Center for Educational Statistics.

Levin, H. M., & Driver, C. E. (1997). Costs of an educational voucher system. *Educational Economics, 5*, 265-283.

Metcalf, K. K., Muller, P., Boone, W., Tait, P., Stage, F., & Stacey, N. (1998). *Evaluation of the Cleveland Scholarship Program: Second-year report, 1997-98.* Bloomington: The Indiana Center for Evaluation, Indiana University.

Moe, T. M. (1995). *Private vouchers.* Stanford, CA: Hoover Institution Press.

Nathan, J. (1996). *Charter schools: Creating hope and opportunity for American education.* San Francisco: Jossey-Bass.

Natriello, G., McDill, E., & Pallas, A. (1990). *Schooling disadvantaged children.* New York: Teachers College Press.

Peterson, P. E., Myers, D., & Howell, W. G. (1998). *An evaluation of the New York City School Choice Scholarships Program: The first year.* Washington, DC: Mathematica Policy Research.

Steinberg, A. (1997). *Real learning, real work.* New York: Routledge.

Sullivan, D. J. (1974). *Public aid to nonpublic schools.* Lexington, MA: Lexington Books.

9

Myths and Misunderstandings

**Health Policy, the Devolution Revolution,
and the Push for Privatization**

MICHAEL S. SPARER

For more than 200 years, policy makers and policy analysts have struggled to determine an appropriate division of labor between local governments, the states, the federal government, and the private sector. What are the tasks that should be performed by public officials? Which tasks are best performed by the private sector? What role should government play in regulating or reimbursing functions best implemented by the private sector? Which level of government should be responsible for particular tasks? How should the different levels of government work together when performing shared tasks?

The current bias in American politics is in favor of devolution, decentralization, and deregulation. There is a bipartisan consensus, for example, that the federal government should delegate more power to the states. Welfare policy illustrates the point. In 1996, Congress abolished the nation's main cash assistance welfare program (Aid to Families with Dependent Children), which had existed since 1935, and replaced it with a new initiative (Temporary Assistance to Needy Families). The motivation was the (debatable) policy assumption that the new law would provide states with more authority over the nation's welfare system, and that the states would use their increased authority to develop innovative welfare reform initiatives.

The bias in favor of privatization is equally powerful. The argument here is threefold.[1] First, government should no longer perform or pay for certain services.

For example, there arguably is no need for government-owned radio stations; the only appropriate government role is to regulate the performance of private-sector media outlets. Second, government should pay for other services but should opt out of the direct provision of such services. The obvious example is prison administration; many states are hiring private firms to run correctional systems. Third, government should use competition and market mechanisms to encourage efficiency in the provision of public services. This strategy is illustrated by the local government that uses competitive bidding to select a refuse collection contractor. The goal is not to replace government-owned refuse companies but to require such companies to compete with the private sector (and to abandon public provision of services if the public employees cannot survive the competition).

I consider the issues of devolution and privatization through the lens of health care policy. Is the federal government delegating to the states increased authority over the nation's health care system? What are the pros and cons of devolution? What does privatization mean in the context of health care? Are governments at all levels seeking to privatize health care services? Are there innovative efforts to create public-private partnerships in the health care arena? What lessons are suggested by the implementation of these initiatives?

There are two sections here. The first is a discussion of health care federalism. What is the intergovernmental balance of power over health care policy, how has that balance changed over time, and is there really a devolution revolution in the health policy arena? The second is a discussion of privatization and health policy. The focus here is on state efforts to persuade or require Medicaid beneficiaries to enroll in managed-care delivery systems. Will these efforts lead to the privatization of the Medicaid program or, on the contrary, does Medicaid managed care lead to an increased (albeit different) government role?

THE EVOLUTION OF INTERGOVERNMENTAL
HEALTH POLICY PARTNERING

For much of the nation's first 150 years, there was a strong bias against federal health and welfare programs. The nation's social welfare system was shaped instead largely by the principles that governed the English poor law system. Social welfare programs were a local responsibility, and assistance was to be provided only to the deserving poor (those who were outside of the labor pool through no fault of their own). National welfare programs were unwise and perhaps even unconstitutional. The only exception was the Civil War pension program, which provided federal funds to Union veterans, but even this initiative was administered and implemented at the local level. National health insurance was not even debated until 1912, when Theodore Roosevelt and the Progressive Party urged its adoption, but the proposal was quickly labeled "un-American" and was easily defeated. Subsequent proposals by Franklin Roosevelt and Harry Truman fared no better.

Lacking both federal leadership and federal dollars, state and local governments tried to provide a social and medical safety net. Local governments established almshouses (or poorhouses) for the indigent, aged, and disabled. Local governments also created public hospitals and public health clinics that provided medical care to the poor. Several states developed institutions for the mentally ill and the developmentally disabled. Overall, however, the quantity and quality of government health and welfare programs was generally inadequate.

During the 1930s, Franklin Roosevelt argued that a decentralized and limited government could not respond effectively to the economic depression. Roosevelt proposed a series of national reforms and federal programs. One idea was a federal welfare system for persons unable to work. A second proposal was national health insurance. Not surprisingly, Southern Democrats, who chaired key committees in Congress, opposed both the welfare and the health care initiatives. The Southerners worried that the social welfare programs would undermine the Southern sharecropper economy and provide too many benefits to children of former black slaves (Quadagno, 1988).

Given the strong opposition, Roosevelt decided to compromise. He first abandoned his proposal for national health insurance.[2] He then agreed to a bifurcated welfare system (that still exists today), under which the federal government finances and administers popular social insurance programs (such as Social Security) and the states administer, set policy for, and help finance the politically unpopular welfare programs (like Temporary Assistance for Needy Children).

The New Deal compromise was important not only for its substantive programs, but also for establishing the principle that the federal government has an important role to play in developing and supervising social welfare programs. In this new political environment, federal officials soon enacted a host of health care initiatives. In the mid-1940s, for example, Congress significantly expanded the federal program that provided federal dollars to encourage medical research. Around that same time, Congress enacted the Hill-Burton program, under which federal dollars were used to stimulate hospital construction and modernization. Congress also enacted some small, but important, initiatives to provide federal funds to those states willing to pay health care providers to care for welfare recipients.

The most significant federal initiative was enacted in 1965 when Congress, following Lyndon Johnson's landslide election, enacted Medicare and Medicaid. Medicare provides a fixed set of health insurance benefits to nearly 36 million of the nation's aged and disabled. It is considered a social insurance program, providing an earned set of benefits. It is financed and administered by the federal government (and its fiscal agents). Medicaid, in contrast, provides health insurance to more than 35 million of the poor. It is generally considered a welfare program, providing benefits primarily to the so-called deserving poor. It is funded jointly by the federal and state governments, and it delegates to state officials significant discretion over most policy decisions.

Interestingly, however, as the federal role in health policy increased, so too did the role played by state and local governments. Many of the new federal programs were to be implemented by state administrators and funded partly by state treasuries. Examples of this are the Hill-Burton program and Medicaid. State officials were also increasing their regulatory oversight of the emerging private insurance industry. By the mid-1960s, for example, most states required commercial insurance policies to cover certain conditions (from substance abuse to podiatry) and some states even regulated the rates that insurers paid for hospital care. States also administered workers' compensation systems, medical malpractice systems, and medical education and licensure systems. Meanwhile, local governments built more public hospitals and public health clinics, expanded public health regulatory initiatives, and, in more than a dozen states, helped to administer state Medicaid programs.

Governments' growing involvement in the nation's health care system was accompanied by a growing amount of intergovernmental bickering and battling. Medicaid politics illustrates the point. Before the late 1980s, for example, federal Medicaid law provided states with broad authority to set eligibility criteria. The result was wide interstate variation in coverage. Between 1988 and 1990, however, Congress required the states to liberalize Medicaid eligibility rules governing pregnant women and children. As a result of these federal mandates, the number of children on Medicaid nearly doubled between 1987 and 1995, growing from 10 million to 17.5 million (The Kaiser Commission on the Future of Medicaid, 1997). At the same time, however, Medicaid costs increased at unprecedented rates, rising from $54.1 billion in 1988 to $157 billion in 1995. State officials blamed the cost increases on the federal mandates.[3] Federal regulators disputed the claim and suggested that states themselves were largely responsible for the cost increases. There was significant intergovernmental tension.

CHANGES IN THE INTERGOVERNMENTAL
HEALTH POLICY PARTNERSHIP

The 1990s are considered by many to be the "decade of devolution" (DiIulio & Nathan, 1998). The assumption is that federal policy makers are delegating increased authority to state and local governments. Medicaid policy again illustrates the argument. Congress stopped imposing new eligibility and reimbursement mandates in the early 1990s. By the mid-1990s, there was a decline in the number of Medicaid beneficiaries (attributed largely to the declining welfare rolls). Around the same time, federal regulators increasingly provided states with waivers from federal Medicaid requirements. States used their increased discretion to encourage or require beneficiaries to enroll in managed care.

Congress then accelerated the trend with a provision in the 1997 Balanced Budget Act that eliminates the requirement that states receive federal permission before requiring most beneficiaries to enroll in managed care. The Balanced Budget Act also provides states with increased authority to set payment rates to Medicaid providers. The era of federal Medicaid micromanagement is evolving into a period of more autonomous state programs.

Medicaid policy notwithstanding, however, the evidence suggests that the rhetoric of devolution exceeds the implementation. Consider welfare reform, cited by many as the most prominent example of the devolution revolution. In 1996, Congress enacted the Personal Responsibility and Work Opportunity Reconciliation Act (PRWORA) in an effort to remake the nation's welfare system. The centerpiece of the new law is the Temporary Assistance to Needy Families (TANF) program, which replaced the 60-year-old Aid to Families with Dependent Children (AFDC) program. The most commonly cited difference between the two welfare programs is that TANF is a block grant (therefore presumably providing states with increased discretion) whereas AFDC was an entitlement program (providing beneficiaries with an enforceable right to benefits as long as they met the statutory requirements).

State officials soon discovered, however, that the federal strings tied to the TANF dollars are nearly as restrictive as the rules governing the old AFDC program. The main difference is that the new rules discourage states from providing coverage to certain groups of the poor, whereas the old rules encouraged expanded coverage. The new welfare law mandates strict work requirements, imposes time limits on the receipt of benefits, and requires unwed teen parent beneficiaries to live in an adult-supervised setting and be in school. Richard P. Nathan (1997) suggests that the framework of the new law is now conservative rather than liberal. Nathan notes that the old law "placed pressure on conservative states to provide benefits" and that the new program pressures "liberal states to terminate welfare benefits and put teeth into work and related family and school behavioral requirements" (pp. 2-3).

The limits of the devolution revolution are also apparent in the health policy arena. Three federal laws illustrate the point.

The Employee Retirement Income Security Act (ERISA). The federal ERISA, enacted in 1974, prohibits states from enacting laws that relate to employee benefit programs unless such regulation is part of the traditional regulation of insurance. One result is that states cannot require employers to provide health insurance to their employees. The employer mandates enacted by Massachusetts, Oregon, and Washington were thus null and void.[4] ERISA also prohibits states from regulating the activities of those companies that self-insure. These companies, which employ more than 50% of the nation's privately insured workforce, are thus immune from state benefit mandates,[5] insurance taxes,[6] and information disclosure rules.

The State Child Health Insurance Program (S-CHIP). The S-CHIP, enacted
as part of the 1997 Balanced Budget Act, provides states with $20.3 billion in
federal funds over the next 5 years[7] to expand insurance programs for young-
sters.[8] The program is a response to the continued erosion of the private insurance market that has led to a growing number (anywhere from 7.3 million to 11
million) of uninsured children.[9] States can choose to use the federal funds to liberalize their Medicaid eligibility, they can use the funds through a separate state
program, or they can do a combination of the two.

Three points about S-CHIP and the devolution revolution are important.
First, S-CHIP dollars have prompted most states to develop expanded child
health insurance initiatives. The federal dollars are fueling the focus on kids.
Second, the federal Health Care Financing Administration is required to
approve all S-CHIP plans. States had until June 30, 1998, to submit a plan for
first year funding. Third, states are required to provide state funds to match the
federal dollars. Several states are reluctant to participate because of the cost-
sharing requirement. State policy makers are all for child health expansions so
long as federal dollars fund all or most of the cost.

The Health Insurance Portability and Accountability Act (HIPAA). Prior to
1996, most insurance reform efforts were enacted at the state level. The background is that more than three quarters of the nation's 40 million or so uninsured
either work in a small business or are self-employed (or are the dependents of
such workers). The first goal is to make health insurance more available. For
example, states have enacted legislation that requires insurers to provide insurance to all applicants (so-called guaranteed issue provisions) and to renew the
policies of all current subscribers. The second goal is to make insurance more
affordable. One example are state-run or state-regulated purchasing alliances.
These alliances seek to pool small business employees in an effort to increase
purchasing leverage. Another example is to allow insurers to sell no-frills policies, presumably at a lower cost, rather than the more comprehensive policies
states often require.[10]

There is little evidence, however, that these state initiatives have made a dent
in the problems of the uninsured. Health insurance is more available, but it is not
significantly more affordable. The cost is still too high.

Over the last couple of years, however, the federal government has made
some initial efforts to regulate the health insurance industry. One example is the
HIPAA, enacted by Congress in 1996. The HIPAA is the first effort to establish
uniform rules governing the availability of health insurance. A second example
is the 1996 federal law requiring health plans to cover 48-hour hospital stays for
women following the birth of a child. Congress even seems poised to enact a
managed-care bill of rights (that would preempt similar state declarations). The
recent spate of federal activity suggests the irrelevance of the devolution revolution to the insurance regulation policy arena. On the contrary, this is one issue

area in which federal officials may well reverse a long-standing deference to state activity.

OLD FEDERALISM IN NEW BOTTLES

Over the last 60 years, the states and the federal government have each dramatically increased their role in the nation's health care system. The intergovernmental division of labor has become increasing blurred. Under Medicaid, for example, each state develops its own program, guided and governed by a variety of federal rules. During the 1980s, federal micromanagement grew more intense. During the 1990s, the level of federal oversight lessened. The administrative balance of power seems to shift regularly.

There is little to suggest a devolution revolution in health care policy. The intergovernmental partnership is instead becoming increasingly complex. Rather than delegating more authority to the states, Congress is expanding its health policy agenda. The S-CHIP program and the HIPAA illustrate the point. At the same time, however, states play important roles in every new federal health policy initiative. This tradition will surely continue.

In my view, these are positive trends. States alone cannot solve the nation's major health care problems (Sparer, 1998a). The federal government needs to play a leadership role. There are, however, enormous differences between the states. Health care programs need to respect these differences. Finding the right balance is an ongoing challenge.

MANAGED CARE AND THE MYTH OF PRIVATIZATION

The connection between health care and the privatization movement is not immediately apparent. The private sector already is the largest employer of health care providers. Private health insurers pay for most of the nation's health care bill. The managed-care industry is comprised primarily of private-sector firms. Several private organizations (such as the National Commission on Quality Assurance) audit the quality of care delivered by managed-care organizations. Private-sector researchers conduct most medical research. The pharmaceutical industry is comprised nearly exclusively of private-sector companies.

The health care industry, in short, is primarily owned and operated by nongovernmental organizations. This is not similar to prisons, refuse collection, or national defense. This is a public good delivered mainly by private agents.

In this service environment, government's role is threefold. First, local governments own and operate public hospitals and public health clinics.[11] These facilities are part of the nation's medical safety net; the patients served are generally poor or uninsured or beset by social and medical problems. Second, government pays for health insurance for some of the poor (through Medicaid), the aged and the disabled (through Medicare), and other targeted populations (through programs like S-CHIP and high-risk pools). Third, government regulates and supervises the behavior of private-sector actors in the health care system. These activities range from developing the rules to govern alleged medical malpractice to enforcing guidelines for the education and licensure of health care providers.

In each area that government acts, there are questions about the appropriate government role. Should government sell public hospitals to private firms? New York City is trying to do so (without much luck so far). One obstacle is the ongoing question about whether prospective purchasers will be guided by the same mission as the current public institutions. Should government encourage greater reliance on private insurance and less dependence on public coverage? Most public officials would say yes, but public dollars will always be needed to subsidize the care of the poor and the disabled. Can government expect managed-care companies to subsidize the cost of graduate medical education? The likelihood that private-sector companies can be persuaded to pay for this sort of public good is quite slim.

There seem, indeed, to be remarkably few efforts to further privatize the health care system; the tasks that government now performs are those that private firms are generally unwilling to perform.

One effort that received much publicity is a program implemented by a handful of states that seeks to encourage middle-class consumers to buy private long-term care insurance. The states are interested because Medicaid has become, by default, the main third-party payer of long-term care costs.[12] The insurers are interested so long as they can limit their liability and cap their costs. The strategy is to enable persons who purchase a limited private long-term care policy to receive Medicaid coverage when their insurance expires, even if they have more assets than are generally allowed. In New York, for example, consumers who purchase 3 years of private long-term care insurance receive Medicaid during their 4th year in a nursing home even if their assets exceed Medicaid levels. The private insurers liability is thus capped, but Medicaid saves too (because most beneficiaries do not live long enough to receive the Medicaid coverage).

Interestingly, however, there is not much of a market for this public-private insurance product; enrollment levels are disappointingly low. There are several explanations for these results. The first problem is cost; the product is still relatively expensive (on average more than $2000 a year). A second issue is nursing home unpopularity; few consumers are willing to spend scarce dollars on a product that most hope never to use. The availability of public dollars is a third problem; many prospective purchasers expect that Medicaid will cover future long-term care costs and that their private dollars will be transferred (with the aid of estate planners) to children and other heirs.

Despite the woeful tales of these various privatization initiatives, there is still much rhetoric that celebrates privatization in the health care arena. The rhetoric usually focuses on Medicaid and Medicare managed care. The assumption is that managed-care initiatives delegate to the private sector the task of organizing and supervising beneficiary care, and that government's role is thereby significantly diminished. Ironically, however, the tasks performed by government increase rather than decrease under both Medicaid and Medicare managed care. The assumption that Medicaid and Medicare are now being privatized is a myth.

MEDICAID BEFORE MANAGED CARE:
THE PUBLIC-PRIVATE PARTNERSHIP

Since its enactment, Medicaid has involved a public-private partnership. The nature of that relationship has changed, however, with the rise of managed care. Under the old (pre–managed-care) regime, the public-private partnership was relatively straightforward. Government officials established the program rules; they determined which individuals received Medicaid coverage, which medical services were covered, and how much participating health care providers were paid. Government also performed three key administrative roles, determining which applicants met the eligibility requirements (and issuing Medicaid cards to those who were eligible), paying the bills incurred by eligible beneficiaries, and supervising the quality of care delivered by participating providers. Government was generally uninterested, however, in the ownership status of the health care providers that actually delivered the care. Some such providers were publicly owned (most notably the public hospitals) but more were part of the private sector (and most of these were nonprofit institutions with a mission to serve the poor).

Although much criticized, the old Medicaid did much good. First, beneficiaries received an insurance card that enabled them to receive covered medical benefits from any willing medical provider. The program thereby provided the poor with increased access to care. Second, safety net health care providers used Medicaid revenue to subsidize the health care delivered to the uninsured. Third, the system was relatively inexpensive to administer. Government officials determined eligibility and paid bills and did little else.

At the same time, however, the old Medicaid had problems. Three issues stand out. First, Medicaid eligibility rules were so restrictive that less than half of the poor received coverage. There also was significant interstate variation in eligibility coverage, raising important concerns about program equity. Second, Medicaid reimbursement rates were very low, especially to office-based primary care providers. As a result, few primary care physicians chose to participate in the program, and most beneficiaries received primary care, if at all, in the emergency room of the local safety net hospital. Third, government officials did little to ensure that beneficiaries received good quality care. Even the so-called "Medicaid mills," which compensated for the low rates by treating an unacceptably high volume of Medicaid beneficiaries, generally operated with little government oversight.

In short, the old Medicaid contained an implicit but unfortunate bargain; government paid very low rates, but those providers willing to accept the low rates could operate with relatively little government oversight.

MANAGED CARE AND THE NEW MEDICAID: SHIFTING POWER TO THE PRIVATE PARTNER?

During the early 1990s, nearly every state legislature began efforts to encourage or require Medicaid beneficiaries to enroll in managed care. These efforts have increased the percentage of Medicaid beneficiaries in managed care from 9.5% in 1991 to 40.1% in 1996 (Holahan, Zuckerman, Evans, & Rangarajan, 1998). These initiatives have important implications for beneficiaries and providers. The initiatives are also changing the nature of Medicaid's public-private partnership.

The new Medicaid is largely motivated by the assumption that managed care will improve access to care and quality of care while simultaneously reducing costs. The argument is straightforward. Managed-care organizations (both commercial health maintenance organizations [HMOs] and provider-sponsored health plans) will compete for the Medicaid business. Government will offer contracts to the best health plans. The health plans will hire and regulate medical providers (under rules set forth in contracts between the health plans and the government). Beneficiaries will choose between several competing plans. Each plan therefore has an incentive to provide good quality care at a reasonable price.

The managed competition is expected to change the health delivery system. No longer will beneficiaries receive primary health care in hospital emergency rooms. This pattern of care delivery is inefficient and unnecessarily expensive; treating an ear infection in a hospital makes little sense. Instead, each client will have a primary care provider. The provider will both deliver care (in a more efficient setting) and act as a gatekeeper to the rest of the health care system. Access and quality will improve. Costs will decline. Marketplace competition will ensure what government regulators have not—accountability, quality, and cost savings.

There is little doubt that the managed-care revolution has changed Medicaid's public-private partnership. First, government (usually) shifts the risk of unexpected health care costs to managed-care organizations (most of which are private-sector organizations). The shift is accomplished by paying the health plans a set fee per client (a so-called capitated payment). This reverses the traditional reimbursement system under which Medicaid paid most providers a set fee for every medical service.[13] Under the old system, the more care a beneficiary received, the more government paid. Under the new system, government's expenditures are fixed; the health plan that incurs costs above the capitation rate loses money.

Second, the new Medicaid privatizes various tasks previously performed by public entities. One example is provider payment. The managed-care plans, not the government, set provider reimbursement rates and pay claims for reimbursement. Similarly, health plans are generally given the task of reducing the geographic maldistribution of health care providers (the fact that there are too few physicians willing to practice in low-income or rural communities and too many who are anxious to practice in upscale neighborhoods and wealthy suburbs). This delegation occurs via the requirement that managed-care plans have enough providers under contract in medically underserved communities to ensure that beneficiaries have adequate access to care. To meet this requirement, health plans might have to build new clinics in low-income communities. Health plans, especially commercial HMOs, could also require affiliated physicians, who previously avoided the poor, to accept Medicaid enrollees.

Finally, managed-care initiatives change the way in which government regulates the health delivery system. Under the old Medicaid, government regulated provider behavior through statutes and administrative regulations. In contrast, under the new Medicaid, government regulates via contracts with health plans. The contracts set forth the terms and conditions under which health plans can participate in the program. These include capitalization requirements, provider network requirements, access and quality guidelines, and so forth. Government officials then work to enforce (or renegotiate) the various contract provisions. The result is ongoing bargaining rather than fixed administrative rules.

Despite these important changes in the public-private partnership, the assumption that managed care privatizes Medicaid is a myth. On the contrary, government's role actually increases when it implements a managed-care initiative. No longer is government a passive payer of bills, generally uninterested (or at least uninvolved) in the actual product purchased with the Medicaid dollar. Instead, government now needs to be a smart purchaser, distinguishing between competing health plans, setting capitation rates, regulating health plan behavior, determining which beneficiaries should be in managed care, determining how quickly the transition from fee for service should take place, determining which benefits should be in the managed-care package, determining which should remain in fee for service, and evaluating the quality of care that beneficiaries receive. Medicaid managed-care initiatives require more administrative infrastructure than does the old fee-for-service system. The increased cost is one reason that the savings from Medicaid managed care are less than expected.

DIVIDING UP THE BENEFICIARIES

State managed-care initiatives focus on welfare mothers and their children; very few include the aged and the disabled. The explanation is threefold. The first is the policy assumption that managed care offers the greatest benefit to young mothers and their children (providing a primary care provider to those who have gone without). The second is the political reality that both the aged and the disabled are organized, influential, and often unhappy about efforts to mandate managed care. Welfare moms, in contrast, are usually less organized, less influential, and less opposed to managed care. The third is the organizational fact that the health plans are less experienced in treating both the aged and the disabled, and therefore less anxious to enroll these populations.

To be sure, fiscal pressure is encouraging states to experiment with managed care for both the aged and the disabled; these groups comprise approximately 30% of Medicaid beneficiaries but spend more than 70% of Medicaid dollars. Nonetheless, progress here is likely to be slow. Washington state, for example, abandoned an effort to require both the aged and the disabled to enroll in managed care only months after beginning the effort. As a result, states increasingly operate two very different Medicaid programs, a fee-for-service system for both the aged and the disabled, and a managed-care initiative for healthy young families.

DIVIDING UP THE BENEFITS

No state requires managed-care plans to provide every Medicaid-covered service. Beneficiaries instead receive some services through their health plans and others through the ongoing fee-for-service system. There are three reasons for the mixed-model approach. First, federal law entitles beneficiaries to receive certain services (such as family planning) from any available provider. Second, health plans traditionally have not provided certain services (such as nursing home coverage), and states are reluctant to force plans to provide unfamiliar benefits. Third, state policy makers sometimes decide that certain services (such as mental health and dental services) should be carved out of the managed-care initiative and delivered instead through an alternative delivery system (either the fee-for-service system or a separate and specialized managed-care system).

For all of these reasons, even welfare mothers and their children, who receive most of their care via their managed-care health plan, still must use the traditional fee-for-service system. State programs must maintain an administrative infrastructure adequate to support both systems.[14]

SETTING CAPITATION RATES

When implementing a managed-care initiative, Medicaid regulators need to decide whether to pay health plans a capitated fee to cover all services in the benefit package or to instead pay health care providers a case management fee and have other services billed on a fee-for-service basis. The trend today favors capitation payment systems.[15] There is no consensus, however, on the best methodology for determining the right capitation rate. On the contrary, there are few policy subjects in the world of Medicaid managed care that are more controversial.

One approach is to have separate rates for every participating health plan. The rates could be generated through a process of competitive bidding or through a series of direct negotiations. A second approach is to set a single rate for all health plans in a particular geographic region (adjusted up or down based on the demographics of enrollees in particular plans).

Under either approach, however, there is often controversy over the amount actually paid. Consider state X, which in the year before its managed-care initiative spent $100 per Medicaid beneficiary per month and in the first year of its initiative paid a health plan $95 per month to provide beneficiaries with a comprehensive benefit package. Is the state paying the right capitation amount? Maybe it is and maybe it is not. If the health plan enrolls a low-cost client, who would have cost the state only $80 in the old fee-for-service world, then Medicaid has paid too much; it has lost $15. Conversely, if the plan enrolls a high-cost client, who would have cost the state $120, then Medicaid has saved $25.

Given this variation, Medicaid rate setters must balance the risk of overpayment (and the audits and criticism that follows) with the risk of underpayment (and the likelihood that commercial HMOs will exit the Medicaid managed-care marketplace). Perhaps the only way Medicaid officials can avoid this double whammy is to develop accurate risk adjustment systems, under which the amount paid depends in large part on the risk status of the beneficiary. So far, however, no state (and no private-sector consultant) has developed an accurate risk adjustment methodology. States can (and do) pay separate rates for separate demographic categories (more for the disabled, less for young children) but states cannot effectively differentiate within the categories (more for the high-risk youngster and less for the low-risk). State officials are now working hard (helped by the ever-present private consultants) to improve risk adjustment systems.

HELPING CLIENTS CHOOSE HEALTH PLANS

Medicaid law generally requires that beneficiaries be able to choose between competing health plans. The marketing and enrollment process is thus critical. Health plans hope to distinguish their product from their competitors and to persuade beneficiaries to enroll. Beneficiaries need to sort through their options and choose a health plan (and a primary care provider). Government needs to minimize (or eliminate) marketing fraud, maximize the likelihood that beneficiaries will be informed consumers, and implement enrollment procedures that are simple and clear. Developing a system that encourages these outcomes is not easy.

One approach is to have Medicaid workers inform beneficiaries of their managed-care options during a face-to-face presentation. Health plan marketers are not permitted to participate in the process or to engage in any direct marketing. A second model is to permit health plans to engage in direct marketing and direct enrollment. In these states, health plan marketers knock on doors in low-income communities, attend health fairs and other community gatherings, and set up shop in local welfare offices. The third approach is to hire a private-sector contractor to handle the marketing and enrollment functions. There are even a handful of companies that specialize in Medicaid marketing and enrollment.

Marketing and enrollment is one policy arena in which state philosophy on privatization is important. In some states, there is a clear effort to hire private-sector companies to conduct marketing and enrollment (pursuant to terms and conditions set forth in a Medicaid contract). Other states prefer to keep closer control over the marketing and enrollment process, and utilize government workers in the task. In all states, however, Medicaid managed care works well only if the state finds the right balance between permissible marketing and regulatory oversight. Finding that balance is not easy.

REGULATING QUALITY OF CARE

There is an economic incentive to underserve in all capitated payment systems. The health plan (or the provider) receives the same fee regardless of the amount of care delivered. Health plan profits rise when service delivery levels decline.[16] The opposite was true under fee-for-service Medicaid; the greater the number of medical services provided, the greater the Medicaid fee.

In an effort to counter the incentive to underserve, states develop elaborate systems to monitor and evaluate quality of care. States first develop a host of quality and access rules that become part of the health plan's contract (these rules cover everything from provider network requirements to permissible waiting times for appointments to acceptable grievance procedures for disgruntled beneficiaries). States require health plans to develop an internal quality-of-care protocol. State regulators conduct quality-of-care audits (usually consisting of chart reviews of a random sample of health plan enrollees). States even hire independent (private-sector) organizations to conduct additional quality-of-care reviews. Taken together, these efforts constitute a focus on quality far beyond anything that existed in the old fee-for-service world. These efforts also require states to significantly increase the administrative infrastructure devoted to quality-of-care issues.

SUPPORTING THE MEDICAL SAFETY NET

The growth of Medicaid managed care could have serious adverse consequences for many safety net health care providers. These providers could lose Medicaid enrollees (as beneficiaries enroll in health plans in which safety net providers do not participate), receive less Medicaid revenue per client (as health plans ratchet down reimbursement), and be left with a costlier and sicker patient population (as mainstream HMOs attract the low-cost Medicaid client but leave the safety net provider with the high-cost client and the uninsured).

In response to this uncertain environment, safety net providers have two options. First, these providers can contract with as many health plans as possible (or at least as many as will offer a good contract). Second, providers can create their own managed-care health plans (and compete directly for a managed-care contract). Most institutional providers (such as hospitals and community health centers) implement both strategies. Implementation is not easy. Providers often lack leverage to negotiate good contracts. Providers often lack sufficient capital to meet state capitalization requirements or perform other start-up tasks. Providers are often unskilled in maneuvering through the new world of risk sharing.

Several states have adopted programs to aid safety net providers in the transition to managed care. There are four main strategies (Sparer, 1998b). The first consists of efforts to ease the licensure requirements for safety net managed-care plans. California temporarily exempts such plans from state capitalization requirements, whereas New York imposes an alternative set of requirements. The second consists of programs to provide supplemental funding to safety net health plans through either special start-up grants or higher capitation rates. The third consists of efforts to ensure minimum levels of enrollment, primarily by assigning to the safety net plans those persons who do not voluntarily choose a plan. The fourth consists of laws that encourage or require commercial health plans to offer contracts to local safety net providers.

Each of these safety net protection strategies poses some risk to good public policy. Will low capitalization rates allow undercapitalized health plans into the market? Will supplemental funds paid to safety net plans encourage commercial health plans to exit the market? Will beneficiaries be assigned to health plans that they do not wish to join? Will government regulators impose inappropriate restrictions on health plan contracts? These questions are best answered during actual implementation. States need to create new administrative infrastructure to monitor, supervise, and adjust. These are new tasks for the public sector.

PUBLIC-PRIVATE PARTNERING IN HEALTH CARE: ADDING UP THE SCORE

We have examined the issues of devolution and privatization through the lens of health care policy. Three conclusions are clear. First, the devolution revolution is more rhetoric than reality. Congress is expanding its health policy agenda and states are key players in every new federal health policy initiative. This pattern is not likely to change soon.

Second, health care is a public good delivered mainly by private agents. In this environment, government's main task is to perform those functions that private firms are unwilling to perform. For example, government owns and operates hospitals and clinics that serve the poor and the uninsured. Similarly, government pays for health insurance for those too poor or too sick to purchase private insurance.

Third, government policy makers are anxious to shift to the private sector some of these public functions. The Medicaid managed-care initiatives illustrate the point. States hope to introduce managed competition into the Medicaid market. The plan is to have commercial HMOs and provider-sponsored health plans compete for the Medicaid business. The assumption is that the new Medicaid marketplace will provide beneficiaries with more choice and better quality at a lower cost.

These efforts have shifted certain tasks previously performed by public entities to the private sector. Health plan behavior is regulated increasingly by formal contracts. Government is shifting the risk of unexpected health care costs to managed-care organizations. At the same time, however, Medicaid regulators have assumed a host of new administrative tasks, such as setting capitation rates, helping clients choose between competing health plans, and establishing programs to protect the medical safety net. Indeed, despite occasional rhetoric to the contrary, Medicaid managed care is increasing government's role in health care for the poor; it is not privatizing health care for this population.

In the end, health care policy is a particularly slippery lens through which to view issues of devolution and privatization. Both the intergovernmental division of labor and the public-private partnership have become increasingly blurred. This pattern is not likely to change soon.

NOTES

1. This typology is set forth in Brecher and Spiezio (1995, pp. 1-2).

2. The only health care program that was enacted as part of the New Deal was a small initiative that funded maternal and child health clinics.

3. During this same era, Congress also required states to (a) provide children on Medicaid with an expanded benefit package and (b) increase the reimbursement paid to safety net medical providers (such as public hospitals and community health centers).

4. The only state with an employer mandate is Hawaii. Congress granted the state a waiver from the ERISA barrier because the mandate was in place prior to the enactment of the federal law. Congress has refused to give other states a similar waiver.

5. Every state requires health insurers to include certain benefits in their medical benefit package. As a result of ERISA, these state mandates apply only when companies purchase insurance from traditional insurance companies.

6. More than 30 states impose special taxes on insurance companies and use the proceeds to subsidize insurance for high-risk populations. Self-insured companies are immune from these tax initiatives.

7. The program appropriates an additional $19.3 billion for the following 5 years.

8. States can spend no more than 10% of its federal dollars on outreach, administration, or direct payments to providers.

9. The number of children with employer-based coverage has dropped from 66.7% in 1987 to 58.6% in 1995.

10. Other strategies include caps on increases in insurance premiums, state-subsidized insurance for high-risk individuals, and tax credits for businesses that insure previously uninsured employees.

11. The states and the federal government also own and operate public hospitals, including state institutions for the mentally ill or the developmentally disabled and federal Veteran's Administration hospitals.

12. Employer-sponsored health insurance rarely covers long-term care. Individuals can buy their own private long-term care insurance policy, but few do so, primarily because of the cost. Meanwhile, Medicare, the insurance program explicitly created for both the aged and the disabled, pays

only for the first 100 days of nursing home care and pays only if the care immediately follows a hospitalization.

13. There are some Medicaid managed-care initiatives in which Medicaid pays primary care physicians an extra fee to manage beneficiary care. In these systems, Medicaid continues to pay on a fee-for-service basis, but there is a gatekeeper managing client care.

14. In some states, there is a third or even fourth delivery system, such as a separate managed-care system for dental services or mental health services.

15. Primary care case-management programs are most common in rural communities where there are often too few managed-care organizations to support a competitive managed-care market.

16. Health plan managers suggest that there also are incentives to provide good and timely care, especially in the case of primary and preventive care. The short-term costs of promptly providing primary care are sometimes less than the long-term costs of delaying the onset of care.

REFERENCES

Brecher, C., & Spiezio, S. (1995). *Privatization and public hospitals: Choosing wisely for New York City*. New York: The Twentieth Century Fund Press.

DiIulio, J. J., Jr., & Nathan, R. P. (1998). Introduction. In F. J. Thompson and J. J. DiIulio (Eds.), *Medicaid and devolution: A view from the states* (p. 1). Washington, DC: Brookings Institute.

Holahan, J., Zuckerman, S., Evans, A., & Rangarajan, S. (1998). Medicaid managed care in thirteen states. *Health Affairs, 17*, 43-63.

Kaiser Commission on the Future of Medicaid. (1997, November). *Medicaid facts*. (Available from the Kaiser Commission on the Future of Medicaid, 1450 G Street, NW, Suite 250, Washington, DC 20005).

Nathan, R. P. (1997, October 30). The newest new federalism for welfare: Where are we now and where are we headed? *Rockefeller Reports*, 2-3.

Quadagno, J. (1988). From old-age assistance to supplemental security income: The political economy of relief in the South, 1935-1972. In M. Weir, A. Orloff, & T. Skocpol (Eds.), *The politics of social policy in the United States*. Princeton, NJ: Princeton University Press.

Sparer, M. S. (1998a). Devolution of power: An interim report card. *Health Affairs, 17*, 7-16.

Sparer, M. S. (1998b). Safety net providers and the new Medicaid: Choices and challenges. In Thompson & DiIulio (Eds.), *Medicaid and devolution: A view from the states* (pp. 154-184). Brookings Institute.

10

From Welfare State to Opportunity, Inc.

Public-Private Partnerships in Welfare Reform

MARK CARL ROM

The American Welfare State is not dead yet, but it is fading away. Its replacement, Opportunity, Inc., seems to be growing brighter by the day. These two forms of governance, Welfare State and Opportunity, Inc., differ in their methods, goals, and not the least, rhetoric. The Welfare State delivers benefits to recipients in order to cushion them from the harshness of markets. Opportunity, Inc., in contrast, seeks to assist clients in becoming independent actors within markets.

The Welfare State is not inherently provided by the government, nor is Opportunity, Inc. provided by the private sector. As part of the Welfare State, private firms can simply deliver benefits. Opportunity, Inc. does not intrinsically consist of private firms. Governmental agencies, too, can act to empower citizens to become economically independent.

However, the transition from Welfare State to Opportunity, Inc. often does, in fact, involve the transfer of responsibility for social service delivery from governmental agencies to private firms. Federal, state, and local governments are all creating public-private partnerships (most often, through contracts) to operate social welfare functions; as measured by the numbers of partnerships, services, and dollars, these efforts are growing (General Accounting Office [GAO], 1997).[1] This observer, and most others, thinks that these trends will continue. In one policy domain after another—pensions, education, transportation, criminal justice, and environmental protection to name a few examples—we are moving away from having governmental agencies actually delivering services toward service delivery by private firms. Even when governmental agencies retain the authority over these programs, they increasingly behave as if they were private-sector actors. In addition, both private and public agencies are focusing increasingly on social service results, rather than processes, and both are placing more emphasis on improving the lives of citizens by empowering them; it appears that this is often accomplished by forcing them to become empowered.

The most dramatic step in the move toward Opportunity, Inc. occurred in the Personal Responsibility and Work Opportunity Reconciliation Act (PRWORA) of 1996. This act terminated the discredited Aid to Families with Dependent Children (AFDC) program, creating in its place the Temporary Assistance for Needy Families (TANF) program. Under TANF, there are two steps toward Opportunity, Inc. that are the most important. In the first, private firms have many more opportunities to run much larger segments of welfare programs. In TANF, private firms are allowed to operate the entire program, and in certain jurisdictions, they do so. In the second, TANF focuses much more than previous welfare programs on enhancing economic opportunity rather than providing continued economic assistance. The major goals of TANF are to get its clients off the welfare rolls and into the workforce. The agencies that deliver TANF, for their part, are now judged by how well they accomplish these goals, not just by how well they process paperwork. In short, we are moving away from the state delivering welfare to recipients and toward having private firms working with clients to increase the opportunities available to them.

This step did not exclusively favor private for-profit firms. The PRWORA contains a charitable choice provision that specifically addresses the use of contracts, vouchers, and other mechanisms to arrange for charitable, religious, or private organizations to provide services for TANF, Medicaid, supplemental security income (SSI), and food stamps. The law requires that religious organizations be permitted to receive funding on the same basis as any other private-sector provider. And anecdotal evidence indicates that religious organizations are increasingly entering into partnerships with governments to provide welfare services (Yates, 1998).

This article focuses on the recent shifts in American welfare policy. In doing so, it addresses several questions. What is the Welfare State in the United States? What is Opportunity, Inc., and what are the main reasons for moving toward it? How is Opportunity, Inc. transforming the Welfare State? How does the shift from AFDC to TANF exemplify this transformation? What are the experiences of the state that has most aggressively created public-private partnerships? What are the main issues now for governments as they seek to create public-private partnerships for social services?

THE WELFARE STATE

The Welfare State, most broadly defined, provides a wide array of services to citizens to protect them from the vicissitudes of life. These services include, among many others, health care; education; housing; food; and income support to children, adults, and the elderly. Governments in the United States spend over a trillion dollars each year on these social welfare programs. The largest of these programs include Social Security, which provided over $500 billion in pensions for the elderly in 1997 (Social Security Administration, 1998); Medicare, which spent an additional $200 billion on medical care for the elderly in that year (Health Care Financing Administration, 1998); and public education, which costs state and local governments over $400 billion annually (Bureau of the Census, 1997).

However, these social welfare programs are not what we usually call welfare in the United States. That term, now most often used pejoratively, is reserved for programs intended to provide assistance to the poor. The largest such welfare program by far is Medicaid, which provides medical care to low-income persons who are aged or blind or disabled, to poor families with children, and increasingly to certain other pregnant women and children at a cost of over $300 billion a year (House of Representatives, 1996). The next largest welfare efforts are the food stamp program, which helps poor families supplement their food budgets, and the SSI program, which provides income support to the poor who are elderly or blind or disabled. Food stamps and SSI each cost federal and state governments about $30 billion annually (see House of Representatives, 1996, pp. 257-326, 856-879).

Even though Medicaid, food stamps, and SSI are the largest welfare programs in the United States, none of them is the welfare program that has generated the most public visibility and controversy. That honor goes to the AFDC program that was terminated in 1996 and replaced by the TANF program.

AFDC was widely seen as the quintessential welfare state program. AFDC was created as a minor and uncontroversial element of the Social Security Act of 1935 with the intention that it would be a temporary program to provide income support to widows and their families. It did not turn out that way, however. Fifty years after its creation, AFDC provided assistance to more than 14 million Americans. The vast majority of the parents it assisted were not widows, but parents who were divorced, separated, or never married. Only a small percentage of the mothers receiving AFDC had paid employment, even though most other mothers now do earn income by working. AFDC did have a work element, the so-called Job Opportunities and Basic Skills (JOBS) program, but only about 10% of AFDC adults actually participated in it. At any given time, almost two thirds of adults receiving AFDC had been "on the dole" for 8 or more years. Finally, almost two thirds of the recipients were non-White minorities (see House of Representatives, 1996, pp. 473, 474, 505). In short, a large proportion of adult AFDC recipients were minority single mothers with little earned income who remained on the rolls for years. For these reasons, AFDC came to be seen as a program that discouraged marriage and work, encouraged out-of-wedlock childbearing and dependency, and primarily served people of color (Rom, 1997a). The critics of AFDC held that welfare recipients became dependent upon the government because, in part, the government did little to encourage independence. The failures of AFDC were thus jointly placed at the feet of welfare recipients and welfare administrators.

Presidents since Richard Nixon, and more recently congressional Republicans, consequently had vowed to get rid of this politically unpopular program. When the Republicans took control of the Congress in 1994, they pressured, and ultimately succeeded, in calling President Clinton's campaign promise to "end welfare as we know it." In 1996, the Congress approved, and Clinton signed, the bill to end AFDC and create TANF in its place (Rom, 1997b).

The key elements of the Welfare State are the governmental agencies' establishment of program standards, determination and monitoring of recipient eligibility, and provision of benefits. At implementation, programs are typically evaluated by their accuracy in delivering benefits to the properly enrolled recipients in the legal amounts. A successful program delivers checks (or medical care, or other benefits) in the right amount, to the right persons, and at the right times.[2] The AFDC quality control system, for example, did not examine whether the program helped recipients become economically independent; it did measure the error rates in correctly calculated recipient income and benefits (House of Representatives, 1996).[3] For the Welfare State, what matters is that benefits are provided to alleviate suffering.

OPPORTUNITY, INC.

Opportunity, Inc. differs from the Welfare State in several important ways. First and foremost, it seeks not to ease misery but to transform lives by promoting responsibility and improving performance, both for welfare clients and for program administrators. Although this does not necessarily call for private-sector service delivery, several arguments are typically made in favor of using private firms to deliver social services (Allen et al., 1989; Curtis & Associates, 1999b; Nightingale & Pindus, 1997; General Accounting Office [GAO], 1995).[4]

CULTURE

One reason that private service providers can be superior to governmental ones is that governmental agencies are stuck in a welfare state rut, used to delivering checks to recipients but not demanding performance from clients. For welfare reform to work, the traditional welfare culture must be changed, both for welfare recipients and for welfare agencies. A main goal of TANF is to move individuals from welfare rolls to employment rolls; this requires that caseworkers have the desire and ability to help clients find jobs. As Judy Gueron, President of the Manpower Development and Research Corporation (1995) has noted, in order to achieve results of [large] magnitude, it is necessary to dramatically change the tone and message of welfare.... When you walk in the door of a high-performance employment-focused program, it is clear that you are there for one purpose—to get a job. Staff continually announce job openings and convey an upbeat message about the value of work and people's potential to succeed. (p. A19)

Although there is no inherent reason why governmental agencies cannot provide high-performance employment-focused programs, it can indeed be difficult to transform existing welfare offices into them. It is easier, perhaps, to hire private-sector firms that already operate such programs.[5]

VALUES

A second, related, argument in favor of public-private partnerships in service delivery is that popular opinion supports such partnerships. Public opinion about welfare programs has been strong and consistent over time (Mead, 1992; Public Agenda, 1996). The salient points have been that the public generally believes that the welfare system is broken, that the poor should be helped to become economically self-sufficient, and that the poor should have to work. The corollaries of these views are that the government has neither been able to make welfare work nor help the poor, mainly because it has not really been able to enforce work requirements. From these views, it is easy to move to the idea that the private sector is the remedy, that private firms are better equipped to promote self-sufficiency, and that private partners will have the ways and means to get welfare clients jobs.

BEHAVIOR

Governmental bureaucracies—at least in the popular view—are slow, rigid, and uniform. Private firms, in contrast, are seen as nimble, innovative, and flexible. These views, surely, are stereotypes, as these characteristics have more to do with incentives and organizational design than they do to whether the organization is public or private. However, it does seem likely that governmental agencies, on average, are more burdened with rules and more restricted by personnel policies than private firms are. Private firms may find it easier, on average, to shift directions, to grow or shrink, or to respond to different market segments (i.e., welfare clients with differing needs).

RESULTS

Two issues are at stake here. The first, more controversial one, is whether private entities produce better social service results—for welfare clients, this means enhanced skills, higher wages, better jobs, and safer childcare or housing among others—than do government agencies. The second issue concerns the consequences for public or private agencies that fail or succeed in producing desirable results.

The evidence on the former is mixed. To be sure, private firms are claiming great successes in reducing welfare caseloads and placing welfare clients in jobs, but then again, governmental agencies appear to have similar good fortune. More generally, the few studies that compare public and private performance do not unequivocally conclude that one is superior to the other (Nightingale & Pindus, 1997).

However, the consequences of poor performance are, at least in principle, clearer for private firms. If they do not perform to the standards of the contract, the contract will not be renewed. If a public agency does not perform, the response is less clear. Should it be penalized for its poor performance or given additional resources to handle its tasks better?

COSTS

Private entities are expected, as a matter of course, to provide social services at a lower cost than governmental agencies. Lower costs are anticipated due to the presumed higher efficiency of private firms. As with performance, the evidence is not completely clear on this point. Studies showing the private sector as more efficient than the government are biased in several ways, which make this conclusion less solid than the proponents of the private sector might prefer. As a result, it is worth considering—as the state of Wisconsin did, as we shall see later—the relative advantages of private and public entities in providing social services.

FROM WELFARE STATE TO OPPORTUNITY, INC.

In virtually every area of social welfare policy, the United States is considering, or experimenting with, public-private partnerships to deliver services. Not all the experimentation is new. In Medicare and Medicaid, for example, the government has always relied on private firms to actually deliver medical care, although the form of these partnerships is being revised with the advent of managed care (Sparer, 1999 [this issue]). There is every indication that the government will increasingly rely not only on private firms to deliver services, but also to make decisions about what services should be provided and when they should be provided. One current proposal, for example, would change Medicare by moving the government out of the business of paying doctors and hospitals directly for medical care; instead, the government would help beneficiaries buy their own coverage from HMOs and other insurance plans (Hager, 1999). For Social Security too, political debate is now focused on ways to enhance its long-term solvency by investing in private equity markets. This section, however, will focus on public-private partnerships in the following four welfare programs: food stamps, child support enforcement, child welfare, and employment and training.

FOOD STAMPS

The food stamp program intends to help low-income families have nutritionally adequate, low-cost diets. These families are expected to spend 30% of their own counted monthly income on food, with food stamps making up the difference between this amount and the amount necessary for an inexpensive but satisfactory diet. The federal government pays virtually all food stamp benefits, but the states have substantial responsibility for administration. In 1997, the program cost about $25 billion and served about 23 million recipients each month, with participation falling substantially from its peak of 28 million in 1994 to under 20 million by October 1998 (Department of Agriculture, 1998c).

Historically, food stamps were, literally, paper stamps distributed each month by the government. The PRWORA mandated that all states convert from paper coupons to electronic benefits transfer (EBT) by the year 2002 (Cates, 1998). By October 1998, 33 states and the District of Columbia had EBT systems operating (statewide in only 27 states), with the other states either conducting trial runs or selecting contractors (Department of Agriculture, 1998a). With EBT, each food stamp recipient is given a plastic card (like a bank card) and a personal identification number (PIN); benefits are credited to the recipient's account each month. When a recipient buys groceries, the card is electronically read, the grocer's account is credited for the purchase, and the buyer's account is debited.

In 1993, Maryland became the first state to have a statewide EBT system in place. Food stamps, TANF, and general assistance benefits, as well as child-support payments, are all included in Maryland's EBT program. Many other states are also experimenting with EBT systems that link various governmental assistance programs. A Wyoming pilot project, for example, is using microchip-equipped plastic "smart cards" to carry food stamp benefits, WIC certification and benefits, and immunization records. In one county, the smart card also carries information from Medicaid's early and periodic screening, diagnosis program, Maternal and Child Health Services, and Head Start information (Cates, 1998). The vast majority of states are using private contractors to develop and implement their EBT systems. Citibank is by far the dominant firm in the EBT field, with the vast majority of the states using Citibank as the prime contractor (the status of state EBT projects is outlined in Department of Agriculture, 1998a).

The EBT system has clear benefits for grocers and the government; the advantages for these two are obvious. Retailers and bankers like EBT because it simplifies accounting and reduces labor costs because there are no coupons to sort, count, and bundle. The federal government also saves time and money because EBT eliminates the printing, transporting, safeguarding, distributing, accounting, and destroying of food stamp coupons. It has been estimated that by 2002, EBT (for other programs in addition to food stamps) will save the federal government nearly $200 million a year (Stegman, 1998).

More importantly, recipients can benefit from EBT. Surveys have shown that most participants prefer the EBT system to the paper coupon system it replaced. Recipients have reported that they like the convenience and security of EBT. They no longer have to go to the food stamp office to pick up their food stamps. They can draw their benefits as needed, instead of receiving a month's allotment at one time. If the card is lost or stolen, it cannot be used by anyone who does not know the PIN, and it can be easily canceled and replaced. Many recipients have also said that EBT reduces the stigma associated with food stamp coupon use (Department of Agriculture, 1998b).

EBT also can help the poor move into the financial mainstream—at least if they are given the incentives and the abilities to do so (Stegman, 1998). To credit benefits to welfare clients, the federal government will create electronic bank accounts for those who do not have them (a large proportion of welfare clients do not). With this foot in the door of a bank, low-income individuals might be further encouraged to use other bank services, such as savings and checking accounts, that help promote economic self-sufficiency. As one analyst puts it, "It is hard to imagine a mother moving from welfare to work, and staying off welfare, without a bank account and without building up some cash reserves for emergencies. This is why the widespread adoption of measures to encourage personal savings and asset-building by the dependent poor is so important" (Stegman, 1998). Still, it is worth worrying about whether the move to EBT will also induce those who are least-equipped to understand and trust the technology to withdraw from the food stamp program.

Federally insured private banks will be invited to compete for these accounts. Federal law does not require banks to offer other low-cost services (such as free checking accounts) to the program beneficiaries, however. Organizations such as the National Consumer Law Center are accordingly concerned that the winning banks will ultimately impose stiff fees on these low-income users, thereby effectively skimming off tax dollars intended for use by the poor.

Although most states are using for-profit firms increasingly to develop and implement their food stamp EBT systems, a much smaller number of states are conducting outreach efforts so that eligible persons actually know how to obtain benefits. These outreach efforts, moreover, are typically contracted through nonprofit community service agencies rather than through for-profit firms. Tennessee, for example, has awarded two outreach contracts, for a total of $50,000, to Manna and West Tennessee Legal Services (Food Research and Action Center, 1998). It appears that, as states are becoming more efficient in delivering benefits, they are also becoming less aggressive in their efforts to inform the poor of their eligibility for them.

CHILD SUPPORT ENFORCEMENT

At any one time, about 25% of all American children live in a single-parent family, and it has been estimated that almost half of the children born in the United States will live with a single parent at some time during their youth. To ensure that these children receive financial support from both parents, the federal and state governments have established a child support enforcement system intended to help locate the absent parents, establish paternity, establish child support awards, and collect payment. The federal government sets standards and provides financial incentives; the states design and implement the programs (for a discussion of the child support enforcement system, see House of Representatives, 1996, p. 529-624).

Since 1986, federal law has specifically encouraged states to consider using private firms for such functions as locating absent parents, and maintaining tracking and payments systems (Nightingale & Pindus, 1997). By 1995, at least 20 states, and many more local governments, were using private firms for one or more of these functions, and several more were planning to do so. The preferred target of the privatization efforts is child support collection, especially from hard to locate parents, although nine states had contracts for full-service child support services for at least a portion of their caseload, and six more had plans to do so.[6] In the typical case, the contractor gets to keep a portion (ranging from 8% to 24%) of the money that it collects, with the remainder passed back to the state (GAO, 1995; see also Melia, 1997).

According to a GAO study, these arrangements benefit the custodial parent, who receives more support income than otherwise; the federal and state governments, which receive partial reimbursement for their welfare expenditures; and the contracting firms, which find it worthwhile to track down and collect from the deadbeats (1995). They also put more pressure on absent parents to provide financial support for their children.

CHILD WELFARE

Sadly, many parents prove ill equipped to raise their children. In 1996, there were over 3 million reports of child abuse and neglect (Craig, Kulik, James, Nielsen, & Orr, 1999). When children are abused or neglected, they may enter the child welfare system, which tries either to improve the functioning of the family or to find another family (through foster homes or adoption) that can care for the children. The state, not federal, government have primary responsibility for child welfare, although there are over 40 federal programs to support state efforts (House of Representatives, 1996).

Since the 1970s, the states, for their part, have increasingly turned to private firms (mainly nonprofits) to deliver child welfare services. State agencies have contracted for such services as investigation, substitute care (e.g., foster homes), and therapeutic services (Nightingale & Pindus, 1997). In New York City, for example, fully 70% of the children in foster care are now served by contract agencies (Giuliani, 1996, as cited in Nightingale & Pindus, 1997). The child welfare systems in Kansas, Michigan, and Texas are largely privatized, and each state reports much higher adoption rates (rather than having children in temporary foster care) and lower child abuse rates (Craig et al., 1999). Other states are beginning to experiment with managed-care approaches to improving child welfare services at reduced costs; early results are positive, but limited (GAO, 1998).

EMPLOYMENT AND TRAINING

The federal government has sponsored many employment and training programs, and most of these programs have used private agencies to deliver services. In fact, since the 1960s, more federally funded employment and training services have been contracted out than not. The contracts have been for a wide range of services, including intake and eligibility determination, training, and job placement, among others. Most of the contractors for these programs have been nonprofit or public organizations, including employment services, vocational schools, public school districts, or community colleges. Less often, for-profit firms such as proprietary training schools, firm-sponsored jobs clubs, or job placement companies have provided the services.

The most prominent of the programs, the Jobs Corps, serves economically disadvantaged youths, and it is administered by the federal government but implemented entirely through contractors at 110 sites in 46 states (House of Representatives, 1996). Thirty Job Corps centers are operated by the U.S. Departments of Agriculture and Interior (through interagency agreements with the Department of Labor) on public land. The remainder of the sites are run by nonprofits and for-profits (Nightingale & Pindus, 1997).

"The Jobs Corps is considered one of the more successful employment and training programs, at least in part because of its public-private mix" (Gurin, 1989, p. 191). For the Job Corps, the federal government provides direction, oversight, and monitoring. The contracting is competitive, with the firms given clear performance expectations. The performance expectations appear difficult to "game," as the contractors cannot improve them by "creaming" (i.e., selecting participants based on their ability to succeed) or by actually securing jobs for the applicants (Donahue, 1989).

TANF

Governments thus have been building public-private partnerships for food stamps, child support enforcement, child welfare, and employment and training programs for years. However, perhaps the most dramatic shift from the Welfare State to Opportunity, Inc. was through the termination of AFDC and the creation of TANF. TANF calls for both governments and individuals to change their goals and their behaviors. As the president of the Wisconsin Policy Research Institute (WPRI) explained it,

> if you expect poor people after generations of entitlements to change their behavior, you must also make the administrators accountable to standards in the same way as recipients. If there are no entitlements for the recipients, there should be no entitlements for the bureaucrats. If recipients who don't show individual responsibility can be dropped from the rolls, so should bureaucrats who do not perform at a high standard. (Miller, 1998)

The PRWORA allowed the states to do just that. Previously, some AFDC functions (such as job training, job search instruction, and day care services) had been contracted out, but these were minor elements of the program. The most important functions of AFDC were to determine eligibility, calculate benefit levels, and deliver the benefits. AFDC was, first and foremost, a check-writing program. In addition, because the states were required to conduct intake and eligibility determination, there was relatively little for private firms to do.

That PRWORA ended AFDC as a federal entitlement program has been the most publicized, and controversial, element in welfare reform. However, an equally important change is that under TANF, state or local welfare agencies can now contract out their entire welfare program, including intake, eligibility, and services. As a result, large for-profit companies (such as Ross Perot's former company, EDS; Lockheed Martin; and IBM) have entered the welfare market with a marked enthusiasm for helping the poor. Some of these companies had already established a foot in the welfare door through their work in child support, employment and training, or child welfare programs.

WELFARE BUSINESSES

Prior to TANF, most of the small number of public-private partnerships in welfare services involved nonprofit organizations and a couple of rather small, welfare-oriented businesses (Bernstein, 1996). America Works had contracts worth $7 million in New York City, Albany, and Indianapolis. Curtis & Associates sold training materials and ran job clubs, and they had just over $9 million in welfare-related contracts from 11 states. Maximus was the largest of these businesses, and it specialized in child support, Medicaid managed care, and data systems management in addition to its welfare-to-work efforts.

These companies have expanded enormously under TANF. Curtis & Associates, for example, now has a contract worth more than $9 million in Waukesha, Wisconsin, alone. By late 1998, Maximus had almost 3,000 employees and $140 million in revenues (for a description of Maximus's many social service contracts, see Maximus, 1998a). One indicator of the promise of Opportunity, Inc. is that when Maximus went public during the summer of 1998, its stock quickly rose almost 50%.[7]

In addition, as the stakes grew larger, larger firms decided to play for the stakes. One stock analyst for Lehman Brothers, who estimated that the potential market for welfare-related contracts is over $20 billion a year, noted that "it's a huge revenue target for the private sector to go after" (Cohen, 1998).

Among those seeking welfare contracts was Anderson Consulting (with over $4 billion in annual revenues), which was marketing a profit-sharing approach to welfare. By late 1996, it had contracts in 14 states and two Canadian provinces, mainly to deliver child support and child welfare services. Larger, still, was Electronic Data Systems (EDS), with contracts in 20 states and $12.4 billion in revenues. EDS, it might be remembered, was built almost entirely on governmental contracts, especially for Medicaid billing and welfare reporting, which it pioneered in the 1960s.

Yet the largest, and most controversial, business in the welfare reform market was Lockheed Martin ($30 billion in revenues), best known as part of the military-industrial complex (for a critique, see Hartung & Washburn, 1998). Its Information Management Services Division had child support contracts in 16 states and contracts in 20 states to convert various welfare benefits to electronic debit cards. After TANF was enacted, it launched a major "welfare reform/self-sufficiency" initiative (Bernstein, 1996).

These firms typically claim to save tax dollars while promoting self-sufficiency, and they boast that both goals are met. In Sheboygan, Wisconsin, for instance, Curtis & Associates has been operating full-service case management contracts since 1989, first for JOBS, and later for Wisconsin's W-2 (the name for Wisconsin's TANF program) and Children First programs. Curtis & Associates reports that its caseload of mandatory recipients has fallen 97% (from 1,100 to 40) during this period, and that it has saved over $2 million in 1995 and 1996 alone, without measurable increases in homelessness or child care protection needs. Curtis & Associates reports similar success stories in other contracts around the country (Curtis & Associates, 1999a). Like Curtis & Associates, Maximus reports glowing performance reports (e.g., high placement rates, good wages for its placements, and large savings for the public) for many of its TANF contracts. In northern Virginia, for example, its Fairfax Works program has moved several thousand welfare recipients off the rolls into unsubsidized private employment; Maximus claims that, in Fairfax, it has placed 95% of its welfare clients (Maximus, 1998b).

Despite their glowing press releases, these firms' performances are hardly immune from criticism. In one such story, Maximus received a $12.8 million contract from Connecticut to manage its child care program for working welfare recipients.

But within months Maximus found its operations in the kind of disarray it usually takes government years to achieve. More than 10,000 of the 17,000 bills submitted by child-care providers were 30 days late in being paid. Day-care centers whose bills were past due worried about having to turn away children or let staff go. Parents who tried to contract Maximus encountered what a state administrator called "telephone system collapse." (Cohen, 1998, p.)

In Virginia, EDS agreed in 1997 to pay the state $2.3 million in reimbursements and damages when it failed to deliver on a $45 million Medicaid computerization contract. In Maryland, Lockheed Martin's performance in child support collection fell 22% below its promised performance, whereas a state-run program collected payments at a much higher rate (Cohen, 1998). However, the story continues, this may still have been an improvement over the state of welfare service delivery prior to the contracting.

There is, still, little research explicitly comparing the effectiveness of public versus private welfare services delivery. The GAO, in comparing the cost-effectiveness of public and private child support services, found that performance varied dramatically, with private firms faring better than some states and worse than others (Yates, 1997b). Other studies sponsored by the Council of State Governments and the Reason Foundation found that some savings can be attributed to private contractors, but less so for welfare delivery than other types of services.

WISCONSIN

Rather than just look at firms that deliver welfare services, it is also worthwhile to examine states that have employed these firms. Wisconsin is the clear leader in public-private partnerships in welfare policy. Under AFDC, Wisconsin, like other states, was prohibited from using private firms to perform major welfare functions such as determining eligibility or conducting case management. County governments had de facto monopolies over administration, and they were reimbursed by the state on the basis of their actual costs. In other words, so long as the counties were delivering legally allowed welfare activities, they could simply pass the bills along to Madison, and the state capital was obligated to pay them. These reimbursements included activities within the JOBS program, the work component of AFDC. As the WPRI noted, "for most of the history of the JOBS program, providers were paid for offering services, whether or not those services moved a single individual from welfare to work" (1998, p. 1).

Yet even in the mid-1990s, Wisconsin state and local governments were not delivering the bulk of JOBS services. Wisconsin was moving away from this system in 1994, 2 years before the end of AFDC. In that year, the state adopted performance contracting for JOBS in Milwaukee (where most AFDC recipients lived), and in 1995, performance contracting was adopted statewide. These contracts stipulated that JOBS contractors could earn substantially more if they actually placed welfare recipients in real jobs; if contractors did not, they would earn much less. In the last full year of the program's operation, only 35 of the 72 counties had public agencies delivering JOBS (and many of these agencies had private-sector contractors). In 22 counties, JOBS was delivered by coalitions of public and private entities. Fifteen counties used private contractors exclusively (WPRI, 1998).

This performance-based contracting has been credited for increasing JOBS placements by 30% in Milwaukee in the first year and for lowering welfare caseloads around the state over time (WPRI, 1998; for examples of other nonprofit contracts under TANF, see Yates, 1997a).

The apparent success of the JOBS-contracting experiment encouraged Wisconsin policy makers to apply a similar model to TANF. As with JOBS, Wisconsin pays W-2 contractors a flat fee; if the contractor can deliver all necessary services for less than this amount, it can keep a portion of the surplus. The more quickly the contractor can place welfare clients in unsubsidized jobs, the less money it will have to pay in services.

It is important to note, however, that Wisconsin was less focused on transferring welfare delivery to the private sector than on breaking the monopoly of governmental agencies over welfare delivery. In fact, county governments were given the chance to earn the "right of first selection" (i.e., to win the W-2 contracts without competition) if they met certain performance standards, and all but five counties earned this right. Several counties chose not to exercise this right, however; Milwaukee, by far the most populous county, chose not to even compete for the contract. As a result, about 70% of Wisconsin's W-2 caseload is handled by nongovernmental entities, both nonprofit and for-profit (WPRI, 1998).

In Milwaukee, therefore, the government no longer administers W-2. It was divided into six districts; vendors could bid on one or more districts, and amazingly, five different bidders won.[8] Each bidder won a 6-month start-up contract, with implementation funds to follow. The contracts were fixed sums, so that the winning firms would profit only if they fulfilled the contract at a lower cost. Naturally, the contractors were worried about the financial risks that they faced. For example, the bidders were all concerned about the element in the contract specifying that contractors would face a $5000 fine each time that they failed to serve a welfare client. Negotiating as a group, they all asked the state to be much clearer as to what constitutes such a failure (Yates, 1997a).

Milwaukee's District 1 has an interesting three-way partnership involving the county government, a nonprofit, and two for-profits (as well as five subcontractors).[9] There, the Young Women's Christian Association (YWCA) joined together with the Kaiser Group and CNR Health to form YW-Works, a "limited liability company that is a profit-making venture" (Yates, 1997a).[10] The YWCA is the managing partner, with control over daily operations, and it is the site of most service delivery. As a nonprofit, any revenue in excess of expenses will be reinvested. The Kaiser Group is responsible for training staff, managing the quality assurance systems, developing the case management/team delivery system, and maintaining employer linkages. CNR Health is responsible for the computer systems, employee assistance and disability management, and risk management consultation.

The YWCA had already been providing JOBS services for Wisconsin prior to TANF. The YWCA was interested in bidding to operate the Milwaukee TANF program, but as one YWCA official put it, "we're great at servicing the client. We're not so great at managing a huge system, and we don't have Kaiser's experience with managing the employer interface" (Yates, 1997a). Hence, YWCA made a decision to pursue a joint venture with the Kaiser Group and CNR Health.

Wisconsin's welfare caseload has fallen an astonishing 86% between January 1993, and September 1998 (Department of Health and Human Services, 1999). Wisconsin's aggressive use of public-private partnerships through its W-2 program must be given some of the credit for these declines. It is worth noting, however, that some other states with large caseload declines (such as Wyoming, where caseloads fell by 90%) have continued to rely primarily on governmental agencies to deliver welfare services.

TEXAS

Wisconsin has a long history of social welfare experimentation, whereas Texas does not. Texas nonetheless tried to embark upon one of the most interesting, and controversial, experiments in welfare policy. Yet, where Wisconsin succeeded (at least as it has defined success), the attempt by Texas to develop a public-private partnership failed to get off the ground.

After TANF was enacted, Texas attempted to create the Texas Integrated Enrollment System (TIES). The goal of TIES was to allow a single firm to handle eligibility determination for 15 programs, including TANF, food stamps, Medicaid, and child support, among others.

TIES proponents saw it as an uncontroversial extension of existing policy; after all, private firms already conducted Medicaid claims processing and tracked child support payments as well as other data management functions. Private firms, for their part, were keenly interested in the size of the contracts (potentially $2.8 billion over 7 years). EDS partnered with the Texas Department of Human Services to obtain the contract, whereas Lockheed Martin joined efforts with the Texas Workforce Commission (Nightingale & Pindus, 1997). However, this proposal drew intense opposition from public employees who questioned the appropriateness of the private determination of public benefits, and not incidentally, who feared the loss of their jobs. Strong allegations about Lockheed Martin's efforts to win the contract have also been raised (Hartung & Washburn, 1998).

In 1996, Texas asked the federal government to grant it a waiver to implement TIES. When TANF was created that same year, states were granted the option to use private firms to determine eligibility for that program. Medicaid and food stamps, however, continued to require governmental officials to determine program eligibility. In May 1997, the Clinton administration ruled that federal law prohibited privatization of food stamp and Medicaid eligibility determination, effectively killing the TIES proposal. The Texas legislature subsequently directed state agencies to coordinate their plans for service integration, and these agencies dropped their plans to partner with private vendors. Texas is now pursuing an incremental—and governmental—approach to integrating social services.[11]

KEY ISSUES

Our governments face several challenges as they develop public-private partnerships for welfare services.

TREATING CLIENTS FAIRLY

The first challenge is to preserve the rights of the clients (i.e., citizens) while providing them the assistance that they need to become economically self-sufficient. Some observers have been concerned that contractors, especially when motivated by profit-making goals and priorities, may not be inclined to provide equal access to services for all eligible beneficiaries or will be tempted to provide inferior services to cut costs. Contractors may have incentives to provide services to clients who are easiest to serve (a practice commonly referred to as creaming), leaving the more difficult cases for the government—if they are to be served at all. These are serious concerns. Indeed, some have claimed that the 1996 welfare reforms permitted "one of the largest corporate grabs in history" (quote by Sandy Felder, public sector coordinator of the Service Employees International Union, as cited in Dunlea, 1999). "Obviously, [firms] are not going into [welfare services] with altruistic motives and the intent of losing money. The profit motive is foremost . . . they're licking their chops" (quote by John Hirschi, Texas state legislator, as cited in Dunlea, 1999). As Business Week put it, "in their zeal to make a profit, private companies could harm people by cutting corners—by withholding benefits from the deserving or by providing inferior service" (Garland, 1997, p. 132).

Private firms implementing TANF, at least in Wisconsin, strongly reject these allegations, claiming "we're not in this for the money" (WPRI, 1998, p. 21). As the president of the Kaiser Group put it, "our focus is on the family and on living-wage jobs. It sounds like rhetoric, but that's what I've been doing my whole life. My whole focus here is on [job] retention and living-wage jobs. I'm not necessarily interested in corporate growth. I'm interested in . . . quality service. That's my incentive" (quoted in WPRI, 1998, p. 22). The Kaiser Group, for example, offers a 24-hour hotline for its TANF clients, and its hotline workers are authorized to provide the assistance the client needs to keep working, whether it be a motel voucher, child care, or alternate transportation (WPRI, 1998). It has been suggested, however, that welfare firms are willing to spend extra money on their initial programs to create positive images that can be used later to gain contracts that are more favorable.

One need not believe that Opportunity, Inc. is altruistic to conclude that welfare firms have incentives to provide appropriate services. Even if private firms seek profits, it would be irrational for them to place unprepared workers in jobs to avoid training and benefit costs. The employer would, first, return the new worker to the welfare firm and, second, refuse to accept future referrals. The welfare firm then must bear the cost of working with the current client and the future costs of finding new employers. In short, it is good ethics and good business for welfare firms to serve welfare clients appropriately. As a result, in Wisconsin at least, welfare firms often appear to offer more services than they are contractually obligated to provide in order to better serve welfare clients (WPRI, 1998).

It is also important to note that governmental agencies are not exempt from the charge that they do not provide the services that welfare clients truly need. Liberal critics of American welfare programs have long noted that millions of eligible individuals have neither received the benefits to which they were entitled nor the services that they lack, not the least of which because our governments have been less than enthusiastic about enrolling them.

The solutions to this challenge include such measures as writing contracts with private firms that are worded to give citizens the same access to these programs as they had before or provide governmental involvement in dispute resolutions, and to punish financially those firms that withhold services from potential clients. These measures are difficult to implement and, perhaps, will make private firms less interested in developing partnerships with governmental agencies. The solutions become even more complicated when the partnerships involve religious institutions (Yates, 1998).

CREATING COMPETITION

A second challenge is to obtain real competition between private bidders so that governments can realize the benefits of privatization. It is not clear whether all areas of social welfare will have enough firms willing and able to submit quality bids. In Wisconsin's case, for instance, the state did not release the names of all the bidders, much less the number of for-profit or nonprofit bidders and how their bids compared with the winning bids. In Milwaukee, it appears that there was at least some competition for each of the six TANF districts. Moreover, the GAO found that most state and local program officials it contacted were generally satisfied with the number of qualified bidders in their state or locality, except for those in rural areas and for those with contracts that require a highly skilled staff (1998). Furthermore, it might be expected that, as the market for Opportunity, Inc. matures, there will be greater competition within local contracts as firms gain experience with operating TANF programs.

CRAFTING CONTRACTS

An additional challenge is to develop contracts that specify program results in sufficient detail to hold contractors accountable; this challenge might be especially difficult for relatively inexperienced state and local governments.

Once again, the Wisconsin experience is instructive. The designers of the W-2 program faced, and tentatively resolved, two main contractual problems. First, what kind of performance standards should the contracts contain? Second, how should contractors be held to these performance expectations?

Establishing performance standards was tricky, in part because it had not been done for the AFDC program. The easiest standard to develop, and ultimately the main one established, concerned case-load reductions. W-2 agencies were given incentives to place clients in unsubsidized jobs (so that the agency would need to neither pay clients benefits nor provide them services). Performance standards were not established for client wages, benefits, or job retention. Accordingly, contractors had no particular financial incentives to enhance client wages, benefits, or tenure. Wisconsin did not establish standards for these performance items because they are unimportant, but, as one policy maker put it,

> it was just too difficult to know what the appropriate baselines should be. There was nowhere else in the country we could look because no one had ever done anything like this. And we had not kept very good data on the caseload in Wisconsin to help us determine what reasonable expectations might be. (WPRI, 1998, p. 20)

Contractors are held to performance expectations in two main ways. First, the contractors are capitated; that is, the contractor receives a flat fee from the state to provide all services (including benefits) to the W-2 population within its jurisdiction. If program costs exceed this fee, the contractor must make up the difference; this provides a clear incentive to the welfare firms to keep their costs down. If the firm can deliver W-2—that is, put welfare clients in unsubsidized jobs—for less than the flat fee, it can keep a portion of the money as surplus.[12] The second way that firms were held to performance expectations involved punishments for providing poor services or withholding services. If a W-2 agency fails to provide required services, it is subject to a $5,000 fine for each case of failure (WPRI, 1998).

MONITORING PERFORMANCE

The final challenge is to monitor performance in social service programs, whether provided directly by the government or through a contract. Weaknesses in monitoring performance make it difficult to ensure that all intended beneficiaries have access to services, and determine whether private providers achieve desired program goals and avoid unintended negative consequences. It seems that governmental agencies must ultimately be responsible for this monitoring; it is much less evident how much states are actually doing to monitor their contracts appropriately.

CONCLUSION

Will Opportunity, Inc. prove itself superior to the Welfare State? Will public-private partnerships in welfare programs deliver better services to those who need them most at a lower cost and in ways that enhance self-sufficiency? We wish we had the answers to these questions but, alas, we do not. The superiority of Opportunity, Inc. is based more on theory, ideology, and hope than on proven results. In general, research findings are mixed (GAO, 1997).[13] Private welfare agencies in Wisconsin have had spectacular success in reducing caseloads but, then again, so have governmental ones. The economic conditions in the United States since the mid-1990s have also been most favorable for welfare reform. TANF could not have had a better economic environment. The success of Opportunity, Inc. would be less certain if economic conditions again become hostile for the poor. The real advantage of Opportunity, Inc. over the Welfare State is not likely to be that private firms are better than public ones, but that multiple, competitive entities provide services better than monopolies do.

NOTES

1. There is no register of all such contracts, and it is difficult to estimate precisely how widespread they are. The GAO found that half of the state and local social service agencies it surveyed had increased their use of contracting during the 1990s; the GAO also reports that the Council of State Governments had found that 80% of state social service departments had increased their use of contracting between 1988 and 1993 (GAO, 1997). The size and extent of these contracts also varies dramatically. Consider social services in California's two largest cities, for example. In Los Angeles County, the child support enforcement program spent less than 5% of its $100 million program budget on contracted services in 1996; in contrast, the child care component of San Francisco's Greater Avenues for Independence (GAIN) program spent all of its program funds, or $2.1 million, on privatized services that same year (GAO, 1997).

2. Social Security is the quintessentially successful welfare state program because it has a very low error rate at these three critical functions.

3. By this standard, the state with the worst AFDC program was Texas, which had an overpayment rate of over 10% in 1993 (House of Representatives, 1996).

4. In this article, private firms include both for-profits and nonprofits. There are, to be sure, major differences between them regarding the provision of social services. There are yet greater differences between private firms and governmental agencies, and that is why both for-profits and nonprofits are compared to the government.

5. Again, this does not mean that private firms are inherently superior to governmental agencies. It is also quite difficult to make a dramatic change to the behavior of private firms.

6. Full service contracts involve location, paternity and support order establishment, payment processing, and collections.

7. In March 1999, when this article was written, Maximus (listed as MMS on the New York Stock Exchange) was valued at 26 7/8 a share (although it is down from a year's high of over $40). It has been profitable every year, and it is not just Maximus's outside stockholders who are profiting from its success. After Maximus went public, its founder and CEO, David Mastram, reportedly made $18.8 million in cash while holding another $110 million in stock, which, by contract, he cannot sell for years (Cohen, 1998).

8. The winners were as follows: District 1—a consortium of CNR Health, the Kaiser Group, and the YWCA (named YW-Works); District 2—United Migrant Opportunity Services; District 3—Opportunities Industrialization Center of Greater Milwaukee; Districts 4 and 5—Goodwill Industries; and District 6—Maximus, Inc.

9. Yates (1997a) also provides examples of nonprofit contracts for welfare services in Michigan, Florida, and Indiana.

10. Maximus was the losing bidder in District 1.

11. Texas has also been relatively aggressive in involving the interfaith community in welfare reform (Yates, 1998).

12. In Wisconsin, the contracts were written so that if the welfare agency or firm's costs were less than the contract amount, the agency could retain the 7%. If there were additional savings, the agency could keep 10% of this amount for unrestricted use (e.g., profit); of the remaining 90%, half goes to the state and half stays with the agency for reinvestment in services (WPRI, 1998).

13. Nightingale and Pindus (1997) explain why newly privatized systems compare favorably to the older governmental systems, even if privatization is not necessarily superior.

REFERENCES

Allen, J. W., Chi, K. S., Devlin, K. A., Fall, M., Hatry, H. P., & Masterman, W. (1989). *The private sector in state service delivery: Examples of innovative practices.* Washington, DC: The Urban Institute Press.

Bernstein, N. (1996, September 15). Giant companies entering race to run state welfare programs. *The New York Times*, p. A1.

Bureau of the Census. (1997). *Statistical abstract of the United States, 1997.* Washington, DC: Government Printing Office.

Cates, S. (1998). Electronic benefits transfer. *Welfare Information Network* [On-line]. Available: http://www.welfareinfo.org/electronic.htm.

Cohen, A. (1998). When Wall Street runs welfare. *Time* [On-line]. Available: http://www.time.com/980323/business.when_wall_stree2.html.

Craig, C., Kulik, T., James, T., Nielsen, S., & Orr, S. (1999). *Blueprint for the privatization of child welfare* (Policy Study No. 248) [On-line]. Available: http://www.rppi.org/ps248.htm.

Curtis & Associates, Inc. (1999a). *Current contracts in Wisconsin* [On-line]. Available: http://www.selfsufficiency.com/cWI.htm.

Curtis & Associates, Inc. (1999b). *Six reasons to choose Curtis & Associates, Inc.* [On-line]. Available: http://www.selfsufficiency.com/reasons.htm.

Department of Agriculture. (1998a). *Food stamp program: Electronic benefits transfer (EBT) highlights* [On-line]. Available: http://www.usda.gov/fcs/stamps/fs.htm.

Department of Agriculture. (1998b). *Nutrition program facts: Electronic benefits transfer* [On-line]. Available: http://www.usda.gov/fcs/ogapi/ebtunf~1.htm.

Department of Agriculture. (1998c). *Nutrition program facts: Food stamp program* [On-line]. Available: http://www.usda.gov/fcs/stamps/fspfor~1.htm.

Department of Health and Human Services. (1999). *ACF data and statistics* [On-line]. Available: http://www.acf.dhhs.gov/stats/caseload.htm.

Donahue, J. D. (1989). *The privatization decision: Public ends, private means.* New York: Basic Books.

Dunlea, M. (1999). The poverty profiteers privatize welfare. *Covert Action Quarterly* [On-line]. Available: http://www.caq.com/CAQ59.PrivateWelfare.html.

Food Research and Action Center. (1998). *Food stamp outreach: A survey of state activities* [On-line]. Available: http://www.frac.org/html/news/fsoutreach.html.

Garland, S. B. (1997, May 19). A rich new business called poverty. *Business Week*, 132.

General Accounting Office. (1995, November). *Child support enforcement: States and localities move to privatize services* (GAO/HEHS-96-43FS). Washington, DC: Author.

General Accounting Office. (1997, October). *Social service privatization: Expansion poses challenges in ensuring accountability for program results* (GAO/HEHS-98-6). Washington, DC: Author.

General Accounting Office. (1998, October). *Child welfare: Early experiences implementing a managed care approach* (GAO/HEHS-99-8). Washington, DC: Author.

Gueron, J. (1995, September 12). A way out of the welfare bind. *The Washington Post*, p. A19.

Gurin, A. (1989). Governmental responsibility and privatization: Examples of four social services. In S. B. Kamerman & A. J. Kahn (Eds.), *Privatization and the welfare state* (p. 191). Princeton, NJ: Princeton University Press.

Hager, G. (1999, February 18). A private prescription for Medicare? *The Washington Post*, p. A4.

Hartung, W. D., & Washburn, J. (1998, March 2). Lockheed Martin: From warfare to welfare. *The Nation*.

Health Care Financing Administration. (1998). *Expenditures for health services and supplies under public programs, by type of expenditure and program: Calendar year 1997* [On-line]. Available: http://www.hcfa.gov/stats/nhe-oact/tables/t18.htm.

House of Representatives, Committee on Ways and Means. (1996). *The Green Book.* Washington, DC: Government Printing Office.

Maximus. (1998a). [On-line]. Available: http://www.maxinc.com.

Maximus. (1998b). *Texas awards MAXIMUS Medicaid managed care contract* [On-line]. Available: http://www.maxinc.com/fall97.html.

Mead, L. (1992). *The new politics of poverty.* New York: Basic Books.

Melia, R. (1997). *Private contracting in the human services.* Pioneer Institute for Public Policy Research [On-line]. Available: http://www.pioneerinstitute.org/piopaper/wp03.htm.

Miller, J. H. (1998). Report from the President. *Privatizing welfare in Wisconsin: Ending administrative entitlements—W-2's untold story.* Thiensville, WI: Wisconsin Policy Research Institute.

Nightingale, D. S., & Pindus, N. (1997). *Privatization of public social services: A background paper.* Washington, DC: The Urban Institute.

Public Agenda. (1996). *The values we live by: What Americans want from welfare reform* [On-line]. Available: http://www.publicagenda.org.

Social Security Administration. (1998). *B1-OASDI benefits: Monthly benefits in current-payment status, by program, 1940-98* [On-line]. Available: ftp://ftp.ssa.gov/pub/statistics/1b1.

Sparer, M. (1999). Myths and misunderstandings: Health policy, the devolution revolution, and the push for privatization. *American Behavioral Scientist, 43*, 138-154.

Stegman, M. (1998). Electronic benefit's potential to help the poor. *Policy Brief* [On-line]. Available: http://www.brook.edu/comm/policybriefs/pb032/pb32.htm.

Wisconsin Policy Research Institute. (1998, January). Privatizing welfare in Wisconsin: Ending administrative entitlements—W-2's untold story. *Wisconsin Policy Research Institute Report, 11*, 1.

Yates, J. (1997a). *Case studies on non-profits' involvement in contracting for welfare services* [On-line]. Available: http://www.welfareinfor.org/case.htm.

Yates, J. (1997b). *Privatization and welfare reform* [On-line]. Available: http://www.welfareinfor.org/jessica.htm.

Yates, J. (1998). *Partnerships with the faith community in welfare reform* [On-line]. Available: http://www.welfareinfor.org/faith.htm.

11

Policy Partnering Between the Public and the Not-for-Profit Private Sectors

A Key Policy Lever or a Dire Warning of Difficulty Ahead?

NICHOLAS P. LOVRICH, JR.

Policy partnering between the public and the not-for-profit private sectors has been little studied. This article clarifies this special relationship, outlining the unexpected strengths and the nonintuitive weaknesses of social capital in explaining partnering successes and failures. The criminal justice system of Washington State breaks new ground in policy-partnering studies. I begin by outlining how social capital is central to these developments, which are grounded, ironically, in both cooperation and conflict. Next, I outline the history, evolution, and political ramifications of the social capital concept. This rich concept is relevant across a range of policy arenas. I consider these in turn. I move on to review, as yet unpublished, research of significance for public/not-for-profit private partnering from recent dissertations under my direction, at the Division of Governmental Studies and Services (see appendix). A broader understanding emerges through this review as to when and how social capital facilitates public/not-for-profit private partnering. I come to an understanding of the limits, as well as the strengths, of social capital. Most importantly, I suggest that social capital cannot always play the role of facilitating public/not-for-profit private partnering relationships because social capital is underdeveloped in many areas. Where this social capital is weak, it is very difficult to develop it and sustain an undertaking that is likely to succeed only through a long-term sustained effort.

CRIMINAL JUSTICE AND THE LATE
DISCOVERY OF COLLABORATIVE PROCESSES

In working with courts, corrections, and law enforcement agencies in Washington during recent years, it is clear that most public agencies in these areas are not accustomed to the kinds of sharing of information and organizational resources that are essential to effective multiagency collaboration. The historical norm has been for courts, corrections, and law enforcement agencies to work hard to maintain professional independence from one another (with separate information systems, separate training and professional development processes, etc.). Moreover, they tend to seek and maintain a similar professional distance from their environment—including citizens, citizen groups, and community-based non-profit organizations; the latter of which tend to attract the "bleeding hearts" that are inclined to be critical of law enforcement and the criminal justice system. Such a professional distance was commonly thought to be necessary to maintain proper objectivity in dealing with the world outside of the criminal justice community (Crank, 1997).

The combination of influences—namely, a strong movement toward collaborative problem solving in inclusive, multiagency and multigroup efforts by other state and local government agencies and the attractiveness of federal grants from the National Institute of Justice, the Office of Community Policing Services, and other extramural sources—led to the widespread adoption of collaborative partnerships among criminal justice agencies all across the country.[1] Unprecedented efforts to share information and organizational resources among criminal justice agencies and build bridges to the public and citizen-based groups grew relatively commonplace. Judges running for public office now frequently speak of court outreach and public education goals. Candidates for the position of sheriff invariably indicate their support for some citizen engagement oriented definition of community policing. Now, even the ultra-closed world of Washington State corrections is witnessing the first stages of a dramatic initiative to decentralize the corrections operation into a set of strong regional offices, each of which is mandated to build bridges to its public and devise appropriate means by which information on public support, public preferences, and public concerns will be made determinative of correctional policy in each region. One central aspect of this correctional reform initiative is designed to promote effective collaboration between community corrections, local law enforcement, and prosecutorial personnel by colocating these three groups of criminal justice professionals in neighborhood-based storefronts (or " Community-Oriented Policing [COP] Shops" as they are known in Washington). These COP Shops are themselves set up as neighborhood-based, citizen-operated entities that are coordinated by a nonprofit organization working in cooperation with a municipal police department. The Spokane Police Department, one of 12 COP Demonstration Cities in the nation and recent recipient of the 1998 International Association of Chiefs of Police award for the most outstanding program for cities over

50,000, operates 10 (with 2 more being developed) COP Shops that involve over 700 citizen volunteers providing regular assistance to police agency operations.

The state requires that inclusive county law and justice councils be involved in the collaborative planning of the use of state criminal justice funds. Restorative justice efforts to create and sustain lay, community-based disciplinary processes in lieu of court-based processing of nonviolent criminal offenders are increasingly commonplace across the state. In the Spokane setting, the nonprofit COP Shop organization is a key player in the restorative justice effort. Equally commonplace is the observation that although this collaborative process is indeed capable of leading to the effective development of collective action on tough, shared problems in many cases, in other cases the same process leads to enhanced conflict and prolonged deadlock. The construct of social capital is increasingly seen as a critical element accounting for the success and/or failure of collaborative partnerships; a better understanding of the concept is believed to be essential in making further progress toward the effective use of collaboration among public agencies and the effective operation of productive partnerships between those agencies and community-based nonprofit agencies.

THE POWERFUL APPEAL OF
THE SOCIAL CAPITAL CONSTRUCT

Initially developed by James S. Coleman (1990) as a term that applies to the strength of trusting interpersonal relationships that obtain in a social collectivity, the concept of social capital has been applied (quite creatively) by Robert D. Putnam to the question of governmental performance. His "Bowling Alone" article (1995), his book on the comparison of regional governmental performance in postwar Italy, and a myriad of related studies have all led to the development of an active and stimulating area of research in contemporary social science.[2] Social capital is seen by many researchers as an essential building block for collective action, which itself is irrational from a rational free rider perspective absent a strong sense of reliable reciprocation (social trust) and an affective tie to others in the social network (sense of community). As for ideological predispositions relating to social capital, social liberals of a communitarian bent find the focus on community attributes, civic engagement, other-regarding values, and the building of interpersonal trust and strong social networks an appealing message. Social conservatives, for their part, are also strongly attracted to the argument that firm family ties, healthy neighborhood interactions, respect for the rights of others, and strong churches and civic organizations are more important to governmental performance and community viability than big government intervention and high-cost public-sector programs.

Social capital was discovered by a wide range of scholars interested in governmental performance before its increasingly frequent application to criminal justice phenomena. In the areas of public school performance, the promotion of public health behaviors, the enhancement of environmental sensitivity, and the promotion of economic development, a number of contemporary scholars have fruitfully explored the area of community asset mapping (Kretzmann & McKnight, 1993) and the coproduction of public services (Brudney & England, 1983), and in the process discovered the utility of the social capital concept. Not to be left out, the criminal justice community has similarly explored the utility of the concept (often referred to as social disorder—the obverse of social capital— by criminologists; see Rose & Clear, 1998) for understanding how COP, community corrections, and restorative justice might all be better understood from a social capital perspective.

Although the applicability of social capital analysis is indeed evident in numerous areas of basic criminal justice research and applied policy studies alike, what is less clear is whether the concept provides a key lever for effective governmental performance, or if it instead constitutes an insight into the ultimate futility of government-led efforts to accomplish enhancements in the quality of community life in geographic areas where such enhancements are most needed. Although a debate among scholars continues as to whether America's fund of social capital is in serious decline or being maintained at an acceptable level (Jackman & Miller, 1998), a wide range of public service–oriented elements of local government are increasingly inclined to build reliance on the existing stock of social capital to help solve their public policy problems.

For example, in public education (K-12), the proponents of the site-based management concept assume that parental, local private sector, and local nonprofit sector assets can be effectively tapped to substantially improve school performance. Similarly, local social service agencies, coping in an era with hitherto radical and somewhat mean-spirited concepts of welfare reform, are laboring to enhance public-private partnerships and inclusive collaborative relationships with community-based nonprofit organizations to enhance the rather wide-meshed safety net with which they are working. In like manner, local public health authorities, struggling with the containment of health care costs and the need to stretch their arms out to a growing uninsured population, are seeking to build locally based, broad-scoped collaborate efforts to bring about the synergy needed to find creative solutions to public-health problems.

For their part, in the criminal justice area, local police authorities, state and local corrections administrators, and trial court officials, in ever-growing numbers of locales, are reaching beyond their respective professional boundaries to tap into the same base of local social capital to secure broader civic engagement in their own particular areas of public policy concern. As noted previously, such attempts are nearly always broadly supported, with political conservatives welcoming the focus on the reinforcement of traditional mores and community-regarding values, and welcoming the de-emphasis of big-government programs. On the part of communitarian liberals, the renewed focus on the sense of community and mutual obligation born of common humanity appears to be both timely and correctly directed. A long-standing common refrain among American liberals—ranging from Reisman, Glazer, and Denney's *The Lonely Crowd* (1950); through Mansbridge's *Beyond Adversary Democracy* (1980); Bellah, Madsen, Sullivan, Swidler, and Tipton's *The Habits of the Heart* (1985); Etzioni's *The Moral Dimension* (1988); Kemmis's *Community and the Politics of Place* (1990); to Michael Sandel's *Democracy's Discontent: America in Search of a Public Philosophy* (1996)—is that the hyperindividualism of American legal-constitutional processes and popular culture (Lipset, 1963, 1996) lead to a host of problems in the accomplishment of social goals that require persistent and concerted collective action.

To these scholars and their many supporters, the enhancement of civic institutions, the promotion of public deliberative processes (Yankelovich, 1991), and the building of a sense of community through "civic journalism" (Cappella & Jamieson, 1997) all represent timely and well-directed efforts. DeLeon (1997) sees public agency managers as being key figures in the process of bringing citizens into the policy process in meaningful ways, and argues that they must learn to be effective facilitators of inclusive, collaborative problem solving processes that engage citizens, capable nonprofit organizations, and strategically situated private sector actors in service coproduction efforts (see Whitaker, 1980).

What difference does social capital make in those state and local government settings where public/not-for-profit private partnering is featured as a major aspect of public policy (intended to address a substantive problem of governance)? As with Robert D. Putnam, we will accept the following definition of social capital offered by James S. Coleman (1990):

> Like other forms of capital, social capital is productive, making possible the achievement of certain ends that would not be attainable in its absence. . . . For example, a group [or community] whose members manifest trustworthiness and place extensive trust in one another will be able to accomplish much more than a comparable group lacking that trustworthiness and trust. (pp. 302, 304)

Putnam argues that social capital is build on "trust, norms, and networks" (1993, p. 167), and that it serves to facilitate collective action; he argues further that "spontaneous cooperation is facilitated by social capital" (p. 167). Putnam shares with Barber (1988), Fukuyama (1995), Seligman (1997), and Kramer and Tyler (1996) the belief that interpersonal trust lies at the core of social capital. For Putnam, the concept of social capital connects directly to the American experience through the powerful writings of Alex DeTocqueville. Putnam (1993) notes that "as depicted in Tocqueville's classic interpretation of American democracy and other accounts of civic virtue, the civic community is marked by an active, public-spirited citizenry, by egalitarian political relations, by a social fabric of trust and cooperation" (p. 15).

THE EVIDENCE THAT SOCIAL
CAPITAL MAKES A DIFFERENCE

What empirical and qualitative evidence can be presented from the applied research in public policy recently performed by the Division of Governmental Studies and Services to prove that the level of social capital makes a substantive difference in the performance of local governments? Given the potential importance of social capital phenomena to the many areas of applied research being conducted by the division, no fewer than four recent Ph.D. dissertations have been devoted to the exploration of social capital phenomena as encountered in the work of the research unit. In the paragraphs to follow, the principal findings of each doctoral thesis will be presented in a brief overview.

When Social Capital Fails to Increase School Performance (Simon, 1997). The amount of social capital is not determinative of success in conditions of severe socioeconomic disadvantage. This finding from Christopher Simon is based on a study of K-12 public school performance.[3] He used standardized test scores and parental surveys for all of Washington's more than 290 school districts. Employing an inventive "outlier analysis approach," Dr. Simon compared two sets of above expectation and below expectation school districts.[4] He reports a strong association between advantage and test score performance (a widely observed finding).

Most importantly, a number of school districts within the categories of high, medium, and low levels of advantage are either considerably above or considerably below the predicted score for the school district. In comparing the two outlier groups within each trichotomized level of advantage, he found that in the mid-level advantage pairings and the high-level advantage pairings, the above expectation school districts did indeed demonstrate higher levels of social capital than school districts that were performing below expectation. Parents in the above expectation school districts were more likely to take part in their child's learning, to be engaged in civic affairs, to turn out for local elections, and to support school levies when they voted. Importantly, this pattern of effect was not in evidence in the case of the low-level advantage school districts.[5]

Social Capital Translates Into Public Health District Successes (Grott, 1999). This study explores public health district successes in collaborative problem solving in the integration of client services and in the development of access for uninsured persons to appropriate health care education and clinical services. In Dr. Catherine Grott's dissertation, she reports results from her study of six county public health districts in the state of Montana.[6] She investigated the hypothesis that those counties with higher levels of social capital would be more likely to be successful in their efforts than counties with lower levels of social capital.

Grott found that county public health districts achieved their goals in rather direct proportion to how much interpersonal trust they reported, how much civic engagement they indicated, and how strong a sense of community they felt. Putnam's argument that social capital translates into easier spontaneous cooperation found support in Grott's findings from the public health policy administration area. She used citizen surveys and public agency personnel surveys in each of the counties she studied. Her personal interviews and focus group sessions with personnel in each county public health district tended to confirm the impressions gained from her community and organizational surveys.

Social Capital and Community Policing: Six Cities (Correia, 1998). Mark Correia investigated the character of connections between the nature of COP programs and community level of social capital in six comparable middle-sized cities in five states.[7] He selected six cities from a nationwide survey of nearly 300 police agencies.[8] His 1996 survey focused on the implementation of COP, and employed a set of six highly similar middle-sized cities that differed significantly in their respective community policing programs.

Correia discovered a U-shaped relationship between social capital and commitment to community policing taking place. Implementation effort was high in both high-range and low-range social capital jurisdictions, but low in mid-range social capital jurisdictions. Success in the execution of community policing initiatives was high in high-range social capital jurisdictions, and low in low-range social capital jurisdictions. These findings are based on Correia's exploration of the connections between social capital and community policing. Correia employed a combination of quantitative and qualitative research methods. He collected citizen surveys in each of the six communities (with the same instrument employed in the Grott study) and conducted extensive staff interviews with each police department. His findings were quite unexpected, and his interpretation of results observed deserves some careful consideration.

Community policing tends to be taken seriously in jurisdictions that can succeed at it easily, or in jurisdictions that see COP as a way of enhancing social capital in places where it is seriously lacking.[9] In the mid-range social capital jurisdictions, it seems that the internal opposition to change is sufficient to keep police executives from pursuing COP with any great degree of enthusiasm. Of particular interest in the Correia study was the partial replication of his findings at the neighborhood level in one of his cities. As part of an in-depth case study in this jurisdiction, Correia compared the level of implementation of COP across neighborhoods and found that the success of COP was common in high-range social capital neighborhood settings and the lack of success was common in low-range social capital neighborhood settings. Correia found a strong association between socioeconomic advantage and social capital at the neighborhood level, which brings the findings reported in the Simon study back to mind.

Social Capital: Easy to Reinforce, Difficult to Engender (Fredericksen, 1995). The fourth piece of research to be considered here is that of Patricia Fredericksen.[10] Fredericksen's study explores the possibility of enhancing the social capital of a given community that is going through an economic transition and experiencing substantial growth. The community in question was moving toward the initiation of an inclusive growth-management planning process when community leaders requested that the Program for Local Government Education provide some targeted training in collaborative problem solving directed toward constructive participation in an open, community-wide planning process.[11]

The Program in Local Government Education secured the services of noted nonadversarial dispute resolution trainer Bill Lincoln, a chief trainer for Fisher and Ury (1981) in their Harvard Negotiation Project and a former faculty member of the Federal Executive Institute. Lincoln trained over 150 local leaders representing labor, business, local government, nonprofit, press, civic groups, and social service groups. The training took the form of 6 intensive days spread over two 3-day weekend sessions.

Fredericksen's study entailed participation in and close observation of the experiential training provided. It also included follow-up contacts with all participants at 6, 12, 18, and 24 months. The intention of the study was to determine if this effort to enhance the ability of community group leaders to engage in collaborative, nonadversarial problem solving produced demonstrable, lasting, and favorable effects. The training was oriented toward building trust and exploring collaborative approaches to the development of consensual agreements on quality of life issues. It also demonstrated how this same nonadversarial approach to problem solving (and conflict management) has parallel applications in family, associational group, and community settings. The data for her study included extensive pretraining attitudinal surveys and follow-up interviews in which training participants were asked to indicate how they used the concepts featured in the training in their family, work group, and community activities.

Fredericksen's principal findings were that the training in a trust building–oriented approach to nonadversarial problem solving had quite differential effects on the participants. For those who were inclined to be mistrustful and who were not highly integrated into associational networks, the training had rather limited results.[12] For these participants, the training effects tended to fade quickly over time and were limited to applications in the family setting. In sharp contrast, those training participants that tended to be trusting in outlook and who tended to be engaged in a wide network of groups and associations were inclined to report strong and lasting effects derived from the training. They were inclined to offer examples of the application of interest-based, nonadversarial (win-win) problem solving in family, associational, and community settings alike. It was Fredericksen's observation that the substantial investment made by the Program for Local Government Education in this community leader training effort produced strong evidence that social capital is relatively easy to reinforce if it is already in existence, but it is much more difficult to engender among social actors not predisposed to trust and engagement in social networks.

NAGGING SUSPICIONS: THE POTENTIAL FOR GOOD (AND EVIL) IN SOCIAL CAPITAL–DIRECTED PUBLIC POLICY INITIATIVES

The findings drawn from this research serve to raise some serious questions about how the concept of social capital is best understood vis-à-vis the requirements of effective public policy making in the contemporary governmental affairs setting.[13] This contemporary setting features an ongoing process of policy and program devolution of governmental responsibilities from the federal to state and local levels of government (Staeheli, Kodras, & Flint, 1997), and an active pursuit of the reinvention of government that has occasioned a great deal of exploration of the potentialities associated with public-nonprofit group partnerships and "load shedding" to nonprofit organizations (Galaskiewicz & Bielefeld, 1998; Handler, 1996).

At the outset, one core question arises, namely, if all of these parties—local police and community corrections agency officials, public health district administrators, public school principals and staff, community planners, judges and court administrators, and others—are seeking to tap into a finite fund of social capital, can that base for civic engagement support all of these attempts to draw on it? Given our knowledge that this social capital resource varies in strength from weak to strong across geographical settings, will not such a reliance on civic engagement and networks of trusting associations serve to exacerbate existing social inequities? The Simon, Grott, and Correia dissertations reported highly differential results associated with social capital in three different areas of public policy. These results indicate that, in highly disadvantaged circumstances, the effort to draw energy from social capital community assets is exceedingly difficult, and the fruitfulness of such efforts tends to be very limited. On a related note, if government-led efforts have been made to enhance social capital where it is weak, what is the track record of such efforts?

The Fredericksen dissertation suggests that efforts to bolster social capital are far more likely to succeed in places where social capital is already strong than in places where it is currently weak. The same phenomenon of disproportionate effects across high and low socioeconomic status communities has been witnessed in the area of community problem solving in COP efforts (Thurman & Reisig, 1996).

Perhaps the most important question to be asked about social capital–directed public policy initiatives is the following: Can the fund of social capital be enhanced through sustained efforts by public agencies to get to know their community and establish a community base of operations in partnership with community-based groups and rank-and-file citizens? From the findings reported by Simon, Grott, and Correia, there is good reason to attempt to draw on the existing stocks of social capital in collaborative partnerships directed to community quality of life improvements. Such efforts tend to be broadly supported by conservative and liberal elements alike, and in places where social capital is strong, positive effects are observed in a relatively short period of time. It is important to recognize, however, that in settings where social capital resources are weak, it will be necessary to make a long-term commitment to agency-community partnerships. The lack of immediate successes and favorable outcomes, and the frequent experience of disappointments and setbacks, should all be viewed in the broader context of building the trust necessary to initiate cooperative collaboration. As Putnam correctly notes, "the greater the level of trust within a community, the greater the likelihood of cooperation. And cooperation itself breeds trust. The steady accumulation of social capital is a crucial part of the story behind the virtuous circles of civic Italy" (1993, p. 171). It is likely that the very same phenomenon can occur in American community settings. If the strong dependence on social-capital–directed public policy processes is to avoid an exacerbation of existing socioeconomic inequities, there must be a commitment to concentrate social capital building efforts in disadvantaged areas. It is necessary to note from Simon's findings that social capital building is not likely to serve as a full substitute for broader social investments in the most depressed settings. Nothing observed in the Simon, Grott, or Correia research suggests that social-capital–directed policies provide a fit substitute for more direct forms of community economic, employment service, and health service investments. Social capital is not the cheap and effective solution to the long-term inequities of American society. Without due attention to such inequities, a greater reliance on social-capital–directed public policies could even exacerbate such inequities.

Perhaps one additional question might be considered fairly central to the consideration of social-capital–directed public policy efforts. Do the simultaneous efforts of multiple areas of public service delivery—police, corrections, courts, schools, social services, parks, public works, and so forth—complement one another, or do they instead serve as competitive drains on a depleted common resource? My reading of the social capital literature[14] leads me to suspect that no one public agency, no matter how enlightened its approach, is likely to succeed in building social capital where it is very weak. However, a comprehensive effort with simultaneous endeavors to promote social capital formation by many public agency actors working in partnership with community-based nonprofit organizations serve as a key policy lever in reinventing the government context. As these efforts develop, however, it is critical that social scientists document the progress and setbacks encountered, and that they collect the observations necessary to support and sustain such efforts in socially disadvantaged areas so that the least well-off among us are not made even more detached from our prosperous and democratic country's socioeconomic institutions.

APPENDIX
The Context of the Research:
The Role of the Division of Governmental Studies
and Services at Washington State University

The observations offered here on the critical importance of the role of public sector and nonprofit sector partnerships in the era of the broad-based devolution of governmental programs and policies in contemporary American federalism stem from over two decades of direct experience in working with federal, state, and local government agencies in the Pacific Northwest. As the director of the Division of Governmental Studies and Services at Washington State University since 1977, I have witnessed a veritable sea change in the governmental conceptualization of societal problems, and a corresponding paradigmatic change in the way public-sector agency officials view the roles of their agencies in the policy development process and in the administration of public programs. In this process of dramatic change in problem conceptualization and agency role definition, the concept of collaborative, multiagency partnerships has assumed a contemporary importance far beyond anything it has enjoyed in the past. This development, in turn, has led to the discovery of the widespread utility of the social capital construct in understanding when community-based collaborative partnerships work as intended, and when they do not produce the results hoped for by participants.

Over the course of the past two decades, the Division of Governmental Studies and Services has joined with Washington's three local government associations—the Association of Washington Cities, Washington State Association of Counties, and Washington Association of County Officials—in a multiagency partnership with Washington State University's Cooperative Extension to operate the Program for Local Government Education designed to provide timely training and applied research services for the state's local government elected and career officials. Owing to the high priority of criminal justice issues in the Evergreen State,[15] a major portion of the work done by the Division of Governmental Studies and Services has come in the area of criminal justice policy assessment and program administration in corrections, law enforcement, and court administration. The formal adoption of COP as the official form of law enforcement taught at the state's Criminal Justice Training Commission in the 1991 legislative session reflects well the high level of interest in criminal justice and public order issues in the state—and clearly reflects as well the multiagency, multigroup collaboration emphasis in public policy commonly witnessed in Washington's contemporary governmental affairs. In this regard, the state of Washington is quite typical of the country as a whole; the reinventing of government in the devolution of policy and program authority context is leading to widespread state and local government public agency experimentation with locally focused endeavors to establish effective collaborative partnership efforts to address public policy problems.

In numerous areas of Washington state public policy, there is evidence of a heavy reliance on inclusive collaborative processes to identify problems, to search out win-win (or superoptimal) solutions, and to implement agreements on cooperative efforts arrived at by means of localized multiagency efforts. The early success of the virtually unprecedented Timber-Fish-Wildlife Agreement (Northwest Renewable Resources Center, 1987; Protasel, 1991), bringing together long-time opponents—timber companies, Native American tribes, environmentalists, state and federal natural resource agencies, local governments in timber dependent areas, and recreationalists—into an effective collaborative process, led to the extension of this inclusive collaborative problem-solving approach to policy problem solving and policy development in many other areas of public concern requiring effective collective action. For example, the state's Growth Management Act of 1990 relies heavily on the ability of local governments within each county to come to agreement on a comprehensive land use plan (and associated zoning regulations) that preserves environmentally sensitive areas, concentrates growth within urban-growth boundaries, provides for low- and moderate-cost housing, minimizes travel between work and place of residence, and promotes other quality of life and environmental values deemed to be important to Washingtonians by their state government (Andranovich and Lovrich, 1992).

Similarly, in the area of public education (K-12), a heavy reliance is placed on site-based management principles and the encouragement of the building of strong partnerships between schools and elements of their local communities. In a like manner, in the area of social and health services, the long-standing community-based Community Action Centers and United Way organizations have received a powerful shot in the arm with the advent of welfare reform and recognition of the need for effective "community asset mapping" (McKnight, 1995, pp. 161-172). State-level social assistance, employment and housing policies are aimed at the mobilization of local community resources that promote self-sufficiency among the poorest of the state's population. Nonprofit partnerships with state agencies dispensing both state funds and federal pass-through funds are at the core of Washington's Work First program, and they occupy a strategic role as concrete evidence of community-based buy-ins (required in many federal funding arrangements) for its various low-cost housing and public health services programs.[16]

NOTES

1. Whether the problem be domestic violence, workplace violence against women, traffic safety, DUI enforcement, crime prevention through environmental design, juvenile justice services, the availability of alternatives to incarceration, or the tracking of sex offenders in the community, one is likely to find a multiagency, multigroup effort under way in the criminal justice policy area.

2. See the special symposium issues of the *American Behavioral Scientist* (Edwards & Foley, "Social Capital, Civil Society, and Contemporary Democracy," 1997) and *Political Psychology* (Mondak, "Psychological Approaches to Social Capital," 1998) devoted to social capital.

3. Simon is now on faculty in the Political Science Department at the University of Nevada, Reno.

4. Simon made use of each school district's mean parental education level and a number of socioeconomic indicators to calculate a composite measure of relative advantage for each school district, then regressed the mean test scores for reading, math, and verbal abilities on this variable.

5. We will return to this observation at the conclusion of this set of reflections on the two decades of applied research experienced in the Division of Governmental Studies and Services, and in connection with Cooperative Extension's Program for Local Government Education at Washington State University.

6. Catherine Grott is currently associated with Montana State University at Billings.

7. Correia is now in the Criminal Justice Department at the University of Nevada, Reno. The research reported here is from his 1998 dissertation.

8. These cities have been surveyed by the Division of Governmental Studies and Services every 3 years since the late 1970s to monitor changes in important law enforcement policy and program emphases over the years.

9. This is based on Correia's data and his extensive personal interviews with law enforcement personnel.

10. This material is from her doctoral dissertation. She is now in the Department of Political Science and Public Affairs Program at Boise State University.

11. This effort is described in a brief account in Fredericksen (1996).

12. This was determined by an exhaustive battery of pretraining assessment forms and questionnaires.

13. The research consisted of four recent Ph.D. dissertation efforts stemming from the applied research of the Division of Governmental Studies and Services at Washington State University, and in conjunction with the Program for Local Government Education.

14. This is from my two decades of experience with applied public policy research, and my oversight of the Fredericksen, Simon, Correia, and Grott dissertations.

15. This was the first state to enact a "three strikes, you're out" law in 1993. It was also the first state to establish a means of administrative detention for noncured, convicted sex offenders who have served out their prison terms.

16. The nonprofit Community Action Centers are now such a major partner of county governments throughout Washington (as is the case in many other states as well) that the Program for Local Government Education partnership includes action center managers in its various training and applied research and planning operations.

REFERENCES

Andranovich, G., & Lovrich, N. P. (1992). Local government then and now: The growth management challenge in the 1990s. In D. C. Nice, J. C. Pierce, & C. Sheldon (Eds.), *Political life in Washington* (pp. 159-179). Pullman: Washington State University Press.

Barber, B. (1988). *The logic and limits of trust.* New Brunswick, NJ: Rutgers University Press.

Bellah, R. N., Madsen, R., Sullivan, W. M., Swidler, A., & Tipton, S. M. (1985). *The habits of the heart: Individualism and commitment in American life.* Berkeley: University of California Press.

Brudney, J. L., & England, R. E. (1983). Toward a definition of the coproduction concept. *Public Administration Review, 43,* 59-64.

Cappella, J. N., & Jamieson, K. H. (1997). *Spiral of cynicism: The press and the public good.* New York: Oxford University Press.

Coleman, J. S. (1990). *Foundations of social theory.* Cambridge, MA: Harvard University Press.

Correia, M. (1998). *Social capital, civic engagement, social equity, and community oriented policing: Underlying factors affecting the implementation of COP in middle-sized communities.* Unpublished doctoral dissertation, Washington State University.

Crank, J. P. (1997). Celebrating agency culture: Engaging a traditional cop's heart in organizational change. In Q. C. Thurman & E. F. McGarrell (Eds.), *Community policing in a rural setting* (pp. 49-57). Cincinnati, OH: Anderson.

DeLeon, P. (1997). *Democracy and the policy sciences.* Albany: State University of New York Press.

Edwards, B., & Foley, M. W. (Eds.). (1997). Social capital, civil society, and contemporary democracy [Special issue]. *American Behavioral Scientist, 40* (5).

Etzioni, A. (1988). *The moral dimension.* New York: Free Press.

Fisher, R., & Ury, W. (1981). *Getting to yes: Negotiating agreement without giving in.* Boston: Houghton Mifflin.

Fredericksen, P. (1995). *Community leaders and collaborative negotiation: An analysis of the personal factors that contribute to an individual's perceived utility of cooperative conflict management.* Unpublished doctoral dissertation, Washington State University.

Fredericksen, P. (1996). Community collaboration and public policy making: Examining the long-term utility of training in conflict management. *American Behavioral Scientist, 39,* 552-569.

Fukuyama, F. (1995). *Trust: The social virtues and the creation of prosperity.* New York: Simon & Schuster.

Galaskiewicz, J., & Bielefeld, W. (1998). *Nonprofit organizations in an age of uncertainty: A study of organizational change.* Hawthorne, NY: Aldine.

Grott, C. J. (1999). *Health care reform at the state level: The dynamics of achieving service integration at the local health district level in Montana.* Unpublished doctoral dissertation, Washington State University.

Growth Management Act of 1990, R.C.W. § 36.70A (1998).

Handler, J. F. (1996). *Down from bureaucracy: The ambiguity of privatization and empowerment.* Princeton, NJ: Princeton University Press.

Jackman, R. W., & Miller, R. A. (1998). Social capital and politics. In N. W. Polsby (Ed.), *Annual review of political science* (Vol. 1). Palo Alto, CA: Annual Reviews.

Kemmis, D. (1990). *Community and the politics of place.* Norman: University of Oklahoma Press.

Kramer, R. M., & Tyler, T. R. (Eds.). (1996). *Trust in organizations: Frontiers of theory and research.* Thousand Oaks, CA: Sage.

Kretzmann, J. P., & McKnight, J. (1993). *Building communities from the inside out.* Chicago: Northwestern University Press.

Lipset, S. M. (1963). *The first new nation: The United States in historical and comparative perspective.* New York: Basic Books.

Lipset, S. M. (1996). *American exceptionalism: A double-edged sword.* New York: Norton.

Mansbridge, J. J. (1980). *Beyond adversary democracy.* New York: Basic Books.

McKnight, J. (1995). *The careless society: Community and its counterfeits.* New York: Basic Books.

Mondak, J. J. (Ed.). (1998). Psychological approaches to social capital [Special issue]. *Political Psychology, 19* (3).

Northwest Renewable Resources Center. (1987). From conflict to consensus. *Timber/Fish/Wildlife: A report from the Northwest Renewable Resources Center, 1,* 1-2.

Protasel, G. J. (1991). Resolving environmental conflicts: Neocorporatism, negotiated rule-making, and the timber/fish/wildlife coalition in the state of Washington. In M. K. Mills (Ed.), *Alternative dispute resolution in the public sector* (pp. 188-205). Chicago: Nelson-Hall.

Putnam, R. D. (1993). *Making democracy work: Civic traditions in modern Italy.* Princeton, NJ: Princeton University Press.

Putnam, R. D. (1995). Bowling alone: America's declining social capital. *Journal of Democracy, 6,* 65-78.

Reisman, D., Glazer, N., & Denney, R. (1950). *The lonely crowd.* New Haven, CT: Yale University Press.

Rose, D. R., & Clear, T. R. (1998). Incarceration, social capital, and crime: Implications for social disorganization theory. *Criminology, 36,* 441-479.

Sandel, M. (1996). *Democracy's discontent: America in search of a public philosophy.* Cambridge, MA: Harvard University Press.

Seligman, A. B. (1997). *The problem of trust.* Princeton, NJ: Princeton University Press.

Simon, C. (1997). *Public schools as "coping" organizations: Economic resource allocations and agency outcomes.* Unpublished doctoral dissertation, Washington State University.

Staeheli, L. A., Kodras, J. E., & Flint, C. (Eds.). (1997). *State devolution in America: Implications for a diverse society.* Thousand Oaks, CA: Sage.

Thurman, Q. C., & Reisig, M. D. (1996). Community-oriented research in an era of community-oriented policing. *American Behavioral Scientist, 39,* 570-586.

Whitaker, G. P. (1980). Coproduction: Citizen participation in service delivery. *Public Administra-*
tion Review, 40, 240-246.
Yankelovich, D. (1991). *Coming to public judgment: Making democracy work in a complex world.*
Syracuse, NY: Syracuse University Press.

12

Public-Private Partnerships in the U.S. Prison System

ANNE LARASON SCHNEIDER

Public-private partnerships in the operation of prisons have existed from the colonial period to contemporary times, although the extent of reliance on the private sector and the policy design models have varied somewhat. Drawing on ideas from policy design theory (Schneider & Ingram, 1997), this study will identify the characteristics of the partnerships, the reasons for private-sector involvement, the rationales and claims made by competing perspectives, and the consequences of private-sector involvement.[1]

Prison policy differs from other policy arenas in ways that have implications for the appropriate role of the private sector. First, prisons deliver punishment, whereas most policies deliver benefits or regulations. Other policies that impose costs—such as tax policy—may be unwanted or resented, but no other policy arena actually delivers punishment. Second, the target populations of prison policy are vastly different from most target populations—prisoners are not free, they do not make choices about most events in their daily life, they have virtually no political power, and they are socially constructed as deviant or violent by most of the population. Third, although many policy arenas offer some form of

Author's Note: *The author would like to acknowledge the valuable information provided by Terry Stewart, Director of the Arizona Department of Corrections. All points of view and interpretations of data, of course, are those of the author.*

political capital for elected officials, few, if any, offer such lucrative possibilities as prisons.[2] By inflicting harsh punishment upon criminals who are socially constructed as deviant, violent, and undeserving, elected officials can gain the accolades of the general public without incurring any noticeable political costs from those actually receiving the punishment. The monetary costs of mandatory long sentences are postponed to the future and spread across all taxpayers. Thus, it may be many years after legislation is passed before the full financial impact is felt. Finally, private-sector involvement in prison policy adds significant new target populations to the political arena by introducing businesses, corporations, and stockholders in publicly traded private prisons into the lobbying milieu. These groups have much to gain from a continued expansion of the number of prisoners available—that is, the prisoner "market."

Because of these differences, the politics of policy making may take on different characteristics, and the criteria by which policy should be evaluated must go beyond the usual reliance on effectiveness or efficiency to include the contributions of policy to justice, citizenship, and democratic institutions. It is one question to ask whether private involvement in prison management is more efficient on a per prisoner basis, but quite another question to ask whether the number of prisoners in society as a whole is efficient, or just, or appropriate in other ways for a democratic society.

THE RISE AND DECLINE OF
PUBLIC-PRIVATE PRISON PARTNERSHIPS

The three following basic types of partnerships have been apparent in the history of prisons in the United States: ownership of the facility in which the prisoners are kept; private use of prison labor and taking of profits from their labor; and private management of the facility, including the day-by-day supervision of prisoners.

Case studies of the emergence of prisons in the American states suggest that private involvement began through a convergence of interests among reformers, public officials, and local businesses (Shichor, 1995; Walker, 1980). Humanitarian reformers believed that prisons would be more humane than common forms of punishment in the American colonies—and later in the western frontier— which were death, branding, torture, or other physical punishment. The role of reformers was evident in the founding of the first prison in the Quaker colony of William Penn when the great law of 1682 banned the death penalty for everything except premeditated murder. This prison was a 5 feet by 7 feet cell. Later, the colony rented space from local businesses (Walker, 1980).

Public officials from the colonial period to the early 1900s believed that prisons could be self-supporting or even profitable for the state, and businesses were interested in sharing in those profits. Some states permitted a private individual or firm to build, manage, and handle the day-to-day operation of the prison itself, a system similar to the ones that have generated such intense debate in the 1980s and 1990s. Knepper (1990) reports that in 1825, Kentucky was not making enough money to support its growing prison population and was in desperate financial straits. A businessman, Joel Scott, paid the state $1,000 a year for the work of convicts in a 250-bed facility that he built and operated, with all profits kept for his own company.

In Louisiana (Walker, 1980), the state leased out the entire operation for 5 years and received $50,000 for the lease. Tennessee, in 1866, leased its Nashville prison to a furniture company for 43 cents per day per prisoner, reportedly because it was suffering from severe financial difficulties, and the number of prisoners had greatly expanded after the Civil War ended. California, in 1851, could not keep up with the increased crime attributed to the influx of settlers and was close to bankruptcy (Shichor, 1995), so the state leased its prison for 10 years to two local businessmen.

Oklahoma and Arizona not only viewed the prisons as potential profit-making entities for the state and for local businesses, but considered prisons to be an important part of the state's economic development program (Conley, 1980, 1981; Knepper, 1990). Oklahoma prisoners actually built McAlister Prison, which included an industrial factory and a 2,000-acre farm. Arizona's first territorial governor, Anson P. K. Safford, believed that a territorial prison would show that the territory was civilized and had a stable social environment sufficient to attract eastern businesses (Knepper, 1990). He was able to exploit the racial characteristics of prisoners—claiming that most of them were wild and dangerous Mexicans who preyed on travelers throughout the state, especially near the Mexican border. He also claimed that it would be the first profit-making state institution and that hard work was good for the health of prisoners (Knepper, 1990). Arizona eventually contracted with a private firm, the Arizona Canal Company, to take over the entire daytime operation of the prison. The prison provided all male convicts to the company for 10 years, for 70 cents per day, in the form of future water rights.

All of these forms of public-private partnerships eventually generated serious problems that produced opposition from business, labor, and humanitarian reformers. In some states, prisoners rioted or protested to such an extent that the partnerships were ended. For example, Tennessee ended its lease arrangement only a year after it began, apparently because the inmates burned the furniture factory. Subsequently, they built branch prisons and leased the prisoners to coal mining companies. In 1891 and 1892, free miners raided the prisons and set the prisoners free, reportedly because the competition was hurting them economically (Knepper, 1990). In Alabama, Knepper reported that opponents were worried that private leasing of prison labor would undermine the fundamental principle of restoring the prisoner's sense of obligation to a just society. They were worried that lessees would try to lengthen the sentences of good workers by giving bad reports about them.

Humanitarian reformers in Texas focused on what they viewed as excessive inmate deaths and injuries that were blamed on the private companies and the prisons they operated. California's contract system was accused of bid rigging, having a corrupt trustee system, selling of pardons, and other issues to the point that the Governor physically took control of San Quentin from the lessee—a former member of the legislature—and used the scandal for political advantage (Shichor, 1995). After a court had ruled that the takeover was illegal, the state had to buy the lease back from the private company for $275,000. In Oklahoma, businesses that did not have contracts joined with labor unions to oppose the prison industry system on the grounds of unfair competition (Conley, 1981).

New York passed legislation in 1842 that restricted the use of prison labor so much that it essentially ended public-private partnerships, and by the turn of the century, most other states had followed suit. Finally, in 1935, the social reform legislation initiated by the Roosevelt administration produced the Hawes-Cooper Act that authorized states to prohibit the entry of prison-made goods produced in other states. In 1936, the Walsh-Healy Act prohibited convict labor on government contracts that exceeded $10,000. In 1940, the Sumners-Ashurst Act made it a federal offense to transport prison-made goods across state borders, regardless of state laws. By the beginning of World War II, public-private partnerships in prisons were virtually nonexistent.

THE REEMERGENCE OF PUBLIC-PRIVATE PARTNERSHIPS: PRIVATE PRISONS

Although prison industries have enjoyed a small resurgence, the most discussed form of public-private partnership today is the one popularly called private prisons, in which a private firm operates (and usually owns) a secure adult facility for prisoners and solicits contracts with local, state, or federal governments.[3]

These relationships are different and far more complex than those in the previously discussed historical period. The 19th century experiments with private involvement almost always involved local businesses. In the 1990s, the businesses are national and international corporations—some of which are publicly traded on one or another of the major stock exchanges. Although some of the private prisons have emerged as a result of contracts with the state in which they are located, the more common situation is that a private firm builds a prison in a state and simultaneously attempts to negotiate contracts with the home state—or any other state, county, or federal entity—for prisoners. The firm is usually paid on a per diem basis, either on the number of prisoners it houses for a particular entity or on the number of places it has reserved for that jurisdiction. In the past, the business paid the state for use of its prisoners; today, the state pays the business to manage the prisoners. Some state contracts, such as Arizona's, require that the Department of Corrections place a monitor on site to make critical decisions about disciplinary matters. Most of the state contracts require that private firms offer the service at 5% to 10% below what it would have cost the state. This, of course, creates complicated cost models involving a delicate balancing act between accounting principles and political realities. In Arizona and some other states, the state law actually includes a detailed description of what is to be counted or not counted in the costs of both private and public prisons (Prison Privatization Act, 1998). Arizona legislation requires that private prisons take out large insurance policies to reimburse state agencies that may have to intervene when an escape is in process or a riot occurs.

The growth of private prisons has been dramatic, as the number of places for prisoners in private facilities has increased from 1,345 (0.5% of all prisoners) in 1985 to 106,940 (8.5% of all prisoners) by December 1997 (Thomas, Bolinger, & Badalamenti, 1998). Thomas, Bolinger, and Badalamenti's *Private Adult Correctional Facility Census*, 10th edition (1997), listed 118 facilities located in 25 different states and Washington, DC; Puerto Rico; Australia; and the United Kingdom. The Private Prison Project at the University of Florida currently shows 162 facilities with 132,346 places (Thomas, 1999). Texas has 19 private prisons, the most of any state by far, as well as having the largest prison capacity and the highest number of actual prisoners held. Most of these prisoners, however, are not from Texas. In 1997, almost 6,000 prisoners from 14 different states were "outsourced" from their home state to a private prison located elsewhere. Most of the privately managed facilities are in the South (with 74, 41% of the total); this is followed by the West (with 32, 27% of the total). There are only 5 in the midwestern states, and only 1 of these has contracts that permit it to take prisoners from the state where it is located. There are only 4 in the Northeast, and none has contracts with its home state. The 5 facilities in the Northeast take local prisoners, federal prisoners, and out-of-state prisoners.

SUBGOVERNMENT POLITICS AND
THE GROWTH OF PRIVATE PRISONS

The Corrections Corporation of America (CCA) was the first corporation to enter the private prison business and currently is the largest one. In 1998, CCA officially became Prison Realty Corporation, and it, along with 10 other private prison businesses, is traded on a major stock exchange. The emergence of CCA is well worth describing here, for it is indeed a new model of public-private partnership in the prison business and it offers a fascinating case of subgovernment policy making.

CCA was well connected with political and financial leaders in Tennessee, and it had strong ties to experts in the prison business. One of the founders of Nashville-based CCA was Tom Beasley, a former chair of the Tennessee Republican party, and another was Nashville banker and financier, Doctor R. Crants. Another CCA founder, Don Hutton, was the former head of the American

Correctional Association—the association responsible for the accreditation standards of adult prisons (Shichor, 1995). Several high-ranking political officials in Tennessee owned CCA stock, including Honey Alexander (wife of the Governor, Lamar Alexander); the state insurance commissioner, John Neff; and the Speaker of the House of Representatives, Ned McWherter. He and Mrs. Alexander both divested themselves of CCA shares to avoid conflict of interest (Shichor, 1995; American Federation of State, County, and Municipal Employees [AFSCME], 1998).

In 1985, Tennessee reportedly faced a crisis in its criminal justice system (Folz & Scheb, 1989). The state was under a court order to reduce the number of prisoners from 7,700 to 7,019 within 3 months. The previous year, they had the highest rate of inmate-on-inmate violence of any state in the union. To complicate the situation further, Tennessee faced a significant budget shortfall and a rate of 450 new prison admissions for every 250 releases.

Realizing that Tennessee faced this kind of pressure, CCA offered to pay the state $100 million for a 99-year lease to operate the entire adult correctional system. CCA reportedly offered to invest $250 million in new facilities, and to receive $170 million per year to manage the system, which was approximately the size of the current state budget for prisons. According to the case study by Folz and Scheb (1989), Republican Governor Lamar Alexander was very interested, and it appeared that bipartisan support for privatization was substantial. A public opinion poll showed that 40% of the voters favored it, with 32% disapproving. Intense lobbying, however, scuttled the CCA proposal, with the most active opposition from the Tennessee State Employees Association; Tennessee Bar Association; Tennessee Trial Layers; American Civil Liberties Union; and AFSCME (AFSCME, 1998).

A much more modest bill was adopted during the 1986 session and signed into law, permitting private management of one new medium security facility. The restrictions written into this bill, however, were so unfavorable to business that there was only one firm bid on it (CCA declined). The first state contract in Tennessee was not granted until 1992 (to CCA), during the administration of Governor Ned McWherter, who was elected governor after Alexander. This contract was immediately challenged on conflict-of-interest grounds because another firm, U.S. Corrections Corporation, reportedly had submitted a lower bid (AFSCME, 1998).

CCA also contacted Texas officials in 1984 (Ethridge, 1990). Ethridge, in his doctoral dissertation, reports that Governor Mark White, a Democrat, viewed the private prison possibility as an opportunity to direct some business to a particular group of developers, and after CCA agreed to use those developers, White reportedly assisted CCA in gaining financial support from Merrill Lynch. Criticism about his close ties to the developers was deflected, Ethridge reports, by White's claim that private prisons were part of his economic development program for the state. CCA promised, among other things, a 20% savings in the costs of prison construction and operation. The legislation was passed with bipartisan support, according to Ethridge, although it was not passed until after White had left office and was succeeded by Bill Clements.

The policy-making context in Texas also was described as one of crisis and failed criminal justice policy (Ethridge, 1990). The total admissions to prison in Texas were twice the number of releases (Ethridge), the state had been found in contempt of court for not having obeyed previous orders to reduce overcrowding, Governor Clements reportedly faced a $231 million budget deficit for fiscal year 1986, and the estimates were that $400 million was needed to build enough prisons to meet the court mandate. The only person to speak against the legislation was the legislative coordinator for the Texas State Employee Union (Ethridge), who said that it was morally wrong and involved a fundamental conflict of interest because profit motives were not consistent with the best interests of prisons and the public. He was quoted as follows:

> Because prison contracts are structured on a per diem basis, the interests of the corporation will be to increase occupancy rates, to increase profits. . . . There is also a conflict of interest because corporate correctional officers will seek to maintain an ever increasing incarceration population and will lobby for tougher prison sentencing policies. (Ethridge, p. 82)

In 1987, Texas took the additional step of passing legislation that permitted local governments to contract for private facilities without having a vote of the people, which ordinarily would be required for any capital project. This may have contributed to the fact that Texas now has more private facilities (19) than any other state.

Privatization has also sparked old-fashioned partisan politics in some states. Arizona's Republican-controlled legislature passed legislation authorizing private prisons in 1985 and again in 1986, but both bills were vetoed by Democratic Governor Bruce Babbitt. Another bill was passed in 1987 and signed by Republic Governor, Evan Mecham, but Arizona's public employee union filed suit against the legislation on constitutional grounds and won. Republican-controlled legislatures again passed privatization legislation in 1988 that was vetoed by Democratic Governor, Rose Mofford, who had taken over as Governor after the impeachment of Evan Mecham. Privatization legislation finally succeeded in 1990, when it was approved mainly along party lines in the legislature and signed into law by Republican Governor Fife Symington. The partisan nature of private involvement in prisons is also documented by Gallagher and Edwards (1997), who found that states with Democratic governors and strong labor unions were more resistant to private prison industries.

The private prison subgovernment not only includes business leaders, state-elected officials, political party elites, and correctional experts, but also two influential social science researchers as well. The initial studies by both Logan and Thomas indicated that privatization had reduced the costs of prisons (Logan, 1990, 1996; Logan & McGriff, 1989; Thomas, 1997). Thomas is a member of

CCA's Prison Realty Corporation's board of directors, and his center at the University of Florida had been partially funded by the corporation (Thomas, 1999). Academics on the whole have been very cautious about the privatization of prisons, if not opposed to it (McDonald, 1990; Shichor, 1995; Sparks, 1994); thus, the emergence of research by well-respected academics that shows private prisons to be less expensive or higher quality has been important in legitimizing the arguments presented by businesses and policy makers.

THE RHETORIC, CLAIMS, AND
SCRIPT OF PRIVATE PRISONS

The most common script offered as an explanation for the growth of private prisons is that increasing crime rates, along with mandatory sentences and longer terms, have produced a rapid increase in prisoners. The increase in prisoners produced extensive overcrowding in secure adult facilities during the 1980s—a time when almost all states were faced with serious financial problems and budget deficits. These factors created a crisis in criminal justice policy, and public officials turned to the private sector to reduce the costs of prison operation.

As plausible as this scenario seems, it is simply inaccurate in some respects. There has been a virtual explosion in the number of persons sentenced to secure state and federal facilities, but it is very difficult to sustain an argument that the increase in prisoners has been the logical result of people committing more crimes than in the past. Data on the rate of imprisonment from 1925 to 1973 show that there was virtually no change in the rate of imprisonment, with the rate hovering around 100 prisoners per 100,000 people (Schneider, 1998). From 1973 to 1997, however, the rate increased to an all time high of 446 prisoners per 100,000 people (Bureau of Justice Statistics, 1998; Maguire & Pastore, 1994, 1996). If this were produced by an increase in crime, then one would expect the rate of crime commission to have increased in a similar way, but, except for drug crimes, this is not the case. In fact, victimization survey data on commission of violent crimes has been going down, not up, since 1973 when the first victimization survey was conducted (Maguire & Pastore, 1994). The uniform crime data on murder, which is the most serious and the most precise in terms of definition— shows an up-and-down pattern, certainly not a steady upward trend that could in any way account for the increase in prisoners (Bureau of Justice Statistics, 1998; Maguire & Pastore, 1995).

The increase in prisoners is accounted for by public policy changes, not changes in the propensity of people to inflict harm on others. The policy changes that produced the increase in incarceration and the overcrowding that results include longer sentences, mandatory sentences, three strikes you're out, no parole, no early release, and the huge increase in penalties for drug offenses. The point here is that turning to the private sector to build more prisons or to manage prisons so that the savings can be used to offset deficits, reduce overcrowding, or permit even more growth in incarceration is a policy choice made by elected public officials. There were other choices that could have been made. By the end of 1996, only 18 states had authorized contracts for private prisons within their state, and 32 had not. It must be emphasized that most states cannot prevent a private business from building a prison in the state and contracting with the federal government or with other states to take their prisoners. Unless a state passes legislation prohibiting the prison business, it is subject to finding one of these within its borders at some point in the future.

The policy choices available to states that are alternatives to privatization include reducing the scope of incarcerative sanctions, increasing the number of community-based alternatives, reducing the length of sentences, increasing the number of early release programs, or investing in prevention programs such as early childhood parenting and education.

The second part of the script is that the increase in prisoners produced overcrowding (which is supported by the evidence), and that overcrowding, combined with tight budgets, led public officials to turn to the private sector to build or manage prisons with the promise of a 5% to 20% savings. This savings, presumably, would permit the state to reduce its overcrowding. To examine this claim, I conducted an analysis in which the number of private prison contracts in the state is regressed on the three following possible explanatory variables: the extent of budget health from 1980 to 1986 (as measured by the difference between revenue one year and expenditures the next year, divided by expenditures; see Berry & Berry, 1992), the extent of overcrowding in the state and local prison systems, and the rate of incarceration (Schneider, 1998). The first two variables reflect the expectation that privatization was produced by the combination of an overcrowded prison system and the budget shortfalls characteristic of the 1980 to 1986 period. The third variable, rate of incarceration per 100,000, is a commonly used indicator for the punitiveness of the criminal justice system in the state.

The results show that budget health is statistically significant, but in the opposite direction of the prediction (beta = .36, $t = 2.64$, significance = .012). That is, states with larger budget shortfalls were less likely to turn to the private sector. Overcrowding had no significant relationship (beta = $-.089$, $t = -.66$). On the other hand, states with higher rates of incarceration were more likely to have private prison contracts (beta = .32, $t = 2.4$, significance = .02). The conclusion I draw is that increased privatization was driven by the same kinds of value orientations that produce more punitive criminal justice systems—a generalized sort of conservative, antigovernment, law and order ideology.

The purpose of this paper is not to offer a complete predictive model of the growth of private prisons, but only to examine the efficacy of the rationales that have been offered. Increases in the number of prisoners, overcrowding, and tight budgets were not causal factors that forced states to turn to private prison management. Instead, these trends required the states to confront the punitiveness of the criminal justice policies that had been produced in the decades after the 1960s. These trends established a context within which privatization could be promoted as a solution to a problem. In Kingdon's (1984) terms, it opened a window of opportunity in which a solution (privatization) found the problem that it could help solve.

In Schneider and Ingram's (1993, 1997) framework, privatization gave policy makers the opportunity to gain political capital through the appearance of doing something about the failed criminal justice system and simultaneously open up market opportunities for private business. It offered the attractive political opportunity to continue the negative social construction of prisoners and, at the same time, to develop a new positively constructed constituency of businesses, corporations, and stockholders who could profit from prisons. Support for private prisons also permitted officials to take advantage of the positive valance associated with downsizing government through privatization.

Policy makers in some states turned to privatization, others did not—at least not yet. The rationales used in states that adopted privatization could have been used with just as much credibility, if not more credibility, in states that resisted the privatization movement.

ISSUES, COSTS, AND QUALITY
OF PUBLIC-PRIVATE PARTNERSHIPS

The media coverage of private prisons has tended toward the dramatic, and it is usually unfavorable. More than one state has had the experience of a riot or escape from a private prison within its borders that houses persons who are from other states entirely. Local police and state highway patrol are expected to help quell the riot or find the escapees—at public expense. Ohio discovered that a private prison within its borders was taking prisoners classified as maximum security when they thought that the prison had agreed to only take minimum and medium security prisoners. However, these kinds of problems—riots, escapes, inmate-on-inmate violence—also occur in publicly managed prisons, and there have been far too few studies making reliable comparisons to draw the conclusion that private prisons are more subject to these sorts of problems than public prisons.

Most of the empirical research on private prisons emphasizes cost differences. Although fraught with methodological problems, the current studies are summarized in Table 1. For the most part, these studies show a slight advantage to the private prisons and illustrate (in Texas, at least) that a state may realize a reduction in per inmate cost, over time. It is interesting to note, however, that comparative data are available for only a handful of the private prisons. Following are some of the many methodological issues:

TABLE 1: Summary of Cost Studies

| State | Cost per Inmate per Day | | Year (data) | Comment |
	Private	Public		
Texas	$36.76	$42.70 to $43.13	1990	Study conducted by the Texas Sunset Advisory Commission compared four private prerelease minimum security prisons for males with hypothetical operation by the state (operational costs only)
	$33.95 to $33.61	$39.79 to $38.64	1995 to 1996	Texas Criminal Justice Policy Council report to the legislature in January 1997, for prisoners in the Texas Institutional Division (reported in Thomas, 1998)
	$27.91	$28.96	1996	Texas Criminal Justice Policy Council report to the legislature in January 1997, for prisoners in the Texas Jail Division (reported in Thomas, 1998)
California	$42.67	$36.15 to $45.55	1991 to 1992	Sechrest and Shichor (1993) compared three for-profit community correctional facilities, one operated by a private business, one by a local government, and one by a police department, both of the latter on a for-profit basis under contract from the state
Tennessee	$73.50	$77.50	1985 to 1988	Logan and McGriff (1989) compared two privately operated 350-bed facilities in Hamilton County, Tennessee (these cost figures assume full occupancy)
	$35.39	$34.90 to $35.45	1993 to 1994	Tennessee Select Oversight Committee on Corrections, 1995, studied one private, minimum-maximum security facility for men with two similar public facilities (U.S. GAO report considers this study to have the best methodology)
Washington (Tennessee data)	$33.61	$35.82 to $35.28	1993 to 1994	Washington's Department of Corrections Privatization Feasibility Study (Legislative Budget Committee for the State of Washington, 1996) used the same data from the Tennessee study of 1993 to 1994, but adjusted it as if the facilities were at full capacity
(Louisiana data)	$23.75 to $23.34	$23.55	1995 to 1996	Washington's Department of Corrections Privatization Feasibility Study (Legislative Budget Committee for the State of Washington, 1996) compared two private and one public mixed-custody facilities in Louisiana
Louisiana				Archambeault and Deis (1996; quoted in Thomas, 1998) compared three large medium-maximum security prisons in Louisiana over 5 fiscal years, 1992 to 1996, and found cost savings of 11.7% for the 5-year totals
Arizona	$35.90 to $44.37	$43.08	1995 to 1996	Thomas's (1997) study of Arizona's costs produced an estimate of $44.37 for a private, 450-bed dual gender minimum security prison (Marana) when taking into account the state officials located at the site, but arrived at an adjusted cost of $35.90 after amortizing the costs of constructions, not including the taxes paid by the facility and other adjustments

- How should indirect costs be allocated in the public and private facilities?
- Should the cost of the private and public facilities be based on the actual average daily population or on the number of places the facility is built to hold? What should be done if it is more than 100% full?
- Should the state costs associated specifically with privatization (e.g., having monitors on site) be counted as part of the cost of the private prison?
- Should in kind services provided by one public agency to another be added to the cost of the public prison (e.g., health or mental health programs)?
- Should services provided by the public sector to the private prison, such as capturing escapees or prosecuting inmates for violent acts on one another, be added to the private prison's costs?
- Should the taxes paid by private prisons be adjusted out, as Thomas (1997) has done in his cost studies, on the grounds that these are returned to the state?

In addition, the studies virtually never explain how or why the private prison manages to have lower costs even though they have the added responsibility of making a profit. There is a general perception that the reduced costs are at the expense of employee salaries. The methodologies also suffer because the comparisons, due to necessity, are of only one or two institutions and usually cover only 1 year of data. The natural variability in annual expenditures for any particular prison may be rather high from one year to the next, and differences as simple as the average age (experience) of employees may account for sizable cost differences between institutions.

Quality comparisons are even less common than cost analyses, although there have been some researchers who have made concerted efforts to develop a methodology with solid theoretical underpinnings for quality studies. Logan (1996) compared a New Mexico women's prison, operated under private contract with the prison that had previously housed New Mexico's women inmates, with a federal women's prison in West Virginia. He examined eight dimensions of service (security, safety, order, care, activity, justice, conditions, and management), each with six or eight separate indicators. The data included staff and inmate surveys as well as institutional records. He concluded that the private prison, overall, had a higher level of service quality, even though there were some interesting differences between staff and inmate assessments (with staff preferring the private prison and inmates preferring the public one).

Thomas' (1997) study of Arizona included several qualitative comparisons, but the fact that the private facility (Marana) housed a mixed gender population made comparisons risky. On most of the indicators, there were no differences, mainly because the time periods were so short that some of the more serious kinds of incidents (riots, inmate-on-inmate assaults or murders, staff abuse of prisoners) were not reported from any facility. The privately operated facility (Marana) had fewer jobs assigned per inmate than the medium security (level 2) public prisons (52 compared with 83), and was given lower ratings by the state's annual audits on most of the indicators. The private prison had an overall *good* rating, whereas all of the public facilities received an overall *excellent* rating. It is impossible to know whether these audit data reflect real differences in performance or system bias against private prisons.

Lanza-Kaduce, Parker, and Thomas (1999) conducted a comparative recidivism analysis for the Florida state legislature in which they compared the 12-month recidivism records of persons released from two privately operated facilities and those released from public facilities. The research design involved a sample matched-on-offense category (using 53 specific categories), race, number of prior incarcerations, and age. Multiple measures of recidivism were used, including rearrest, reconviction, and resentencing to incarceration as well as an overall indicator of any recidivism. There was a sample size of 198 in each group. With fewer rearrests (96 compared to 192), fewer reincarcerations (101 to 146), and fewer incidents of any form (172 to 237), the results clearly gave the edge to private facilities. There were similar differences in the severity of the recidivism offense. Finally, the study compared persons in the private facility who had completed their assigned programs and those who had not. The lower recidivism rates in the private prison, compared to the public prison, were due almost entirely to the fact that the private facility had more persons who completed their assigned rehabilitative programs. The noncompleters had recidivism rates almost identical to the persons from the public facilities—giving some powerful indication that successful completion of in-prison programs predicts the reduction of subsequent criminal activity.

A study of several Louisiana prisons (Archambeault & Deis, 1996) included a number of qualitative dimensions. The state-operated facilities were found to have higher quality in terms of preventing escapes, preventing sexual offenses, using urine testing, and having a wide scope of educational and job-related programs. The private facilities were found to have fewer critical incidents, a safer work environment for employees and prisoners, more effective discipline, and better access to programs for prisoners.

The design and methodologies of these studies indicate that on a localized, institutional basis, private prisons appear not to damage or harm the criminal justice system capacity of the state, and it may reduce costs without reducing service, or it may even improve service.

Another empirical question that needs analysis is whether public-private partnerships accentuate the pressure for an ever-increasing supply of prisoners, leading to longer sentences and more intrusive criminal justice practices. It would be naive to believe that private prison corporations are not involved in lobbying, and it would be equally naive to expect that they are only interested in capturing a larger market share from the public-sector prisons. In fact, possible conflicts between the two can be avoided if both work to ensure that there is a ready supply of prisoners to be housed. Prison as the punishment of choice has always been politically attractive, but it is limited due to its long-term cost. Even though the public may be easily swayed by the law and order rhetoric into believing that long prison terms are deserved by those who break the law, the public, nevertheless, does not like to spend money on people they perceive as undeserving, such as prisoners and would prefer to allocate those funds to education or other target populations. Hence, public-private partnerships that permit a large role for the private sector have the potential effect of bringing about a coalition between public and private providers of prisons with both advocating for increasing the scope of duration of prison sentences. Second, private management appears to cost less and therefore can be promoted by elected officials as a way of reducing the costs of the criminal justice system, even though the number of persons imprisoned stays the same or even increases.

The results of a regression analysis (see Schneider, 1998) indicate weak supports for these contentions, although the newness of private prisons and the complexities of the policy-making process are such that caution is in order. The results show that states with more contracts to private prison companies within their jurisdiction in 1996 had higher rates of incarceration per 100,000 in 1997 than states with fewer contracts (beta = .50, t = 3.85, significance = .000), even when budget health was controlled. This conclusion should be taken with caution, however, because the proportion of all prisoners who could be held in private facilities currently under contract or being built is still only about 8%. Furthermore, the time lag in the causal analysis is complicated. Decisions by a state to permit private prisons occur through several legislative sessions and may not result in any private prison contracts for several years after the authorization. The incarceration rate is the product of policy decisions over a long period of time, not simply during 1 year. It is possible that the rate of incarceration and the use of private contracts are both the product of an underlying conservative ideology, but it is also possible that political dynamics are being altered by the presence of private prisons in the state in such a way that the state can continue to increase the proportion of its population it is able and willing to place behind bars.

CONCLUSIONS AND IMPLICATIONS

Public-private partnerships in prison operation is different from most other policy arenas because prisons deliver punishment, and there is no way to turn this into a technical administrative exercise devoid of discretion. When private owners or managers run a prison, they hire the guards and staff, and set the tone for how the prisoners are treated. There is enormous discretion exercised by the caseworkers who are in direct contact with prisoners. There are important differences between delivering service, benefits, treatment, or regulations to a target population and delivering confinement, orders, rules, discipline, and physical pain to a captive population that has no choice and no say in how they are treated.

In terms of the future of public-private partnerships in prisons, I believe this is a policy arena in which we would expect to find pendulum effects similar to those observed during historical experiments with private involvement. Extensive private involvement will give way to public delivery mechanisms that, in turn, will yield to private ones at some future time. A pendulum pattern in public and private delivery systems is expected because prisons are institutions that cannot be managed as effectively as expected by the media, political elites, or general public regardless of whether they are entirely under government control or whether they involve extensive privatization. Perhaps prisons will never be effective enough in producing public safety because public safety is more contingent on societal factors such as families, communities, schools, nonprofits, economic opportunities, and the absence of race and class discrimination. Institutions that cannot produce the level of performance expected and desired by the media, political leaders, and the public will move from the public sector toward partnerships with extensive private involvement, and then back toward the public sector, as the private gives up on them.

NOTES

1. First, policy design theory emphasizes the substance of policy. What is being delivered to whom using what kinds of tools (incentives), with what rules, through which implementation structures, with what goals in mind (both symbolic and instrumental), with what rationales, and with what kinds of underlying assumptions. Second, policy design theory recognizes that policies emerge from a complex context involving the dynamic interplay between political power, social constructions (of events, people, facts), and the rationales that are used to justify various policy choices. Third, our theory of policy design posits the following four evaluative criteria for public policy: efficient problem solving, justice, citizenship, and democratic institutions. Policy design theory is intended to integrate interpretive (constructivist) perspectives with explanatory (positive) perspectives. Because this paper is intended mainly to analyze a particular kind of public-private partnership, the approach will reflect the theoretical underpinnings but not emphasize theory.

2. Political capital refers to the ability of elected officials to manipulate a policy arena to enhance their potential for reelection or election to higher office.

3. For a discussion of the reemergence of prison industries, see the lengthier version of this paper, Schneider, 1998.

REFERENCES

American Federation of State, County, and Municipal Employees (1998). *Corrections corporation of America. Public employee, January, February* [On-line]. Available: http://www.afscme.org/afscme/press/pejf9809.html.

Archambeault, W. G., & Deis, D. R., Jr. (1996). *Private versus public prisons in Louisiana. Report to the National Institute of Justice* [On-line]. Available: http://www.uss.uconn.edu/~wwwsoci.

Berry, F. S., & Berry, W. D. (1992). Tax innovation in the states: Capitalizing on political opportunity. *American Journal of Political Science, 36*, 715-742.

Bureau of Justice Statistics. (1998). *Prisoners and prison capacity* [On-line]. Available: http://www.ojp.usdog.gov/bjs/pub.

Conley, J. A. (1980). Revising conceptions about the origin of prisons: The importance of economic considerations. *Social Science Quarterly, 62*, 249-257.

Conley, J. A. (1981). Prisons, production and profit: Reconsidering the importance of prison industries. *Journal of Social History, 53*, 259-275.

Ethridge, P. A. (1990). *An analysis of the policy process pertaining to the utilization of private prisons in Texas.* Unpublished doctoral dissertation, Sam Houston State University.

Folz, D. H., & Scheb, J. M. (1989). Prisons, profits, and politics: The Tennessee privatization. *Judicature, 73,* 98.

Gallagher, D., & Edwards, M. E. (1997). Prison industries and the private sector. *Atlantic Economic Journal, 25,* 91-98.

General Accounting Office (1997). *Private and public prisons: Studies comparing operational and/or quality of service* (U.S. GAO Letter Rep. GGD-96-158) [On-line]. Available: http://www.securitymanagement.com:80/library /000231.html.

Kingdon, J. (1984). *Agendas, alternatives and public policies.* Boston: Little, Brown.

Knepper, P. E. (1990). *Imprisonment and society in Arizona territory.* Unpublished doctoral dissertation, School of Justice Studies, Arizona State University.

Lanza-Kaduce, L., Parker, K. F., & Thomas, C. W. (1999). A comparative recidivism analysis of releases from private and public prisons. *Crime & Delinquency, 45,* 28-47.

Legislative Budget Committee for the State of Washington. (1996). *Department of Corrections privatization feasibility study.* Olympia, WA: Legislative Budget Committee.

Logan, C. H. (1990). *Private prisons: Pros and cons.* New York: Oxford University Press.

Logan, C. H. (1996). Well kept: Comparing quality of confinement in a public and a private prison. *National Institute of Justice Report* [On-line]. Available: http://www.uc.uconn.edu/~wwwsoci.

Logan, C. H., & McGriff, B. (1989, September/October). *Comparing costs of public and private prisons. A case study* (National Institute of Justice Research in Brief Rep. No. 216). Washington, DC: National Institute of Justice.

Maguire, K., & Pastore, A. L. (Eds.). (1994). *Sourcebook of criminal justice statistics.* Washington, DC: Bureau of Justice Statistics.

Maguire, K., & Pastore, A. L. (Eds.). (1996). *Sourcebook of criminal justice statistics.* Washington, DC: Bureau of Justice Statistics.

McDonald, D. C. (1990). The cost of operating public and private correctional facilities. In D. C. McDonald (Ed.), *Private prisons and the public interest* (pp. 86-106). New Brunswick, NJ: Rutgers University Press.

Prison Privatization Act, 128 Ariz. Rev. Stat. §§ 41-1609, 1681-1684, 1803. (1997).

Schneider, A. (1998, September). *Private prisons as public policy.* Paper presented at the American Political Science Association Annual Conference, Boston.

Schneider, A., & Ingram, H. (1993). Social constructions and target populations: Implications for politics and policy. *American Political Science Review, 87,* 334-347.

Schneider, A., & Ingram, H. (1997). *Policy design for democracy.* Lawrence: University Press of Kansas.

Sechrest, D., & Shichor, D. (1993). Corrections goes public (and private) in California. *Federal Probation, 57,* 3-8.

Shichor, D. (1995). *Punishment for profit: Private prisons/public concerns.* Thousand Oaks: Sage.

Sparks, R. (1994). Can prisons be legitimate? Penal politics, privatization, and the timeliness of an old idea. *British Journal of Criminology, 34,* 14-28.

Tennessee Select Oversight Committee on Corrections. (1995). *Comparative evaluation of privately-managed CCA prison and state-managed prototypical prisons.* Nashville: Tennessee Legislature.

Texas Sunset Advisory Commission. (1991). Information report on contracts for correctional facilities and services. In *Recommendations to the Governor of Texas and members of the seventy-second legislature* (chap. 4). Austin, TX: Author.

Thomas, C. W. (1997). *Comparing the cost and performance of public and private prisons in Arizona.* Phoenix, AZ: Arizona Department of Corrections.

Thomas, C. W. (1998). *Evaluating the potential public policy implication of correctional privatization by the state of Iowa.* Miami: University of Florida.

Thomas, C. W. (1999). *Private prison project* [On-line]. Available: http://web.crim.ufl.edu/pcp/census/.

Thomas, C. W., Bolinger, D., & Badalamenti, J. L. (1997). Private adult correctional facility census (11th ed.). *Private Corrections Project* [On-line]. Available: http://web.crim.ufl.edu/pcp/census/1997.

Thomas, C. W., Bolinger, D., & Badalamenti, J. L. (1998). Private adult correctional facility census (11th ed.). *Private Corrections Project* [On-line]. Available: http://web.crim.ufl.edu/pcp/census/1998.

Walker, S. (1980). *Popular justice: A history of American criminal justice.* New York: Oxford University Press.

13

The Strengths and Weaknesses of Public-Private Policy Partnerships

PAULINE VAILLANCOURT ROSENAU

> The public's attitude here is strikingly pragmatic and nonideological. Do whatever works.
>
> —Yankelovich, D. (1994)

Partnering for policy purposes by government, commercial enterprises, and not-for-profit private organizations in the public and private sectors raises the question of how to evaluate such collaboration. The results of just such an undertaking could help define the appropriate policy role for the private sector and the public sector, suggesting when each should have principal responsibility, where the two can work together, and the extent to which they can share responsibility. Not much is known about the success and failure of public-private policy partnerships. This may be because of a general resistance to conduct systematic policy evaluation (Rom, 1999 [this issue]; Stiglitz & Wallsten, 1999 [this issue]). Politics and discourse seem to drive the process. This article is an attempt to

Author's Note: *The author is indebted to Jessica Neal, research assistant, for her help throughout this project. Her competence, reliability, and attention to every detail made all the difference.*

reach conclusions about the successes and failures of public-private policy partnerships.

There is a certain consensus in the policy literature to the effect that government does some things best, the private sector other things, and the not-for-profit still different things (Ghere, 1996). In theory, public-private policy partnerships could combine the best of each, but do they do that in reality?

The public sector draws attention to public interest, stewardship, and solidarity considerations. It is better at openness to public scrutiny, employment concerns, "policy management, regulation, ensuring equity, preventing discrimination or exploitation, ensuring continuity and stability of services, and ensuring social cohesion (through the mixing of races and classes for example, in the public schools)" (Osborne & Gaebler, 1992, pp. 24-25). The public sector is oriented toward social responsibility and environmental awareness (United Nations Development Programme, 1998). It has local knowledge and experience with difficult-to-serve populations.

The private sector is thought to be creative and dynamic, bringing "access to finance, knowledge of technologies, managerial efficiency, and entrepreneurial spirit" (United Nations Development Programme, 1998). It is better at performing economic tasks, innovating and replicating successful experiments, adapting to rapid change,[1] abandoning unsuccessful or obsolete activities, and performing complex or technical tasks.

The not-for-profit organization (or "third sector") is strong in areas that require "compassion and commitment to individuals." They do well where customers or clients "require extensive trust," or "need hands-on personal attention (such as day care, counseling, and services to the handicapped or ill)." This sector excels when commerce involves "moral codes and individual responsibility for behavior" (Osborne & Gaebler, 1992).

Too much can be made of these differences because both the public and the private sectors have overlapping traditions. Competitive, competent, and efficient public service is crucial to society and central to policy ethics.[2] These values are inherent in the tradition of the neutral civil service. In addition, an accountable private sector is the goal of the emerging field of managerial or business ethics (Showstack, Lurie, Leatherman, Fisher, & Inui, 1996). In practice, partnering is not so straightforward because policy ethics and managerial ethics imply obligations that are not entirely the same.[3]

In examining the results of public-private policy partnerships as outlined in the various policy sectors discussed in this issue, I consider several criteria. I examine how these policy-partnering experiments and experiences measure up on cost and quality performance, equity, access, citizen participation, and democracy in the policy process. Next, I ask whether they increase or decrease government regulation. I also consider the implications of public-private policy partnerships for accountability. I discuss the important challenges to public-private policy partnerships—conflicts of interest, cost shifting from one partner to another, and managing risk and uncertainty. I examine the context and environment of successful public-private partnering and try to learn from a broad range of experiences in a variety of policy sectors.

Partnerships offer the promise of greatest success when the strengths of more than one player are required. The need to balance between public and private (not-for-profit and for-profit), especially when policy is involved, is widely appreciated by those committed to a larger role for the private sector and those committed to a larger role for the public sector. It may well be that there are "things that government can do better than private business, or even that only government can do" ("A Survey of Social Insurance," 1998, p. 4). Partnering holds the promise of a possible compromise in the form of constructive collaboration.

It makes little sense to invent new forms of policy delivery for their own sake rather than because they improve performance in some way. When the government fulfills a public policy function better, in terms of lower cost and improved quality, why partner? When the private sector yields better quality at lower costs without untoward externalities, this should be the preferred organizational form. There is no reason to expect in advance, in the absence of evidence, that the private sector, the public sector, or public-private policy partnerships will be superior. In addition, the performance of all of them may vary from sector to sector.

Partnering takes several forms and Linder (1999 [this issue]) discusses these in this issue. Public-private policy partnerships have in common a shared responsibility for policy that impacts citizens. Authentic partnering, in theory, involves close collaboration and the combination of the strengths of both the private sector (more competitive and efficient) and the public sector (responsibility and accountability vis-à-vis society).

In the real world, public-private policy partnerships may involve little close cooperation, and may even border on pure privatization. Other extreme, minimalist partnerships are loosely organized and closely contractual. The public and private partners may even compete with each other. They are partners only in the sense that they collectively provide an essential service. For example, in the health sector, as Sparer (1999 [this issue]) points out, the partnership consists largely of the government paying for the part of the market in which profits are unlikely (poor, elderly, etc.) and monitoring the performance of the private partner in the rest of the market.

Anticipating success or failure in advance of implementing public-private policy partnerships, although desirable, is extremely difficult, and monitoring partnerships for impact and performance is critical. This is part of the learning process, essential to successful policy. Based on evidence and reports presented in this issue and from the broader policy literature, some generalizations appear to be in sight.

COST REDUCTION AND
IMPROVED PERFORMANCE (COST AND QUALITY)

From this review of public-private policy partnerships, I concluded that evidence about cost efficiency is mixed in the policy literature. If cost and efficiency are defined narrowly and externalities (including long-term, nearly unanticipatable consequences) are discounted, then partnering will not increase policy costs. In some cases, it may decrease costs or improve some aspects of performance slightly. This is true when partnering is very loose, and the private and public partners do not work closely together. The most optimistic estimate suggests savings between 30% and 50% when private partners deliver public services (see Zachary, 1996, for a summary of Mercer group study). Kamieniecki, Shafie, and Silvers (1999 [this issue]) found that cost efficiency is probable in an environmental program. Schneider (1999 [this issue]) concludes that, overall, private prisons do cost slightly less than public sector prisons do, and they may even improve service, and reduce recidivism.[4] Levin (1999 [this issue]) suggests that in education, private schools within a voucher system are probably more cost effective than public schools in producing student achievement (until the infrastructure costs of a voucher system are considered; Levin, 1998). He also indicates that there is little evidence that private schools are less costly than public schools for similar students and services (Levin, 1998). Rom (1999) reports equally complex results regarding private provider performance in the welfare sector. Most of the time, externalities offset observed cost advantages (Levin, 1999; Schneider, 1999).

In some cases, efficiency may be achieved by setting aside possible gains in other evaluative criteria such as quality, equity, democracy, accountability, and so forth. For example, Stiglitz and Wallsten (1999) suggest that to achieve optimal results from research and development partnering projects, the best proposals, defined as the ones with commercialization potential, should not be funded; instead, the best among those unlikely to be funded by the private sector should be funded. Research and development partnerships should give priority to projects that "would benefit society but would not be privately profitable without a subsidy."

Sometimes, cost efficiencies vary across the population served. For example, partnering has increased the cost of electricity to small consumers, but at the same time, it has decreased the cost for large consumers (Carlisle, 1998).[5] Large power suppliers see immediate benefits but small businesses suffer (Selz, 1996). Is there reason, in instances such as this, to continue partnering when experience indicates mixed results?

In some policy sectors, the intellectual power and philosophical attraction of partnering is such that even when, on balance, evidence suggests that the private partner's services cost more, they are still purchased. States turn to private health providers (Ku & Hoag, 1998) and the federal government looks to private

HMOs to save money for the Medicare program, but private Medicare costs the government more (Bodenheimer et al., 1999)! Private sector HMOs have made considerable profit in this Medicare market because they enroll a healthier-than-average beneficiary (Morgan, Virnig, DeVito, & Persily, 1997; Riley, Tudor, Chiang, & Ingber, 1996). Monitoring, assessment, and transaction costs also increase the price of public-private policy partnerships to society.

Externalities are important, but they are seldom seriously considered when assessing cost performance. This is because they are so difficult to anticipate, to quantify, and to enter into any cost-benefit analysis of partnering. Sometimes they are simply overlooked. For example, policy-partnering savings may result in lower wages to workers, reduced job security, skimpier benefits, having no pension plan, paying less attention to safety gear, the absence of union representation, the lack of health insurance at reasonable rates, the lack of dependent health insurance coverage, and so forth (Smith & Lipsky, 1992). In the long run, such savings could mean that more such workers without benefits will make claims on government health and welfare benefits. The increased overall costs could be significant. In addition, without health insurance coverage and pensions, taxpayers could end up paying for more services for the poor in the long term. Moreover, the national tax base is undermined, and this adds to the burden of government services, directly and indirectly. Societal social mobility could also be reduced (Zachary, 1996). In another example, Arizona now requires a full-time employee of the state's Department of Corrections to be on-site to monitor private prison disciplinary decisions (Schneider, 1999). This adds to the cost of private prisons but could easily be overlooked in cost accounting.

EQUITY, ACCESS, AND DEMOCRACY

In a democracy, all citizens need to be treated fairly with regards to policy. This is central to our value system (Yankelovich, 1994). How serious are the problems of equity when public-private policy partnerships are created (Graham, 1998)? The case that partnerships increase equity through choice and competition can certainly be made in a convincing fashion (Osborne & Gaebler, 1992). The private sector offers choices in the sense that it is meeting demands for nonstandardized services and providing choices between different kinds of services, "between schools, between training programs, between housing options" (Osborne & Gaebler, 1992, pp. 20, 183). However, the opposite view is equally convincing (Graham, 1994; Graham, 1998). For example, the social goal of access to health insurance may be sacrificed when universal programs, such as Medicare, are restructured to increase choice through competition. One of the unintended effects is the increased cost of services to the sickest and the poorest who need health insurance the most but are the least able to pay for it (Neuman & Langwell, 1999).

Equity considerations are an issue for public-private policy partnerships, although it is not a problem unique to them.[6] Equity of treatment and fair access to services are never certain—abuse is possible from both public and private providers. "You don't have a choice in applying for a welfare check. Because you don't have a choice, you can be mistreated" whether it is the government or a private partner who is responsible (quote from Joseph E. Stiglitz, as cited in Wessel & Harwood, 1998, p. A10). This is certainly the case for prison populations (Schneider, 1999) and welfare recipients (Rom, 1999).

At the same time, many people expect better performance on equity and more democratic considerations from the public sector than from the private sector, attributing to the government a special mission in this respect. As Mintzberg (1996) puts it in the following:

> I am not a mere customer of my government, thank you. I expect something more than arm's length trading and something less than the encouragement to consume. . . . I am a citizen, with rights that go far beyond those of customers or even clients. (p. 77)

He is not alone in questioning the value of partnering for policy matters in which equity considerations have a significant impact. "Private citizens should not have life or death power over other private citizens when you're talking about basic necessities" (quote from Barney Frank, as cited in Wessel & Harwood, 1998, p. A10). The appropriateness of public-private policy partnerships as providers of essential services needs to be studied across a broad range of sectors (Felsenthal, 1997; Jaffe & Brooks, 1998).

Performance of public-private policy partnerships on equity is mixed. In concrete terms, Kamieniecki et al. (1999) observed real problems. Similarly, in educational partnerings with the private sector, mechanisms such as vouchers, which are supposed to increase equity, may fail to meet their goal. "Most analyses of educational vouchers suggest that they would increase inequities" (Levin, 1999 [this issue], p. 135). When schools are made to compete for students under a voucher system and private schools are allowed to charge whatever they wish, they may charge enough to effectively eliminate poor families from sending their children to private schools (Starr, 1990).

Examined together, the articles in this issue raise the question as to whether or not equity concerns are less of a problem when partnerships involve public/not-for-profit private providers (Lovrich) than with public/for-profit private providers (Kamieniecki et al.). However, Rom suggests that solutions to equity considerations become very difficult when, for example, religiously affiliated groups (not-for-profit private providers) provide welfare services, including Temporary Assistance for Needy Families, Medicaid, Supplemental Income, and Food Stamps (see Yates, 1998). Some of these groups are only interested in providing service to their own groups (Rom).

There are other limitations regarding public/not-for-profit private partnerships related to equity and access. These types of partnerships require substantial amounts of social capital. It is easier to increase social capital where it already exists than where it is minimal to begin with. Those in highly disadvantaged circumstances do not have the same levels of social capital in their communities. This means that partnerships are not even possible in places where the not-for-profit private sector is poorly organized or where the social capital is insufficient. The demand for this type of partnership is high, so high that it threatens a depletion of social capital resources, especially where it is already a preciously scarce resource (see Lovrich, 1999 [this issue]).

VULNERABLE POPULATIONS

The difficulties of vulnerable populations with regard to access and equity in the marketplace (Aday, 1993) are not ameliorated when services are delivered by public-private policy partnerships (see Kamieniecki et al., 1999; Levin, 1999; Sparer, 1999). This is a case where societal values regarding policy may take precedent over a strict cost calculation. It is assumed that these sectors of the population deserve special, even preferential, treatment. There seems to be a national consensus involving broad, communal values to the effect that "the poor and the victimized" are deserving of governmental protective measures (Farkas & Johnson, 1996, p. 45), as are vulnerable populations in general (Anonymous, 1991/1992).[7] However, there is no support for making welfare available to the healthy unemployed (Farkas & Johnson, 1996).

Turning provision of goods and services for vulnerable populations over to private, for-profit, companies, even within partnerships, imposes a caveat emptor philosophy that creates problems. Many vulnerable populations are not able to meet the skilled, critical purchaser requirement of the buyer-beware market, whether services are delivered by public-private partnerships or another entity.[8] Private sector companies have moral obligations to investors that take precedent over obligations to customers, and the customers in question are not able to defend themselves because "sellers inevitably know a great deal more than buyers, who can find out what they need to know only with great difficulty" (Mintzberg, 1996, p. 77). This is especially worrisome in the context of intense market competition, such as the one that characterizes the United States today.

Public partners are not immune to pressures that may compromise services to vulnerable populations. These are of a different nature than is the case with private partners. Public providers are under pressure to reduce costs for a variety of reasons, including competition with private partners to serve the same populations, budget cuts, and fiscal austerity measures. State monitoring of Medicaid patients in California nursing homes was arranged to overlook quality regulations in exchange for a lower price (Sparer, 1996).

If partnerships emphasize cost reduction or profit maximization at the price of significant quality compromises, vulnerable populations may not be able to respond appropriately and aggressively. Residents of nursing homes are an example. Minimalist forms of policy partnering, in which collaboration between public and private partners are formal and limited, have failed. "Private accreditation organizations would actually put nursing home residents in jeopardy" (quote from Donna E. Shalala, as cited in Pear, 1998, p. A12). There is evidence that private sector nursing homes do not adequately screen staff and end up employing some workers with criminal records (Love, 1998).[9] Patients in need of mental health care have been "imprisoned in psychiatric hospitals" until their health insurance benefits were exhausted.[10] Kickbacks to doctors for referrals may have compromised the health care of Medicare patients (Bodenheimer et al., 1999; Lutz, 1994). The Columbia/HCA Healthcare Corporation pressured doctors "not to admit the uninsured" (Woolhandler & Himmelstein, 1998). Close monitoring is advised to assure appropriate access to social services as well (see Rom, 1999).[11] In addition, public-private partnerships have not adequately addressed the needs of the uninsured, safety net considerations, and the community perspective (Lane, 1998).

In highly competitive perfect markets, less than competent customers may fall by the wayside.[12] Businesses in the private sector are not altruistic organizations, nor should they be expected to fulfill a welfare function (Buchanan, 1998). The abuse potential is evident when minimalist partnerships involve private partners that provide services for pay to populations that are at a great power disadvantage[13] because they are not able to distinguish successfully between the quality of products offered by the private partner.

DEMOCRACY AND PARTICIPATION

Do public-private partnerships increase or reduce public participation and input into the policy process? There is evidence that partnering can reduce citizen input into the policy process, but at the same time, there is some hope or expectation that partnerships might be structured to increase citizen participation. Kamieniecki et al. (1999) indicate that in environmental policy areas, public-private partnerships may reduce the opportunity for citizen input in the policy process. This takes place as the influence of the private sector partner increases. The reasons for this, and the extent to which it applies to other policy sectors, is not known. It may be structural to the extent that when the private partner administers a policy matter, as with emissions credit sales, there is less appreciation of the value of citizen input. Rosenbaum (1999 [this issue]) suggests that this need not be the case for public-private policy partnerships, and that they could lead to the development of new institutional designs in commercial nuclear power facilities that would include environmental interests and other publicly concerned groups and individuals. On the other hand, some public/not-for-profit private partnerships encourage citizen involvement perhaps to too great an extent (Lovrich, 1999).

REGULATION AND PUBLIC-PRIVATE
POLICY PARTNERSHIPS

Does partnering result in decreased regulation? The answer is not necessarily, and this is a surprise. It seems logical that as the policy role of the private sector in providing public services increases with partnering, government regulations would be reduced. As J. A. Dunn (1999 [this issue]) indicates, public-private partnerships can sometimes be used instead of adversarial regulatory processes (e.g., the Partnership for a New Generation of Vehicles between the Clinton Administration and the U.S. auto manufacturers). Similarly, this was the case with the sale of emissions credits (Kamieniecki et al., 1999). However, partnering can also lead to the opposite situation. Sparer (1999) suggests that increasing the role for private partners only augments the need for federal regulation in Medicaid programs.

Partnering cannot be defined as a success if it results in lower quality of public policy services, the need for more government oversight, and the need for expensive monitoring, even if it appears to reduce costs. This may be the case for nursing homes, where residents need to be protected because private providers seek to "maximize profits at the expense of patients" (Iglehart, 1996). The same is true for the education sector, in which the infrastructure required for monitoring the mix of public and private education providers may be greater than the marginal savings attributed to private schools (Levin, 1999).

Experience from many countries suggests that where, on normative grounds, an adequate level of services and special programs (such as those targeted to the disabled) are as important as cost savings, regulation may be required to assure that these societal goals are reached through partnering arrangements (Saltman & Figueras, 1998). For example, regulation might be the only means to assure that private educational institutions take socialization to civic responsibility seriously, but the costs of such regulation might be prohibitive (Levin, 1999). Regulation can, more realistically, be employed to compensate for inadequate consumer information in imperfect markets, such as those of utilities (Davis, 1996) and health care (Moran, 1997; Rice, 1996; Sparer, 1996). In addition, as previously mentioned, many advocacy groups urge government regulation as a way to assure protection of vulnerable populations (Anonymous, 1998).

Regulation is sometimes employed to level the field of competition if the competition involves public and private providers of policy relevant goods and services. When the public and private sectors partner to provide essential services collectively by competing with each other, such competition is closely regulated (Colton, Frisof, & King, 1997). For example, in the education sector, regulation assures fair competition between private and public schools by monitoring quality.[14]

Economists feel regulation is one way to control for imperfect markets. To the extent that public-private policy partnerships must function in imperfect markets, the need for regulation remains. Regulation functions to "prevent an opportunistic race to the bottom" (Kuttner, 1997, p. 138) and to "keep the profit motive in check" (Anders, 1996, p. 257). Regulation also discourages dishonest practices vis-à-vis customers, which might be put in place to gain advantage over competitors. This is especially important if the private partners "ideologically and financially oppose seeing themselves as having any special responsibilities to the public" (Colton et al., 1997; Hassan, 1996). When public responsibilities are in question, there is a call to "regulate loss ratios, profit margins, stockholder yields, and executive compensation" (quote from Burt Margolin, as cited in Iglehart, 1996). However, even in international markets usually assumed to be independent of any state responsibility, it appears that government is expected to assure confidence in times of crisis (Soros, 1998).

Although reducing big government is, certainly, one of the principal incentives for partnering, results appear to be modest. Regulation is not withering away, and it may even be increasing in some policy sectors along with the trend toward partnering, both in the United States (Sparer, 1996, 1998) and Europe (Saltman & Figueras, 1998; Supiot, 1996).[15]

ACCOUNTABILITY AND DEMOCRACY

Public-private policy partnerships must be accountable if they are to fulfill policy objectives successfully. A central principle of democratic theory is that leaders and government be held accountable for their actions. When critical public functions are entrusted to partnerships, substantial policy responsibility may be granted to nongovernmental agencies. They may make policy decisions usually reserved in a democracy to elected officials or state representatives. Partnering for welfare services is an example (see Rom, 1999). In another example, as Schneider (1999) points out, the private partner is making public policy when privately employed guards decide whether a prisoner should go to solitary confinement or whether she or he should be left to possible abuse or injury by a cell mate. Accountability is central to the ability of partnerships to perform these responsibilities.

Historically, public provision of essential services and the monopoly status given to those providers were justified on the basis of the exceptional importance of the product. The private sector did well for routine matters. The public sector was assumed to be better when urgent matters dictated the need for cooperation rather than competition (Rosenau, 1999). Today, private sector partners are responsible for the provision of many essential services, and the public accepts this as a relatively normal state of affairs.

Accountability of public-private partnerships is tested when the interruption of essential services causes substantial public disruption. "Society simply cannot afford to allow them to fail, to be mismanaged, or to be marked by consumer abuses" (Colton et al., 1997, p. 391). Special cases of public responsibility include essential services (Bonbright, Danielsen, & Kamerschen, 1988) such as water supply, pesticides that threaten human hormonal systems (Cushman, 1998), air pollution, food supply, and public health functions (Voelker, 1998; see quote from Quentin Young on public health).

In cases of partnering for policy purposes, anecdotal evidence of failed accountability abounds, although systematic studies comparing accountability performance are few. For example, Corrections Corporation of America is reported to have explicitly misinformed city and state officials about the security risk of inmates housed in a Youngstown-based private prison. Corrections Corporation of America did not promptly notify the police when five murderers escaped; instead, the company attempted to cover it up. The company's accountability seems lacking, and the local mayor characterized Corrections Corporation of American as the "most deceitful, dishonest corporation I have ever dealt with" (Jaffe & Brooks, 1998, p. A8).[16] If the same event happened in a public prison, would accountability dynamics have been different?

Partnering for the provision of electricity speaks to mixed results, and it raises problems related to accountability in another policy sector. In an attempt to compete on price, some private sector providers have failed to assure services, which resulted in serious losses to consumers. Electricity blackouts and power shortages are examples (Carlisle, 1998; Holden, 1996). During emergencies, prices have risen 100-fold, while private companies capitalized on shortages. They have been accused of deliberately holding back supplies to increase prices or to embarrass a rival supplier (Kranhold, 1998; Kranhold & Emshwiller, 1998), even in situations in which populations were at risk (Salpukas, 1998a, 1998b).[17] Are these isolated events, or are they systemic manifestations of failed accountability?

On the most general level and in the abstract theoretical sense, it is difficult to argue that the public or private partner is more accountable, or that partnering for policy increases or decreases accountability. Hard evidence is absent, and both sides make convincing cases. Stiglitz and Wallsten (1999) propose that sovereign governments, as public partners, are probably less accountable in that they "cannot bind themselves with contracts in the same way that private partners . . . can" (pp. 57-58). This is because it is also the role of government to enforce contracts. Examples of failed government responsibility abound, especially in countries where a government's tenure in power is sometimes unpredictable, where the transition from one government to another is not peaceful, or where long-term credibility is yet to be demonstrated. However, at least in theory, in countries with responsible political parties, the failure of a public sector partner could have electoral consequences for the party in power.[18] If the private sector partner fails in its contracts or commitments for public responsibilities, recourse is equally complicated. Sometimes justice can be had through the judiciary, but this route can be expensive and lengthy.

The government (the public partner) is the provider of policy relevant public goods and services of last resort (accountable) in two senses. First, the state steps in when private capital is unavailable (for any number of reasons, including the absence of market incentives) or withdrawn, but an important social good needs to be accomplished. This is the basis of public-private partnerships in the field of applied technology research and development (Stiglitz & Wallsten, 1999). In another example, private capital lacked appropriate market incentives to develop cleaner and more fuel-efficient vehicles. The Clinton administration was reluctant to force the issue through new regulations that were likely to generate hostility and opposition from the automobile industry, so Washington offered public funds and an implicit 10-year hiatus in new federal fuel economy regulations to engage Detroit in the partnership to develop a new generation of cleaner, more fuel-efficient vehicles (see Dunn, 1999).[19]

Second, when partnerships fail through bankruptcy, inability to meet agreed upon goals, and so forth, government (the public sector) is the provider of last resort, at least when partnering involves essential public services.[20] In the end, there is the often unspoken consensus between public and private partners to the following effect: Government is expected to fulfill the policy responsibilities of failed private sector partners (Lovrich, 1999). For example, if privatization of pension plans were to be adopted on a national scale, and they fail because of a stock market crash or the bankruptcy of the private pension plan provider, "the state would have to step in" ("A Survey of Social Insurance," 1998, p. 10). The same is true for health care because when people become so sick that they lose their private health insurance, "they return to the state scheme" ("A Survey of Social Insurance," 1998, p. 19; Sparer, 1998). The state has served the same role for public sector utilities with the "stranded costs" from nuclear power (Salpukas, 1997).

Although there may be no easy solution to the accountability challenges associated with public-private policy partnerships, the articles in this issue point to some trends. Accountability is more likely to be assured when partnerships are structured in specific ways. Partners must be "assigned specific responsibilities and given incentives and resources to fulfill those responsibilities" (Stiglitz & Wallsten, 1999, p. 57). Goals must be clearly articulated (Kamieniecki et al., 1999). In cases such as education and health, in which social purposes are important, accountability does not appear to emerge from market forces alone (Levin, 1999; Sparer, 1999).

The questions for the future are several. Are these accountability issues merely a matter of transition—will more experience lead to resolution by prevention in terms of setting up mechanisms by which policy relevant goods and services will be assured? Is the accountability problem linked to the nature of policy-partnering patterns to date—namely, a high prevalence of minimalist partnering arrangements? Would closer public-private partnering and cooperation between partners remedy the situation and lead to more responsible policy results (Holden, 1996)? Is the accountability problem related to conflicts of interest inherent in partnering to fulfill policy functions? This is the topic to which we now turn.

CONFLICTS OF INTEREST AND
PUBLIC-PRIVATE POLICY PARTNERSHIPS

Although combining the strengths of private and public partners is important, such partnerships can also be a source of conflict of interest. One study suggests that the organization of public-private policy partnerships "requires special attention" because the public and private sectors have different orientations (Reijniers, 1994, p. 13). The private sector is oriented toward

- achieving returns on the invested funds;
- daring to take business risks;
- having to anticipate market and competitive developments;
- and realizing a corporate goal.

The interests of the public sector are in

- legislation, regulations, and authorities;
- political opinion and political influence;
- democratic decision-making processes;
- the minimization of risks;
- and the realization of a social goal (Reijniers, 1994).

Reconciling responsibilities of private capital with general obligations to the public may not be easy in all cases. Partnering for policy goals is probably more successful, and conflicts of interest are minimized when the terms of the partnerships are designed to "fulfill public objectives, within the limits of available public resource constraints. . . . When the partners have separate interests, however, more attention needs to be placed on the incentive-accountability structure" (Stiglitz & Wallsten, 1999, p. 57).

When the interests of the public and private partners are aligned and they share objectives, things work more smoothly than when the opposite is true. However, even in these cases, conflict of interest may result, and at great cost to society. When tangible economic benefits accrue to both the public (government) and private partners, the public interest is not always well served. Schneider (1999) points out in her discussion of the Corrections Corporation of America, that this is the case when a coalition of businesses (in need of a ready supply of prisoners) and politicians (for whom prison projects give a tough-on-crime image that they believe will gain votes) find their interests aligned. Here, the total cost of incarceration may go up because of the greatly increased cost to the public of incarcerating people who do not need to be incarcerated. Even if the per capita cost (per prisoner) is lower in private prison systems, the overall cost to taxpayers is much higher because of the conflict of interest between the public-private partners on one side and those of society (and taxpayers) on the other.[21]

Avoiding conflicts of interests and harmonizing the public and private sector orientations is a difficult task to the extent that there is, too often, and perhaps for structural reasons, an absence of a moral standard in market competition, the venue of public-private policy partnerships (Hirsch, 1976; see Lie, 1997 for a summary of a moral critique of the market). Stiglitz and Wallsten (1999) argue that as concerns center on applied technology policy, partnering might be best focused on topics that "would be privately unprofitable but socially beneficial because of high spillovers" (p. 58). It might be that conflicts of interests are reduced in such partnering circumstances.

The need to keep information confidential for proprietary reasons raises a conflict of interest question for some public-private policy partnerships.[22] Maintaining proprietary rights while carrying out a public policy role may constitute a conflict of interest vis-à-vis the public's right to full information (Totty, 1997). The private sector is weak on transparency, but this is required if public scrutiny, a taxpayer's right, is to be assured. Proprietary information is important in the private sector if one is to do better than one's competitors (Stiglitz & Wallsten, 1999). Thus, a potential conflict of interest results when policy partnering requires that those providing services be responsible to the public. Private partners may simply refuse to disclose information, about contracts with workers for example (Totty, 1997), and often enough, they have good reason to refuse if they want to avoid helping their competitors.[23] In another example, managed-care companies partner with government to provide services to Medicaid and Medicare programs, and they are not obligated to make public the contracts they negotiated with doctors. These contracts contain incentives designed to influence how doctors treat patients (Bodenheimer & Grumbach, 1995). Such commercial secrets may mean that the proprietary nature of information can interfere with consumers obtaining the full information they require to make an informed decision to purchase.

SEEKING CERTAINTY AND PASSING THE BUCK

Managing risk and uncertainty are critical to the success of any public organization or private enterprise competing in the marketplace. Both risk and uncertainty interfere with the optimal performance of public-private policy partnerships. For example, the health care costs of the sickest 5% of the population are close to $48,000 per person per year. It is less than $300 per person per year for the healthiest 50%; the national average is $4,000 per person per year (MacStravic, 1998). The health care costs of 90% of Medicare patients average $1,340 per person per year. However, the remaining 10% average $28,120 per person per year (Moon & Davis, 1995). The incentives for health insurance companies to avoid the sickest are great—insuring too many of the sickest would lead to bankruptcy. This is called *cream skimming*, and it is a serious problem for public-private policy partnerships.[24]

Cost shifting of the less profitable part of the market to the public sector partner is one effective way to reduce risk. It is done routinely in education, health, airlines, postal service, and others. There is a strong financial incentive to take only the most profitable portion of the market that one serves, be they healthy patients (Sparer, 1999), high socioeconomic status students (Levin, 1999), or white collar workers, and leave the rest without service or with poorer quality service. Cost shifting from the private sector to the public sector increases the private partner's profits and increases the fiscal responsibility of the public sector partner.[25]

> With a mixed public-private system, there is a great danger that the private providers will gravitate towards the services where it is easy to make a quick profit, leaving the public sector carrying the inherently unprofitable activities, and once again, being dubbed "inefficient." (Barker, 1996, p. 155)

The postal service is an example of cream skimming and cost shifting of a relatively recent origin. The view that uniform service at a uniform price requires a public monopoly no longer holds. Competition with private providers such as Federal Express has made for better and quicker (but not cheaper) service than the Federal Postal Service, especially in major metropolitan areas. Mail delivery in rural areas, which cannot be served at a profit, are simply neglected by the private sector. The taxpayers end up subsidizing the cost of providing regular mail service to these areas where the private providers cannot be expected to provide service.[26]

Today, public sector partners also seek to reduce risk and increase certainty, although the mechanisms are sometimes different from those employed by the private sector (Raffel, 1997). The financial interests of the state are at risk when providing public goods and services, and there is a large element of uncertainty involved. One of the advantages of public-private policy partnerships is that they can be structured to permit closer budgetary oversights. Governmental concerns with balancing the budget over the last decade suggest that fixed expenditures are preferred.

In pursing fiscal certainty, government partners with private sector providers for services (prison, health, education, etc.) to populations for a specific price and a set term. In the prison system, this leads to per diem per prison payments to owners of private prisons. In the health sector, the Medicare program is being reformulated to shift risk to patients (who must choose the best plan) and its private partners (capitated managed care payments).[27] Sparer (1999) explains how insurance companies shift risk to doctors through capitation (Bodenheimer & Grumbach, 1998).[28] Government also seeks to shift the actual care of patients to family members (Fisher, 1998; Leon, Cheng, & Neumann, 1998; Rimer, 1998).

The situations in which cost shifting is likely to occur are predictable. When partnering is minimalist in character, when joint accountability and responsibility are weak, and when fiscal pressures in a highly competitive market are

strong, cost shifting to reduce risk makes sense to both public and private partners seeking to achieve their goals.

The solution to cost shifting in policy-partnering situations is known. Cost
shifting or cream skimming disappears when public-private policy partnerships
are required to make goods or services or both available to all possible purchasers, or to all those eligible to receive them.[29] For example, "simply by requiring
that insurers and prepaid plans take all comers," the current practice of seeking
out "low-risk patients and dumping the rest on the public sector would end"
(Osborne & Gaebler, 1992, p. 313). The same principle applies in other policy
sectors. Rom (1999), for example, suggests that contracts with private partners
in the welfare sector can be written in such a way as to discourage cost shifting.

THE CONTEXT AND STRUCTURE OF SUCCESSFUL
PARTNERING FOR POLICY FUNCTIONS

In general, public-private policy partnerships are likely to be successful in
certain contexts, if they are structured in specific ways. They perform well if
there is broad community or societal consensus in the value of the policy goals.
The agreement of the business sector is as critical as having a "cohesive society
and masterful government" (Mead, 1998). Political will, political feasibility,
electoral support, and political constituency agreement enhance the chances of
success and survival for partnerships. In the case study of applied technology
partnering, it was shown that scientific merit is not sufficient to ensure success.
Stiglitz and Wallsten (1999) observe the following:

> Programs that attempt to select projects only on their economic and scientific mer-
> its may never develop a constituency and, thus, political support. Such programs
> may either be eliminated or changed to build support. This creates a potential
> Catch-22 situation: A program that allocates funds to reward constituencies may
> be popular, but will be less effective at correcting a market failure, whereas a pro-
> gram that attempts to correct a market failure may never develop a constituency
> and ultimately be canceled. (pp. 61-62)

In general, partnering success is more likely if (a) key decisions are made at
the very beginning of a project and set out in a concrete plan, (b) clear lines of
responsibility are indicated, (c) achievable goals are set down, (d) incentives for
partners are established, and (e) progress is monitored. This can be accomplished only at the highest level of corporate and public organizational levels
(Nagel, 1997). It approximates the type of arrangement Dunn (1999) refers to in
his discussion of Partnerships for a New Generation of Vehicles, and it requires
substantial planning involving both partners.

Success in partnering to provide essential public services may require cooperation as much as competition between the public-private partners. This is
because the

benefits of an activity are available to all and cannot be captured by the party generating the benefits. In such situations, the private sector faces economic incentives that will cause it to invest in that activity at a level below what is socially optimal. (Rettig, 1997, p. 140)

This appears to be the case for the education sector as well as for research and development. Partnerships are made more difficult in education because private and public schools are competitors for students. Private schools often attract clientele by putting down the public schools. The choice is increased, but collaboration to reach broad social goals is limited.[30]

Success of public-private policy partnerships may be greater if such partners are not competing in tight market situations. Highly competitive market conditions do not provide incentives for cooperative ventures between public and private sectors working toward shared goals (Hirsch, 1976). This may explain the partnering success between public and not-for-profit private partners (Lovrich, 1999) where market considerations are less of a consideration. These types of partnering experiences are reported to be increasingly common (Lowry, 1995) and successful. This is perhaps because the goals of all those involved are aligned (Hinnant, 1995) and potential conflicts of interest less likely to develop.

SUMMARY, SYNTHESIS, AND CONCLUSIONS

Business and government have much to learn from each other, and public-private policy partnerships encourage this type of exchange. In the policy sectors considered in this issue, partnering at a distance, or minimalist partnerships, appear to be the norm. This type of relationship between public and private partners is one of limited contractual obligation rather than that of mutual accountability. Few authentic, fully integrated, coaccountable examples of partnering were observed. Side-by-side production of policy functions is far more common in these policy sectors. This means that the real benefits of public-private policy partnerships may not be entirely evident as yet across the whole range of policy sectors. There appears, however, to be some movement toward closer partnerships, involving joint financing and responsibility, in some areas (transportation, energy, and applied technology research).

When the profit motive is absent, as in the case of partnering between public and not-for-profit private partners, more consequential and significant forms of partnering are possible. Public/for-profit private policy partnership may be more difficult, especially when organizational structures constitute zero-sum financial relationships between partners. Where partnering takes place in less competitive market contexts, efforts to seek financial certainty and shift risk to the other partner will be reduced.

Public-private partnerships improve short-term cost performance in several policy sectors studied here, but only to a very small degree. Long-term calculations are more complicated and could shift the balance in the other direction. Externalities could also easily overturn any savings. Quality performance is mixed on noneconomic performance variables.

When government is an active public partner with the private sector, it is assumed that democracy and equity concerns are assured. In most of the articles in this issue, across a range of policy sectors, this was not the case. Public-private partnerships have not resolved problems with regard to equity, access, participation, and democracy. In fact, public-private policy partnerships may achieve cost reductions at the price of democracy and equity. There is, however, a potential for future public-private policy partnership consortiums to increase public trust and improve on democracy and equity concerns. Developing them in this direction will not be easy, as those left out are hard to bring in, and it will be difficult to convince them to participate for a number of reasons.

There is no evidence that the minimalist forms of public-private partnerships that exist today can increase access or successfully provide services to vulnerable populations without risk to quality and without being closely monitored. Services to vulnerable populations are expensive. If there is no potential for profit, then the private partner, in all fairness, cannot be expected to assume such responsibilities (Buchanan, 1998). In addition, the use of public-private policy partnerships to provide essential services to vulnerable or captive populations may incur increased expenses related to monitoring that escape consideration in calculating overall costs.

Public-private policy partnerships do not seem to reduce regulation as has been hoped, and instances of increased regulation are reported. Partnering appears to shift the nature of government's role away from that of simply providing services. Instead, government moves to partnering for the provision of services and the monitoring of the marketplace.[31] This sometimes results in a situation in which government is one of many providers, each competing for customers. Although the initial goal was to reduce regulation, in the end, regulation appears to be required to assure fair competition between private and public providers who partner in this minimalist sense.

Policy accountability is not inevitably improved by public-private policy partnerships. It is likely to be greater when responsibilities and goals are clearly indicated in advance, and when contracts are closely crafted for this end. This is seldom the case in minimalist partnerings in which partners merely compete with each other.

Conflicts of interest are a source of problems for public-private policy partnerships. They threaten to undermine performance. Stockholders' interests must come first when the private partner is a for-profit organization. This makes for divided loyalty, and it conflicts with public policy obligations to society. If a partnership involves a private, not-for-profit organization in partnership with a public sector partner, then this type of conflict of interest is less of a problem, but different conflicts of interest may be present. The worst case scenario, and it is to be avoided, is one in which vulnerable populations (children, the elderly, the disabled, and the cognitively impaired) are dependent on providers whose main motive is to make a profit or reduce costs in a context of low regulation and little attention to monitoring quality (Wessel & Harwood, 1998). It can, of course, involve either a public or a private provider partner.

In light of this evaluation based on the research and analysis presented and summarized in this issue, the following recommendations seem reasonable. When cost considerations are the main concern, and when externalities are expected to be limited and a short time frame is in place, public-private policy partnerships may be appropriate. When one or more of these conditions do not hold, when partnering is minimalist in form, when accountability is critical, when vulnerable populations are the policy focus, when cost shifting presents problems, and when societal normative choices are more important than costs, public-private partnering may not be the best approach to policy.

NOTES

1. Due to inefficiency or other reasons, the public sector may fail to keep up with increased demands. The response may be to set up a partnership with the private sector (Hartung & Washburn, 1998; Iglehart, 1996). Schneider (1999) suggests that this is what brought about the increase in private prisons.

2. High bankruptcy rates (4,500 in 1998) for private sector businesses (American Bankruptcy Institute, 1999) and government bailouts of private enterprises suggest that the private sector does not have a monopoly on efficiency and effectiveness.

3. For example, what is often a legitimate business expense is often not an expense that is justifiable to taxpayers. In the end, these types of fundamental differences can create problems for a public-private policy partnership (Ghere, 1996).

4. Media sources suggest that this is not the case everywhere; in private prisons that have saved money, such as Louisiana, instances of "brutality, cronyism, and neglect" call into question the value of saved resources (Butterfield, 1998). This should not be taken to mean that government always does a good job. Abuse in public prisons, for example, is also a problem (Nieves, 1998).

5. Competitive strategies for market share in utilities has, in the short term, resulted in partnerships reducing costs to small consumers at a loss to the provider in order to assure deregulation of previously public sector services. Prices to small consumers are expected to return to higher levels in the long term (Salpukas, 1997). Ironically, the opposite appears to be the case in telephone services. Short-term effects may include higher telephone bills for households, although it is hoped that this will reverse in the long run (Landler, 1997).

6. Partnering is not a means to redistribute wealth, and when that is the agreed upon goal, it is a poor choice of policy mechanism. "The private sector can channel voluntary redistribution through charity, but only the state can legally take money from the rich and give it to the poor. Any reform of the welfare state must spell out how much redistribution that will involve" ("A Survey of Social Insurance," 1998).

7. It is essential to the legitimacy of according special treatment that the status of persons receiving special consideration must not be the result of their own action. This includes those who are the victims of natural catastrophe, floods, earthquakes, hurricanes, and so forth. It includes those unemployed through no fault of their own. For example, the person's company went bankrupt because the general economic situation changed (Levinson, 1996). It encompasses the sick and the ill who are struck by cancer and genetic disease, as well as children and the cognitively impaired.

8. Juveniles in private prisons are another population that has been reported in the popular press to be victimized by irresponsible private partners of the state (Butterfield, 1998). The market competition model does not apply here because the purchaser of services and the recipient are not the same.

9. The situation was so bad that Congress adopted legislation requiring the FBI to do criminal background checks on new nursing home employees (Omnibus Consolidated and Emergency Supplemental Appropriations Act, 1999).

10. Tenet Healthcare Corporation (formerly National Medical Enterprises) paid "about $100 million to former patients" (Eichenwald, 1997; Lutz, 1993, p. 3).

11. Advocacy groups are a commonly proposed remedy. Children have a natural advocate if the parent is a critical consumer. This mechanism fails when parents cannot play this role or when the elderly outlive their spouse and children. But what about those who are in both of these categories and have no advocate, or those whose advocate is incompetent or makes poor choices?

12. This situation is not uncommon, even in the general population. One study reports that only 11% of Medicare recipients "have adequate knowledge to make an informed choice" among various Medicare managed-care options. As much as "30 percent . . . know almost nothing about HMOs" (Hibbard, Jewett, Englemann, & Tusler, 1998). Many patients are not able to report if services billed were actually provided because of the complexity of medical care. "Consumers do not seem able to evaluate the usefulness of medical services and to make the type of decisions that economic theory calls for them to make" (Rice, 1997).

13. This includes all those who cannot make complex purchasing decisions for themselves because of cognitive limitations (some of the elderly), age (children), or legal status (see Schneider, 1999). The chronically ill and the disabled have successfully organized lobbying groups, but they are still in need of special protection.

14. At the same time, it results in the blurring of distinction between public and private schools altogether (Starr, 1990).

15. Some forms of privatization are said to even increase "government penetration of the private sector" (Starr, 1990).

16. Similar abuse of private police functions have also been noted, which calls into question the advisability of institutions such as bounty hunters laws. They are neither partnerships nor privatization, but they are an abuse of legal statutes that have resulted in the deaths (punished by a minimal 6-month jail sentence) of innocent citizens ("Bounty Hunters Kill Couple," 1997).

17. The same problems have been documented in other countries as well (Moffett, 1998).

18. Private partners may not find this of much assurance if they are left bearing the financial costs of an unanticipated change of government and a shift in policy.

19. "Although there was plenty of capital available to the auto industry, they had no profit incentive to invest in cleaner, more fuel efficient models because their customers did not make purchase decisions on those characteristics. Indeed, Detroit's most profitable vehicles are its less clean, less fuel-efficient SUVs [sport utility vehicles]. Market incentives dictate they invest capital in developing new lines of ever-bigger behemoths and not worry about the future of the environment" (Dunn, 1998).

20. Whether this is fair to taxpayers or not is another complicated consideration.

21. Much of this analysis resulted from e-mail correspondence with Dr. Anne Schneider, March 9, 1999. My thanks to her for pointing out the importance of this type of conflict of interest.

22. Private means "what is hidden or withdrawn." Public means what is "open, revealed, or accessible." (Weintraub & Kumar, 1997).

23. Warden raises the possibility that health plans may not "want to release information indicating good performance in areas of high-tech or high-risk care, for fear of attracting expensive new enrollees" (1996, p. 117).

24. Cream skimming, in this context, is defined as the tendency of the private partner to avoid difficult and expensive clients, and actively seek out those who are less expensive to serve.

25. In certain situations, it is almost impossible to know if a so-called partnership that permits clients to choose services from either a private or public provider results in overall savings or not. This is the case when private providers can pick and choose which customers they will serve. If less

desirable customers are discouraged or rejected, directly or indirectly, by private providers, while public providers must take all comers, including those not desired by the private providers, any comparison of cost efficiency would be difficult. Education and health are some cases in point.

26. Providing health coverage to some groups is unlikely to produce profits for a private company. Examples of these groups include the elderly (sickest), Native Americans (high rates of chronic health problems typical of poverty), the military (high-risk professions), and prisoners. Cost shifting from the private sector to the public sector, directly or indirectly, is employed to assure health care for these populations.

27. "In the past several years the federal government has attempted to privatize the Medicare system, which covers 39 million elderly and disabled individuals, by encouraging HMOs to take on and manage the health care risk for a fixed reimbursement or capitation" (Kumar, 1999).

28. It makes little difference whether the public sector is partnering with other public providers (federal to state) or with private sector providers. Block grants to the state achieve much the same goal.

29. When not-for-profits (private or public) have provided services, in the past, this sometimes happened automatically.

30. In some states, the public sector is required "to pay for busing to private schools, textbooks in the secular subjects, and provide categorical grants for special education and remedial education. The schools are required to provide separate rooms for the latter without religious symbols. In general, the public schools send teachers to work in those rooms" (H. M. Levin, personal communication, September 15, 1998).

31. In any case, there is a real dilemma as to what exactly is "irreducibly governmental at a time of boundary-challenging and boundary-blurring" (Starr, 1990).

REFERENCES

Aday, L. A. (1993). *At risk in America: The health and health care needs of vulnerable populations in the United States*. San Francisco: Jossey-Bass.

American Bankruptcy Institute (1999). *Bankruptcies break another record in 1998* [On-line]. Available: http://www.abiworld.org/release/latest.html.

Anders, G. (1996). *Health against wealth: HMO's and the breakdown of medical trust*. Boston: Houghton Mifflin.

Anonymous (1991/1992). The responsive communitarian platform: Rights and responsibilities. *The Responsive Community, 2*, 4-18.

Anonymous (1998). Assisted living gains popularity among senior citizens. *CNN Interactive* [On-line]. Available: http://cnn.com/health/9808/13/assisted.living/index.html.

Barker, C. (1996). *The health care policy process*. Thousand Oaks, CA: Sage.

Bodenheimer, T., & Grumbach, K. (1995). *Understanding health policy, a clinical approach*. Stanford, CA: Appleton and Lange.

Bodenheimer, T., & Grumbach, K. (1998). *Understanding health policy, a clinical approach*. Stanford, CA: Appleton and Lange.

Bodenheimer, T., Grumbach, K., Livingston, B. L., McCanne, D. R., Oberlander, J., Rice, D. P., & Rosenau, P. V. (1999). *Rebuilding Medicare for the 21st century. A challenge for the Medicare Commission and Congress*. San Francisco: Health Access Foundation.

Bonbright, J., Danielsen, A., & Kamerschen, D. (1988). *Principles of public utility rates*. Arlington, VA: Public Utilities Reports.

Bounty hunters kill couple in case of mistaken identity. (1997, September 2). *The New York Times*, p. A13.

Buchanan, A. (1998). Managed care: Rationing without justice, but not unjustly. *Journal of Health Politics, Policy and Law, 23*, 617-634.

Butterfield, F. (1998, July 15). Profits at juvenile prisons earned at a chilling cost. *The New York Times*, pp. A1, A14.

Carlisle, T. (1998, December 3). Electricity deregulation lengthens Alberta nights. *The Wall Street Journal*, p. A18.

Colton, R., Frisof, K. B., & King, E. R. (1997). Lessons for the health care industry from America's experience with public utilities. *Journal of Public Health Policy, 18*, 389-400.

Cushman, J. H. (1998, August 31). E.P.A. to hunt dangers in everyday products. *The New York Times*, pp. A1, A14.

Davis, V. W. (1996). *Telecommunications service quality*. Columbus, OH: National Regulatory Research Institute.

Dunn, J. A., Jr. (1998). Driving Forces: The Automobile, Its Enemies and the Politics of Mobility. Washington, DC: Brookings Institution.

Dunn, J. A., Jr. (1999). Transportation: Policy-level partnerships and project-based partnerships. *American Behavioral Scientist, 43*, 92-106.

Eichenwald, K. (1997, July 30). $100 million settlement seen in tenet suits. *The New York Times*, p. D1.

Farkas, S., & Johnson, J. (1996). *The values we live by: What Americans want from welfare reform*. New York: Public Agenda.

Felsenthal, E. (1997, May 21). Convict's suit threatens privatized jail service. *The Wall Street Journal*, pp. B1, B10.

Fisher, I. (1998, June 7). Families provide medical care, tubes and all. *The New York Times*, pp. A1, A21.

Ghere, R. K. (1996). Aligning the ethics of public-private partnership: The issue of local economic development. *Journal of Public Administration Research and Theory, 6*, 599-621.

Graham, C. (1994). *Safety nets, politics, and the poor: Transitions to market economies*. Washington, DC: Brookings Institution.

Graham, C. (1998). *Private markets for public goods; raising the stakes in economic reform*. Washington, DC: Brookings Institution.

Hartung, W. D., & Washburn, J. (1998, March 2). Lockheed Martin: From warfare to welfare. *The Nation, 266*, 11-16.

Hassan, M. M. (1996). Let's end the nonprofit charade. *New England Journal of Medicine, 334*, 1055-1057.

Hibbard, J. H., Jewett, J. J., Englemann, S., & Tusler, M. (1998). Can Medicare beneficiaries make informed choices? *Health Affairs, 17*, 181-193.

Hinnant, C. C. (1995). Nonprofit organizations as inter-regional actors: Lessons from southern growth. *Policy Studies Review, 14*, 225-227.

Hirsch, F. (1976). *Social limits to growth*. Cambridge, MA: Harvard University Press.

Holden, B. A. (1996, August 19). Did competition spark power failures? *The Wall Street Journal*, pp. B1-B2.

Iglehart, J. K. (1996). Averting disaster: A conversation with the Los Angeles County "health czar." *Health Affairs, 15*, 86-91.

Jaffe, G., & Brooks, R. (1998, August 5). Hard time: Violence at prison run by Corrections Corp. irks Youngstown, Ohio. *The Wall Street Journal*, pp. A1, A8.

Kamieniecki, S., Shafie, D., & Silvers, J. (1999). Forming partnerships in environmental policy: The business of emissions trading in clean air management. *American Behavioral Scientist, 43*, 107-123.

Kranhold, K. (1998, July 16). Power agency to investigate market turmoil. *The Wall Street Journal*, p. A4.

Kranhold, K., & Emshwiller, J. R. (1998, July 24). New rules blamed for power shortages. *The Wall Street Journal*, p. A2.

Ku, L., & Hoag, S. (1998). Medicaid managed care and the marketplace. *Inquiry, 41*, 332-345.

Kumar, A. N. (1999, January). Greater financial strength seen for health insurers and managed care industry in 1999 despite concerns. *Standard & Poor's* [On-line]. Available: http://www.standard andpoors.com/ratings/insurance/commentary.htm.

Kuttner, R. (1997). *Everything for sale: The virtues and limits of markets.* New York: Knopf.

Landler, M. (1997, March 30). Rising phone bills are likely result of deregulation—lawmakers are angered—free market rules mean end of subsidies that have let millions afford service. *The New York Times,* pp. A1, A13.

Lane, D. G. (1998). Summit participants say public/private partnership must evolve. *Behavioral Healthcare Tomorrow, 7,* 12.

Leon, J., Cheng, C. -K., & Neumann, P. J. (1998). Alzheimer's disease care: Costs and potential savings. *Health Affairs, 17,* 206-207.

Levin, H. M. (1998). Educational vouchers: Effectiveness, choice, and costs. *Journal of Policy Analysis and Management, 17,* 373-392.

Levin, H. M. (1999). The public-private nexus in education. *American Behavioral Scientist, 43,* 124-137.

Lie, J. (1997). Sociology of markets. *Annual Review of Sociology, 23,* 341-360.

Linder, S. H. (1999). Coming to terms with the public-private partnership: A grammar of multiple meanings. *American Behavioral Scientist, 43,* 35-51.

Love, A. A. (1998, September 14). Study: Nursing homes screen workers poorly. *Houston Chronicle,* p. 3A.

Lovrich, N. P., Jr. (1999). Policy partnering between the public and the not-for-profit private sectors: A key policy lever or a dire warning of difficulty ahead? *American Behavioral Scientist, 43,* 177-191.

Lowry, R. C. (1995). Nonprofit organizations and public policy. *Policy Studies Review, 14,* 107-114.

Lutz, S. (1993, September 6). NME execs say firm's secure, but S & P cuts rating. *Modern Healthcare, 3,* 16.

Lutz, S. (1994, July 4). NME to pay fine of $379 million. *Modern Healthcare, 2,* 13.

MacStravic, S. (1998). Who's your best customer? *Managed Care Quarterly, 6,* 1-6.

Mead, L. M. (1998, September). *Statecraft: The politics of welfare reform in Wisconsin.* Paper presented at the meeting of the American Political Science Association, Boston, MA.

Mintzberg, H. (1996). Managing government, governing management. *Harvard Business Review, 74,* 75-83.

Moffett, M. (1998, April 27). Sour juice: In Brazil, a utility dims public's enthusiasm for privatization. *The Wall Street Journal,* pp. A1, A10.

Moon, M., & Davis, K. (1995). Preserving and strengthening Medicare. *Health Affairs, 14,* 31-46.

Moran, D. W. (1997). Federal regulation of managed care: An impulse in search of a theory. *Health Affairs, 16,* 7-21.

Morgan, R. O., Virnig, B. A., DeVito, C. A., & Persily, N. A. (1997). The Medicare-HMO revolving door—the healthy go in and the sick go out. *New England Journal of Medicine, 337,* 169-175.

Nagel, J. H. (1997). Editor's introduction: Radically reinventing government. *Journal of Policy Analysis and Management, 16,* 349-356.

Neuman, P., & Langwell, K. M. (1999). Medicare's choice explosion? Implications for beneficiaries. *Health Affairs, 18,* 150-161.

Nieves, E. (1998, November 7). California examines brutal, deadly prisons. *The New York Times,* p. A7.

Omnibus Consolidated and Emergency Supplemental Appropriations Act, Pub. L. No. 105-277, 112 Stat. 2681 (1999).

Osborne, D., & Gaebler, T. (1992). *Reinventing government: How the entrepreneurial spirit is transforming the public sector.* New York: Addison-Wesley.

Pear, R. (1998, July 22). Clinton urges crackdown on nursing home abuse. *The New York Times,* pp. A1, A12.

Raffel, M. W. (1997). Dominant issues convergence, decentralization, competition, health services. In M. W. Raffel (Ed.), *Health care and reform in industrialized countries* (pp. 291-301). University Park, PA: The Pennsylvania State University Press.

Reijniers, J.J.A.M. (1994). Organization of public-private partnership projects. *International Journal of Project Management, 12*, 137-142.

Rettig, R. A. (1997). *Health care in transition: Technology assessment in the private sector.* Santa Monica, CA: RAND.

Rice, T. H. (1996). Containing health care costs. In R. M. Anderson, T. H. Rice, & G. F. Kominski (Eds.), *Changing the U.S. health care system* (pp. 81-100). San Francisco: Jossey-Bass.

Rice, T. H. (1997). Can markets give us the health system we want? *Journal of Health Politics, Policy and Law, 22*, 383-426.

Riley, G., Tudor, C., Chiang, Y. -P., & Ingber, M. (1996). Health status of Medicare enrollees in HMOs and fee-for-service in 1994. *Health Care Finance Review, 17*, 65-76.

Rimer, S. (1998, June 8). Families bear a bigger share of caring for the frail elderly. *The New York Times*, pp. A1, A17.

Rom, M. C. (1999). From Welfare State to Opportunity Inc.: Public-private partnerships in welfare reform. *American Behavioral Scientist, 43*, 155-176.

Rosenau, P. (1999). *The competition paradigm.* Unpublished manuscript.

Rosenbaum, W. A. (1999). The good lessons of bad experience: Rethinking the future of commercial nuclear power. *American Behavioral Scientist, 43*, 74-91.

Salpukas, A. (1997, February 1). Subsidizing competition in utilities. *The New York Times*, p. A19.

Salpukas, A. (1998a, July 15). Deregulation fosters turmoil in power market. *The New York Times*, pp. B1, B7.

Salpukas, A. (1998b, October 25). A California vote could rewrite U.S. electric bills. *The New York Times*, pp. A1, A13.

Saltman, R. B., & Figueras, J. (1998). Analyzing the evidence on European health care reform. *Health Affairs, 17*, 85-108.

Schneider, A. L. (1999). Public-private partnerships in the U.S. prison system. *American Behavioral Scientist, 43*, 192-208.

Selz, M. (1996, October 3). Electric-utility deregulation is seen as costly for small-business owners. *The Wall Street Journal*, p. B2.

Showstack, J., Lurie, N., Leatherman, S., Fisher, E., & Inui, T. (1996). Health of the public; the private-sector challenge. *Journal of the American Medical Association, 276*, 1071-1074.

Smith, S. R., & Lipsky, M. (1992). Privatization in health and human services: A critique. *Journal of Health Politics, Policy and Law, 17*, 233-253.

Soros, G. (1998, September 15). The crisis of global capitalism. *The Wall Street Journal*, p. A22.

Sparer, M. S. (1996). *Medicaid and the limits of state health reform.* Philadelphia, PA: Temple University Press.

Sparer, M. S. (1998). Devolution of power: An interim report card. *Health Affairs, 17*, 7-17.

Sparer, M. S. (1999). Myths and misunderstandings: Health policy, the devolution revolution, and the push for privatization. *American Behavioral Scientist, 43*, 138-154.

Starr, P. (1990). The new life of the liberal state: Privatization and the restructuring of state-society relations. In J. Waterbury & E. Suleiman (Eds.), *Public enterprise and privatization* (pp. 22-54). Boulder, CO: Westview Press.

Stiglitz, J. E., & Wallsten, S. J. (1999). Public-private technology partnership: Promises and pitfalls. *American Behavioral Scientist, 43*, 52-73.

Supiot, A. (1996). Work and the public/private dichotomy. *International Labour Review, 135*, 653-663.

A survey of social insurance; privatising peace of mind. (1998, October 24). *The Economist, 349*, 3-22.

Totty, M. (1997, January 22). Privatization push creates an ethics obstacle course. *The Wall Street Journal*, p. T1.

United Nations Development Programme (1998). *Public-private partnerships* [On-line]. Available: http://www.undp.org:80/ppp/index.html.

Voelker, R. (1998). Activist Young says "gathering storm" will propel a single-payer movement. *Journal of the American Medical Association, 280,* 1467-1468.

Warden, G. L. (1996). Chaotic, shifting relationships of purchasers, plans, and providers. *Health Affairs, 15,* 116-117.

Weintraub, J., & Kumar, K. (1997). *Public and private in thought and practice: Perspectives on a grand dichotomy.* Chicago: The University of Chicago Press.

Wessel, D., & Harwood, J. (1998, May 14). Capitalism is giddy with triumph: Is it possible to overdo it? *The Wall Street Journal,* pp. A1, A10.

Woolhandler, S., & Himmelstein, D. U. (1998). *For our patients, not for profits: A call to action.* Cambridge, MA: The Center for National Health Program Studies, Harvard Medical School.

Yankelovich, D. (1994). How changes in the economy are reshaping American values. In H. J. Aaron, T. E. Mann, & T. Taylor (Eds.), *Values and public policy* (pp. 16-53). Washington, DC: Brookings Institution.

Yates, J. (1998). Partnerships with the faith community in welfare reform. *Welfare Information Network* [On-line]. Available: http://www.welfareinfo.org/faith.htm.

Zachary, G. P. (1996, August 6). Two-edged sword: More public workers lose well-paying jobs as outsourcing grows. *The Wall Street Journal,* pp. A1, A6.

About the Contributors

RONALD J. DANIELS is Dean and Professor of Law at the University of Toronto. His research and teaching interests encompass corporate law, law and economics, the legal profession, and privatization of government services. He has published extensively in these areas, including, most recently, *Corporate Decision-making in Canada* (1995, with R. Morck).

JAMES A. DUNN, JR., is Associate Professor of Political Science and Public Administration, Rutgers University—Camden. He is the author of several books, including *Driving Forces: The Automobile, Its Enemies, and the Politics of Mobility* (1998) and *Miles to Go: European and American Transportation Policies* (1981).

SHELDON KAMIENIECKI has taught at the University of Southern California since 1981. He is currently Professor and Chair in the Department of Political Science and Director of the Environmental Studies Program in the College of Letters, Arts and Sciences. His books concerning environmental issues include *Public Representation in Environmental Policymaking: The Case of Water Quality Planning* (1980); *Controversies in Environmental Policy* (1985, edited with Robert O'Brien and Michael Clarke); *Environmental Regulation Through Strategic Planning* (1991; with Steven Cohen); *Environmental Politics in the International Arena: Movements, Parties, Organizations, and Policy* (1993); and *Flashpoints in Environmental Policymaking: Controversies in Achieving Sustainability* (1997, edited with George A. Gonzalez and Robert O. Vos). He is the co-editor of a major book series for the MIT Press on American and Comparative Environmental Policy.

HENRY M. LEVIN is David Jacks Professor of Higher Education and Affiliated Professor of Economics at Stanford University. Dr. Levin's publications include more than 200 articles and thirteen books, including *Resource Guide for Accelerated Schools* (1993), *Effective Schools in Developing Societies* (coeditor, 1993), *Comparing Public and Private Schools* (coeditor, 1987), *Schooling and Work in the Democratic State* (co-author, 1985), and *Public Dollars for Private Schools* (coeditor, 1983). He is the former editor of *Review of Educational Research*.

STEPHEN H. LINDER is Associate Professor of Management and Policy Sciences/Health Services at the University of Texas-Houston Health Science Center's School of Public Health. He teaches courses in social and political theory, policy design, and qualitative policy analysis. His current writing focuses on policy discourse. He has published widely in the professional journals in the general area of policy sciences and public health.

NICHOLAS P. LOVRICH, JR., is the Claudius O. and Mary W. Johnson Distinguished Professor of Political Science and has served as the Director, Division of Governmental Studies and Services, at Washington State University for the past twenty-one years. He is the author or coauthor of a number of books, including most recently (with Russell J. Dalton, Paula Garb, John C. Pierce, and John M. Whiteley) *Critical Masses: Citizens, Nuclear Weapons Production, and Environmental Destruction in the United States and Russia* (1999). He has served as Editor-in-Chief of the *Review of Public Personnel Administration* since 1990.

MARK CARL ROM is an Associate Professor of Government and Public Policy at Georgetown University. He is also the Acting Executive Director of the Georgetown Graduate Public Policy Institute. He has published the books *Welfare Magnets: The New Case for a National Welfare Standard* (1990), *Public Spirit in the Thrift Tragedy* (1996), and most recently *Fatal Extraction: The Story Behind the Florida Dentist Accused of Killing His Patients and Poisoning Public Health* (1997).

PAULINE VAILLANCOURT ROSENAU is an Associate Professor at the School of Public Health, The University of Texas-Health Science Center at Houston. Previously, she was a Professor of Political Science at the University of Quebec in Montreal for two decades. Rosenau edited *Health Reform in the Nineties* (1994). She is the author of several other books including *Post-Modernism in the Social Sciences* (1992), which has been translated into Chinese, Korean, Spanish, and Turkish. Her last two books received *Choice* Magazine's Annual Outstanding Academic Books Awards (1992, 1994).

WALTER A. ROSENBAUM is Professor of Political Science at the University of Florida and Adjunct Research Professor, Department of Environmental Medicine, School of Public Health, Tulane University. Among his many publications is the fourth edition of *Environmental Politics and Policy* (1998).

ANNE LARASON SCHNEIDER is Dean of the College of Public Programs at Arizona State University. Professor Schneider is the co-author (with Helen Ingram) of *Policy Design for Democracy* (1997) and the author of *Deterrence and Juvenile Crime and Opinions and Policies in the American States*.

DAVID SHAFIE is a Ph.D. candidate in Political Science at the University of Southern California and teaches at California State University, Long Beach.

He is a co-author of *Rethinking California: Politics and Policy in the Golden State.*

JULIE SILVERS is a Ph.D. candidate in Political Science at the University of Southern California. She is currently conducting research for her dissertation, which examines conflicts between transnational corporations and environmental activists in Latin America.

MICHAEL S. SPARER is an associate professor in the Division of Health Policy and Management at the School of Public Health at Columbia University. He practiced law from 1980 to 1988 as an attorney for the New York City Corporation Counsel's Office supervising all phases of litigation in disputes between city, state, and federal governments. Dr. Sparer is author of *Medicaid and the Limits of State Health Reform* (1996).

JOSEPH E. STIGLITZ is a professor of economics at Stanford University. He served at the World Bank as Senior Vice President for Development Economics and Chief Economist from 1997 through 1999. He was an active member of President Clinton's economic team prior to his appointment to the World Bank, serving on the U.S. Council of Economic Advisers starting in 1993. He was named chairman of the council in June 1995. Dr. Stiglitz has authored numerous books and texts, including *Principles of Macroeconomics* (second edition, 1997), *Principles of Microeconomics* (second edition, 1997), *Economics* (second edition, 1997), and *Economics and the Public Sector* (third edition, 1999).

MICHAEL J. TREBILCOCK is Professor of Law and Director of the Law and Economics Programme at the University of Toronto Law School. He is the author of many books, including *The Common Law of Restraint of Trade* (1986), which was awarded the Walter Owen Prize in 1988 for the best legal text in English published in Canada in the previous two years, *The Limits of Freedom of Contract* (1993), and *Exploring the Domain of Accident Law: Taking the Facts Seriously* (1995). He has also co-authored books including *Canadian Competition Policy* (1987), *Trade and Transitions: A Comparative Analysis of Adjustment Policies* (1990), and *International Trade Regulation* (1995).

SCOTT J. WALLSTEN is an economist at Stanford University and The World Bank. From 1995–1996, he was a staff economist at the U.S. Council of Economic Advisers. He was awarded an Alfred P. Sloan Foundation dissertation fellowship for his thesis, entitled "Government-Industry R&D Programs, Economic Geography, and Spillovers," for which he received his Ph.D. in 1998. His current research focuses on industrial organization, regulation, and the economics of science and technology.

Index